The Indian Archaeological Society mourns the untimely death (on 17 December 1974) of Dr. Moti Chandra, who was an Honorary Fellow of the Society.

पुरातत्त्व
पुरातत्त्व
PURĀTATTVA

Bulletin of the Indian Archaeological Society

No. 7 1974

Editor
B.K. Thapar

Assistant Editor
B.M. Pande

D.K. Printworld (P) Ltd.
New Delhi

Cataloging in Publication Data — DK
[Courtesy : D.K. Agencies (P) Ltd. <docinfo@dkagencies.com>]

Purātattva : bulletin of the Indian Archaeological Society, no. 7, 1974 / editor, B.K. Thapar ; assistant editor, B.M. Pande.

p. cm.

Includes bibliographical references.

ISBN 8124602832

1. Archaeology — India — Periodicals. 2. India — Antiquities — Periodicals. 3. India — Civilization — Periodicals. I. Thapar, B.K. II. Indian Archaeological Society.

First Published in 1974
First Reprinted in 2005
ISBN 81-246-0283-2
Price for volume 7 (1974): Rs. 800 US $ 40

Reprint authorised by
Indian Archaeological Society
New Delhi - 110 016

Purātattva is published annually.

Manuscripts (whether in the form of articles or notes or book reviews) offered for publication should be sent to the Editor, Purātattva, Indian Archaeological Society, B-17, Qutab Institutional Area, New Delhi - 110 016.

Published and printed by:
D.K. Printworld (P) Ltd.
'Srikunj,' F-52, Bali Nagar
New Delhi – 110015
Phone : (011) 2545 3975, 2546 6019 Fax : (011) 2546 5926
E-mail : dkprintworld@vsnl.net
www. dkprintworld.com

PURATATTVA

NUMBER 7, 1974

CONTENTS

PURATATTVA

NUMBER 7 1974

Editorial

THIS issue of *Puratattva* appears in a new garb of changed format. The process has involved some inevitable delay, for which we owe an explanation to the readers and crave their indulgence. Some of the obstructive factors of the delay, such as power-shedding by the Electric Supply Undertaking to the Press, the scarcity of metal for block-making as also for casting, the steep rise in the price of paper and above all the paucity of funds, have been admittedly beyond our control. Furthermore, the publication of the *Puratattva*, which is a Bulletin of the Indian Archaeological Society, has hitherto been timed with the holding of the Annual Congress of the Society: the last Congress was held in November 1972 when the last issue of *Puratattva* was published ; the next Conference, scheduled for December 1973, had to be postponed to a future date because of the rail-strike which, in consequence, affected the publication-schedule of *Puratattva*. With a view to ensuring timely publication of the Bulletin, it has now been decided that *Puratattva* should be published every year in December, irrespective of the holding of the Annual Congress of the Society. We earnestly hope that it would be possible for us to keep up to this time-schedule.

* * * * * *

With this issue we also take the opportunity of extending our heartiest congratulations to two of our distinguished archaeologists who were awarded Padma Bhushan on the last Republic Day (26th January, 1974): Professor H.D. Sankalia and Dr. Moti Chandra. It is gratifying to learn that this is not the first time that archaeologists of repute have been awarded such honours by the Government. On earlier occasions, Shri A. Ghosh (1962) and Shri C. Sivaramamurti (1968) were awarded Padma Shri and Professor K. Nilakanta Shastri (1957), Shri T.N. Ramachandran (1964) and Professor Niharranjan Ray (1969), Padma Bhushan.

Warmest congratulations are also due to Dr. Lokesh Chandra who has been nominated as a Member of the Rajya Sabha (1974 –). In this case as well, on earlier occasions, similar distinction was conferred on two renowned historians and archaeologists : Professor Niharranjan Ray (1957-1965) and Professor S. Nurul Hasan (1968 –).

All these scholars are too well known to need any introduction to our readers. Nor will it be felicitous to list their contributions here. Suffice it to mention that each one of them has made significant contribution to the cultural history of India. It is a happy augury that one of them, Professor S. Nurul Hasan, now heads the Ministry of Education, Social Welfare and Culture. The archaeological community, therefore, has reasons to be proud of this recognition by the Government.

* * * * * *

Another noteworthy news which we would like to share with the readers is the appointment of Professor S.B. Deo as Head of the Department of Proto-Indian and Ancient Indian History at the Deccan College Postgraduate and Research Institute, Pune. Professor Deo is no stranger to this prestigious Institute, having worked here, with his customary dedication, in various capacities since 1955, excepting the spells at Kathmandu (1963-65) and Nagpur (1966-74).

* * * * *

Archaeology has been making headlines in this country during the last four months or so. The Report of the Estimates Committee of the Lok Sabha on the

Archaeological Survey of India has been published, which has resulted in some polemics; articles have appeared in the Press, commenting on the working of the century-old Survey ; new goals have been suggested for the old discipline.

Archaeological research in the country has, until recently, been looked upon as a Cinderella, having struggled through conditions seldom affluent. In the circumstances, some of the ills are likely to be of accumulative nature. What the outcome of this assessment will be is not for us to anticipate here, but it is hoped that this criticism, some of which seems to have been overstated, will not obscure the measures that have already been taken or are proposed under the Fifth Five Year Plan.

Two aspects of the criticism, viz., publication and excavation, concern us very closely and as such have to be received with understanding, howsoever disconcerting it may appear to be. Publication, which has reportedly fallen behind field-research, has to be accelerated so that the backlog of excavation-reports is cleared at the earliest. In this connection we may recall that the Archaeology Review Committee (March-April 1965) had observed that the already published reports had set very high standards and had accordingly brought considerable credit to India from many parts of the world. We do not commend such feelings of complacence beyond a reasonable stage, for we know, that among the published reports there are some which are unworthy of international standard. It would be seen, therefore, that promptness is not the only merit of an excavation-report, it has to be sound and adequtely published as well. Constant efforts directed to this end alone can sustain a high standard in an increasingly competitive world. One of such efforts consists of providing informed criticism, through reviews, of the concerned publication. Care, however, should be taken that this tool does not become dangerous.

In excavation, which remains a valuable instrument for increasing our knowledge of India's heritage, the need for a careful strategic planning on regional or on an all-India basis has often been emphasized. The programme has to be worked jointly by the Survey, the universities and the State Departments of Archaeology, so that a sense of common purpose is achieved. It has been suggested that strictly problem-centred projects should be taken up.

The implementation of the recommendations of the Archaeology Review Committee relating to excavation by the Survey's Circles has resulted in the falling-off in the Survey's output of original work. Meanwhile, the Universities have stepped up their excavation-activities. But, for a country of the size and cultural variety of India, the extent of the total effort falls short of the requirement. There are upwards of twenty universities which undertake field-work in archaeology. Unfortunately, however, there is a marked imbalance in the growth of field archaeology in these universities : some of these have fully-equipped Departments for undertaking explorations and excavations, while others have neither adequate expertise nor the proper equipment for such a work. Yet, there is another category where archaeology is taught but not practised. The position of the State Departments of Archaeology is no better: out of a total of twenty-one States, only sixteen have so far set up Departments of Archaeology. A uniform performance of technical skill or a national standard in a collaborated work is, therefore, difficult to achieve. What we need today are fully trained leaders; tuition without experience is of no avail in field-archaeology.

In both these aspects—publication and excavation—the role of the Central Advisory Board of Archaeology, which, among other things, approves the exploration-excavation programmes of all the excavating agencies (Indian and foreign), including the Survey, assumes greater importance. The Standing Committee of the Board which consists of five elected Members of the Board and whose functions include giving of advice to the Board generally on the promotion of archaeological pursuance in the country, should insist on adherence to specific problems of the work proposed. The Committee could also strictly examine the technical competence of the staff, both for field-work as also for the preparation of the report. The procedure must be relentlessly imposed. It is hoped that this increased strictness in the examination of exploration-excavation programmes would prove useful to Indian archaeology in the long run.

B. K. THAPAR

Archaeological and Ethnographic Evidence for the Hafting and Use of Microliths and Related Tools

V. N. Misra

Deccan College Postgraduate and Research Institute, Pune

[*Received on* 23 *September* 1973]

IN spite of long and extensive research on the Stone Age, our knowledge of the methods of hafting and use, and of the functions of tools remains very limited. First, most of the prehistoric stone tool types went out of use long ago with the result that no close equivalents could be found among the tool forms of the present-day stone using societies. Secondly, handles and hafts, being of organic materials, survive only in exceptional circumstances. And finally, most of the stone tools, particularly those belonging to the Palaeolithic Age, have been found in secondary archaeological contexts removed from their original places of manufacture and use and dissociated from materials and situations in relation to which they were used. It is only in recent years that archaeologists have begun to pay adequate attention to the excavation of living sites which afford possibilities of finding stone tools in their original contexts.

Fortunately, the situation is less disappointing with regard to the Mesolithic stone tools. A large number of microlithic and related tools have been found in their stratified contexts, sometimes also in original hafts. The available evidence suggests that most of the microliths, because of their small size, were used as elements of composite tools, after being hafted in wood or bone handles. The artifacts which were generally made from microliths are spearheads, arrowheads, sickles, knives, daggers and adzes. We shall discuss the evidence for each of these types separately.

SPEARHEADS

A number of spearheads are known from Mesolithic sites in Denmark and Sweden. A very fine example of this implement comes from Bussojomosse, Scania, Sweden.[1] The haft, made of bone, is serrated along the left margin, both near the proximal and distal ends. Microliths, which appear to be scalene triangles, are set in grooves on both sides of the haft. They are set end to end and the unretouched side projects off the haft. Four microliths survive on the right side and three on the left, but judging from the empty spaces on both sides there must originally have been several more (FIG.1,*1*).

Three specimens of this class are known from the Mesolithic bog of Svaerdborg in Denmark. These have been described in some detail by Johansen.[2] Two of these are represented by small fragments; one of them had two flint blades still preserved in the grooves, one on each side. The third specimen, nearly complete, measures nearly 22 cm in length in its extant condition and, like other examples of this type, has an oval section. Four narrow bladelets were found in its immediate vicinity and the excavator believes that they were certainly originally fixed in the lateral grooves of the bone haft (FIG.1,*7*). The bone point was cut from a tubular bone and is slightly damaged at its lower end which originally appears to have been pointed. The lateral grooves are of unequal length. On the left side, the groove extends

[1] J. G. D. Clark, ***The Stone Age Hunters*** (London, 1967) p. 104, fig. 105.

[2] K. F. Johansen, K. Jessen and H. Winge, 'Une station de plus ancien age de la pierre dans la tourbiere de Svaerdborg', *Mémoires de la Société Royale des Antiquitaires du Nord* (Nouvelle Serie), 1918-1919, pp. 327-29, fig. 59.

right up to the lower extremity, while on the right side it terminates 5·5 cm above this extremity and is replaced by fine and regular denticulations. This kind of denticulation also occurs no one of the edges, mostly on the basal end, but sometimes also on the upper end of other Danish and Swedish points. In most cases the denticulations are so fine and so carefully done that they appear to have been intended for ornamentation rather than for any particular use.

Johansen also tells us that a different and very rare type of bone point is known from one of the localities at Mullerup in Denmark. It is broad and flat unlike the common type with a thin bone handle, to which the three Svaerdborg examples belong, and of which numerous examples are known from the island of Zealand in Denmark and from Scania.

Bone points with unilateral as well as bilateral inserts are known from the Mesolithic cultures of Central Europe and from the Upper Palaeolithic of Siberia. Kozlowski[1] has described and illustrated such finds from Poland and adjacent countries. In both unilateral and bilateral types, the bladelets used are unretouched and are often intentionally broken on one or both the ends. The unilateral type occurs in the Kunda culture of Estonia and Latvia and in the Neman culture of Lithuania and northern Poland. The bilateral type, more characteristic of Denmark and Sweden, is represented in Poland in the Janislawice culture (FIG.3,*1-2*).

The spear point with blade inserts has its ancestry in the Upper Palaeolithic cultures.[2] It is known from the sites of Afontovo, Verkholenskaya Gora, Mal'ta and Kokorievo in Siberia.

These points are also common in the Isakovo and Serovo Neolithic cultures in Siberia.[3] They are made by fitting carefully shaped blade "inserts" in grooves cut in a long animal bone, usually a rib. In form they are similar to Upper Palaeolithic prototypes, pointed at one end, and abruptly cut off at the other, with a circular transverse section. The Isakovo blades were not secondarily retouched on the edge which was to be inserted in the groove. The side blades are either secondarily retouched to form a series of small, equally-spaced dentations, oriented in one direction, or in addition to the dentation, are retouched from one side to form a unilaterally sloping blade. The dentations are added after the side has been retouched.

The side-bladed spearheads of the Isakovo Culture have an average length of 30-35 cm and a maximum length of 50 cm and their shaft is round. Their position in the graves makes it clear that their points were attached to spears. They were placed parallel to the body with pointed ends upwards, that is, the preserved points were next to the head (Ponomarevo burials nos. 10, 13, 16). In two cases (Isakovo mound burial no. 2 and Ponomarevo burial no. 10), the spearheads lay just above the pelvis. A.P. Okladnikov has proposed that these were short hunting spears of the order of the short spear-axe used by the contemporary Nanaiets and Nikhva, so-called "gida". These may have been put into the hands of the deceased or placed across the body.

Long, leaf-shaped points, made of glass and telephone insulators, by bifacial pressure flaking, and with dentations on both edges, were mounted as spear points by Australian aborigines in Western Australia.[4] There can be little doubt that pressure-flaked bifacial stone points,excavated from Ingaladdi and other older sites, which are clearly the prototypes of glass pieces, were similarly mounted.[5] Another kind of spear, made with stone flakes and known as 'Death spear' is also recorded from Australia.[6] It was made by mounting a series of small, irregularly-shaped and unretouched stone chips on both sides of the head of a wooden stick. No grooves were made and the chips were mounted in resin. One of the artifacts consisted of as many as twenty-two chips. The chips were of stone, usually quartz, and in later stages of glass and chinaware. It has been suggested that these formless fragments were degenerate substitutes for well-made microliths, excavated from older deposits, but this needs to be confirmed by future research. This kind of spear had a wide though marginal distribution in Australia.

ARROWHEADS

Evidence for the use of microliths as tips and barbs of arrows is quite plentiful and comes from many sites in far flung areas. The beginnings of

[1]S. K. Kozlowski, *Pradzieje Ziem Polskich od IX do V tysiaclecia* p. n.e. (Warsaw, 1972), p. 292, fig. IIb, nos. 13 and 14, and personal communication.

[2]H. N. Michael, 'The Neolithic Age in Eastern Siberia', *Transactions of the American Philosophical Society*, vol. 48, no. 2 (1958), p. 43, and personal communication from Dr. S. K. Kozlowski.

[3]*Ibid.*, pp. 42-43.

[4]F. D. McCarthy, *Australian Aboriginal Stone Implements* (Sydney, 1967), p. 42, fig. 23 no. 5; and D. J. Mulvaney, *The Prehistory of Australia* (London, 1969), pp. 16-17.

[5]Mulvaney, *op. cit.*, pp. 116-17, fig. 25.

[6]McCarthy, *op. cit.* (1967), p. 34; and Mulvaney, *op. cit.*. pp. 93-94.

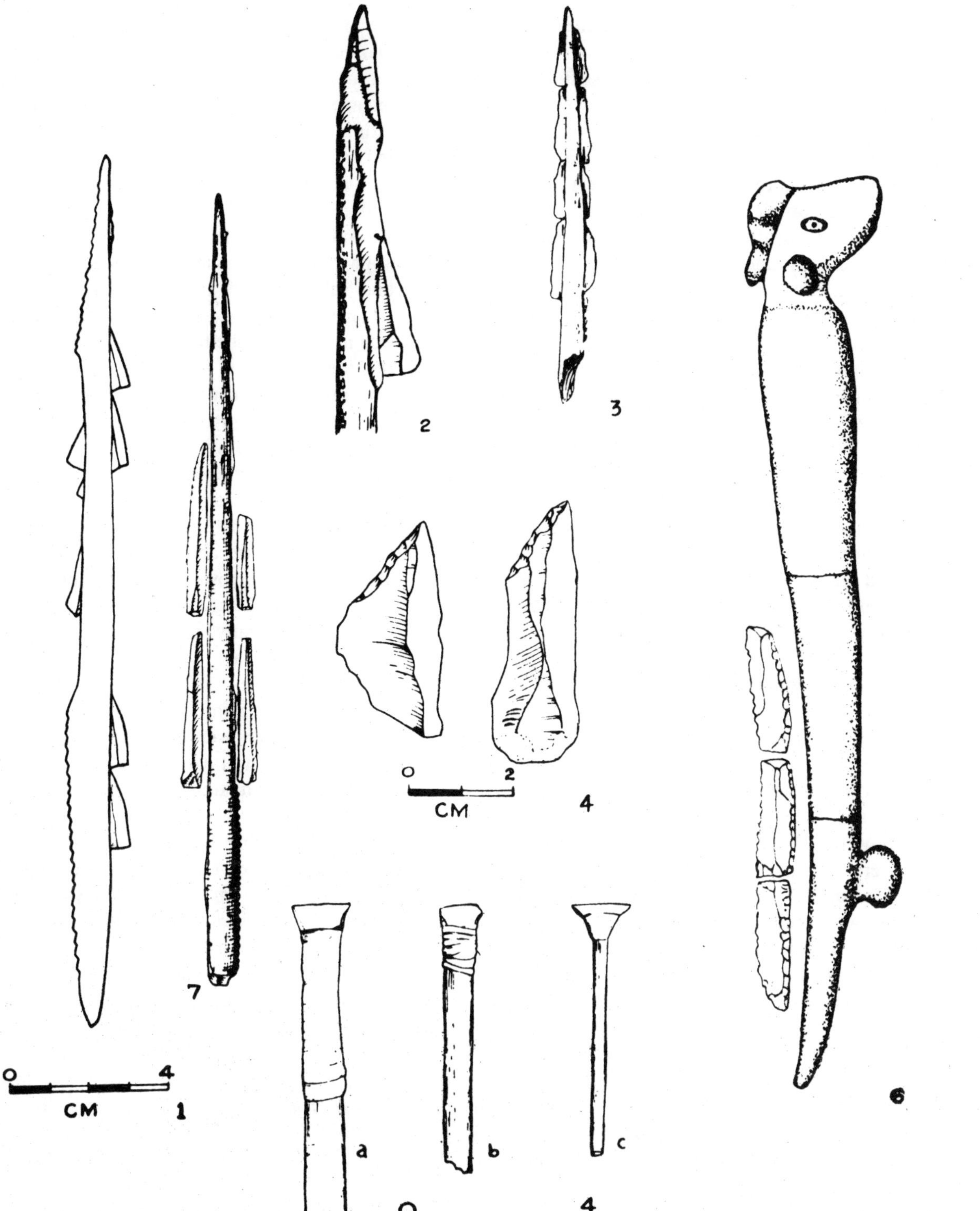

FIG. 1. *1, spearhead from Bussojomosse, Scania, Sweden; 2, arrowhead with flint barb and tip from Loshult, Scania, Sweden; 3, arrow point from Scania, Sweden; 4, obliquely blunted blades from Vig, Zealand, Denmark; 5, chisel-ended arrowheads from (a) Tvaermose, Jutland, Denmark; (b) Petersfehner Moor, Oldenberg, Germany, and (c) Egypt (Middle Empire); 6, grooved sicklehaft from Mugharet el-Kabarah, Israel; 7, spearhead from Denmark*

archery are not at present very clear. It is possible that tanged points of the Aterian culture of north Africa and of the Solutrean culture of France were used as arrowheads, but the evidence is sadly deficient. Conclusive evidence for archery dates from the final or Younger Dryas period (*c.* 8800-8300 B.C.) and comes from the site of Stellmoor in north Germany, occupied by Ahrensburgian reindeer hunters.[1] Remains of a complete tanged point found with two fragments of the shaft in the breast of a reindeer are highly suggestive; indeed the only gap in the evidence is an actual bow (FIG. 3, *12*).

Less conclusive evidence of archery comes from the Hamburgian (13000 B.C.) levels of the same site. Here, splinters of shouldered flint points have been found embedded in reindeer bones, but it cannot be established that these points were released by arrows. From the Hamburgian site of Meiendorf was obtained evidence of holes in the bones of cranes and White Grouse, which match the reindeer antler points. But it cannot be proved that projectiles were used.

Another early evidence of the probable use of bow and arrow comes from Africa.[2] In a Late Pleistocene graveyard at Jebel Sahaba, a little north of Wadi Halfa in Sudanese Nubia, dated to between 12000 and 10000 B.C., were buried many persons who had died a violent death. The bodies show that they had been killed by weapons pointed with microliths or other small stone inserts. One man had as many as one hundred and ten such artifacts associated in such a way as to suggest that they had entered his body as the barbs and points of projectiles and two of them were still embedded in his skull. Stone artifacts were similarly found sticking in the bones of five other burials. From their contexts it is apparent that they were points and barbs of arrows rather than of spears. If they had been mounted as spears the spearhead might be expected to have made a deeper wound where the conical point of the weapon had penetrated.

The earliest known bows come from the bog of Holmegaard in Denmark.[3] These were self bows about the height of a man made from a single length of springy wood like elm or yew and shaped with carefully made grips near the middle of the stave. The forepart of a wooden arrow-shaft is known from the Maglemosian site of Vinkelmose in Jutland, Denmark. The tip of the shaft is an oblique slot for a microlithic point and the base is notched to engage a bow string. The base is also bound by a string. This binding was intended to hold the feathering required to steady the flight of the arrow. Forepart of an actual arrow with a microlith used as a tip and another used as a barb has been found from Loshult, Scania in Sweden. The microliths used appear to be triangles held together by resin. This find shows two distinct functions of the microliths: when mounted on arrow-shafts, the function of the one mounted at the tip was to penetrate and that of the side one, to cut (FIG. 1, *2*).

Transverse arrowheads (*petit tranchet*) were often used as tips of arrows. Actual specimens of these tools, hafted in arrow-shafts, are known from Tvaermose, Jutland (Denmark), Petersfehner Moor, Oldenburg, Germany and from Egypt (Middle Empire).[4] J. de Morgan[5] tells us that in some of the arrows, barbs are also made of similar flint flakes, and that these arrows formed the principal projectile weapon of the Pharaohnic armies. Often, the flakes did not bear any retouch. Chisel-edged flakes, similarly used, are known from Abydos.[6] From Egypt also comes the evidence of representations of chisel-ended arrowheads on monuments which make it clear that they were used for shooting a variety of game. Thus, an undated rock engraving in southern Egypt shows an archer shooting a running ostrich with what are undoubted chisel-ended arrows. Even more enlightening in some ways is the painting on the north wall of the tomb of Antefoker, vizier of Sesostris I which shows the archer shooting down with similar arrows into a netted enclosure crowded with game, among them a bull and a couple of bubale already stricken.[7] The association of chisel-ended arrowheads with Ertebolle middens, and the absence of any other recognizable form of arrowhead, suggests that in prehistoric Europe also they were used to shoot a wide range of quarry.[8] A specimen of a *petit tranchet* was found deeply embedded in a human vertebra from a Neolithic chalk-cut grotto in the valley of Petit-Morin, Champagne, France.[9] Tra-

[1]J. G. D. Clark, 'Neolithic Bows from Somerset, England, and the Prehistory of Archery in North-West Europe', *Proceedings of Prehistoric Society* (New Series), vol. XXIX (1963), pp. 61-62. This article (pp. 50-98) contains a masterly survey of archery in prehistoric Europe together with an exhaustive catalogue of the finds of bows and arrow-shafts in western Europe. The evidence summarized on this subject in the present paper is based largely on this and other writings of Professor Clark cited in this paper elsewhere.

[2]J. G. D. Clark, *The Prehistory of Africa* (London, 1969), p. 160.

[3]Clark, *op. cit.* (1967), p. 93.

[4]J. G. D. Clark, *The Mesolithic Settlements of Northern Europe* (Cambridge, 1936), fig. 51, nos. 1-3.

[5]J. de Morgan, *La Prehistoire Orientale*, Tome I, Generallite (Paris, 1925), pp. 271-72, fig. 42.

[6]*Ibid.*, fig. 42, nos. 4-5.

[7]J. G. D. Clark, *Prehistoric Europe: The Economic Basis* (London, 1952), p. 36

[8]*Ibid.*, p. 36.

[9]*Ibid.*

pezoidal forms of arrowhead are also known from the Neolithic dwellings of Switzerland. These were mounted on their wooden shafts with the help of birch-pitch.[1]

Obliquely blunted blades and flakes were also probably used as tips and barbs of arrows. Two specimens of this type (FIG.1, *4*) and a flint flake were found in the breast region of an aurochs skeleton at Vig near Jyderup in the north-west of the island of Zealand in Denmark.[2] These were probably part of an arrow which got stuck in the breast of the animal, and the microliths remained embedded after the wooden shaft had rotted away. Oblique arrowheads of rhombic shape are common in the Kongemose culture of Denmark, and these were probably used both as tips and barbs of arrows.[3]

A microlithic triangle was found embedded for a third of its length in the vertebra of the skeleton of a young man buried in the Tardenoisian midden on the isle of Teviec off the peninsula of Quiberon in the Morbihan.[4] A bone arrow-point with flint barbs from Scania, Sweden is illustrated by J. Hawkes and Sir Leonard Woolley[5] (FIG.1, *3*). It is broken at the proximal end, and so the complete length and shape are not known. In the extant condition four microliths are seen set end to end on each side as barbs, but possibly originally there were more further down. The microliths appear to be simple bladelets or scalene triangles. It is possible that this specimen was a spear point rather than an arrowhead.

Simple blades with or without retouch are also used as tips and barbs of arrows. An elongated bladelet hafted as an arrowhead is known from Heluan (Lower Egypt).[6] From Abydos in Egypt Morgan[7] has illustrated what appears to be a pressure-worked bladelet used as the tip of an arrowhead.

Bilaterally retouched points, used as tips of arrows, are known from Swiss Neolithic dwellings (FIG. 3, *3*).[8] These were mounted on their wooden shafts with the aid of birch-pitch. From South Africa there is evidence of a unilateral point and an irregular lunate of glass being used to make an arrowhead.[9] The implements were mounted in wax. This was done by a Bushman prisoner in Cape Town at the end of the nineteenth century. Glass and wax were used in this case in place of stone and vegetable gum normally employed by the Bushmen. The explanation for retouch, according to the man, was that it provided suitable surface for the wax to grip without the stone being so deeply embedded in the matrix that it would not come out in the wound. Allchin tells us that several arrowheads of this type are kept in the Pitt-Rivers Museum at Oxford (FIG.3,*7*). Leaf-shaped points mounted as arrowheads in wooden shafts are known from Scotland.[10] In India, use of triangles, trapezes and lunates as tips and barbs of arrows is known from their depiction in rock paintings at Bhimbetka, Lakha Juar, Raisen and Modi in Madhya Pradesh.

The question is often asked as to how such tiny tools as microliths, when mounted on arrow-shafts, could be effective in killing any game. It is to be remembered that apart from the force which is exerted when the weapon is released by a projectile, it is very likely that prehistoric man treated the microliths, which he used to tip and barb his arrows, with poison. The practice of poisoning arrowheads is ethnographically documented from many areas, and some archaeological evidence is also available for it. At the site of Gwisho Springs in Zambia, dated to mid third millennium B.C., were found numerous pods of the shrub *Swartzia,* commonly used for arrow poison by the Kalahari Bushmen. This is considered particularly significant in the light of the fact that all the other plant remains that occurred in any quantity at this site belonged to edible species and had clearly been brought to the site for food.[11]

SICKLES

Yet another use of microliths was in the manufacture of sickles used for the harvesting of cereal crops and other plants and also for household work. The earliest known sickles come from the Natufian sites in Palestine. Two complete and several fragmentary grooved bone sickle-hafts were found at

[1] *Ibid.*, fig. 22, no. 4.
[2] Clark, *op. cit.* (1936), fig. 29.
[3] Clark, *op. cit.* (1963), p. 70.
[4] Clark, *op. cit.* (1952), pp. 35-36.
[5] J. Hawkes and Sir Leonard Woolley, *Prehistory and the Beginnings of Civilization* (London, 1963), fig. 24A.
[6] Morgan, *op. cit.* (1925), fig. 42, no. 2.
[7] *Ibid.*, fig. 42, no. 3.
[8] Clark, *op. cit.* (1952), fig. 22, no. 3.
[9] B. Allchin, *The Stone-tipped Arrow: the Late Stone Age Hunter-gatherers of the Tropical Old World* (London, 1966), p. 203, fig. 41, no. 6.
[10] Clark, *op. cit.* (1963), fig. 15.
[11] Clark, *op. cit.* (1969), p. 157.

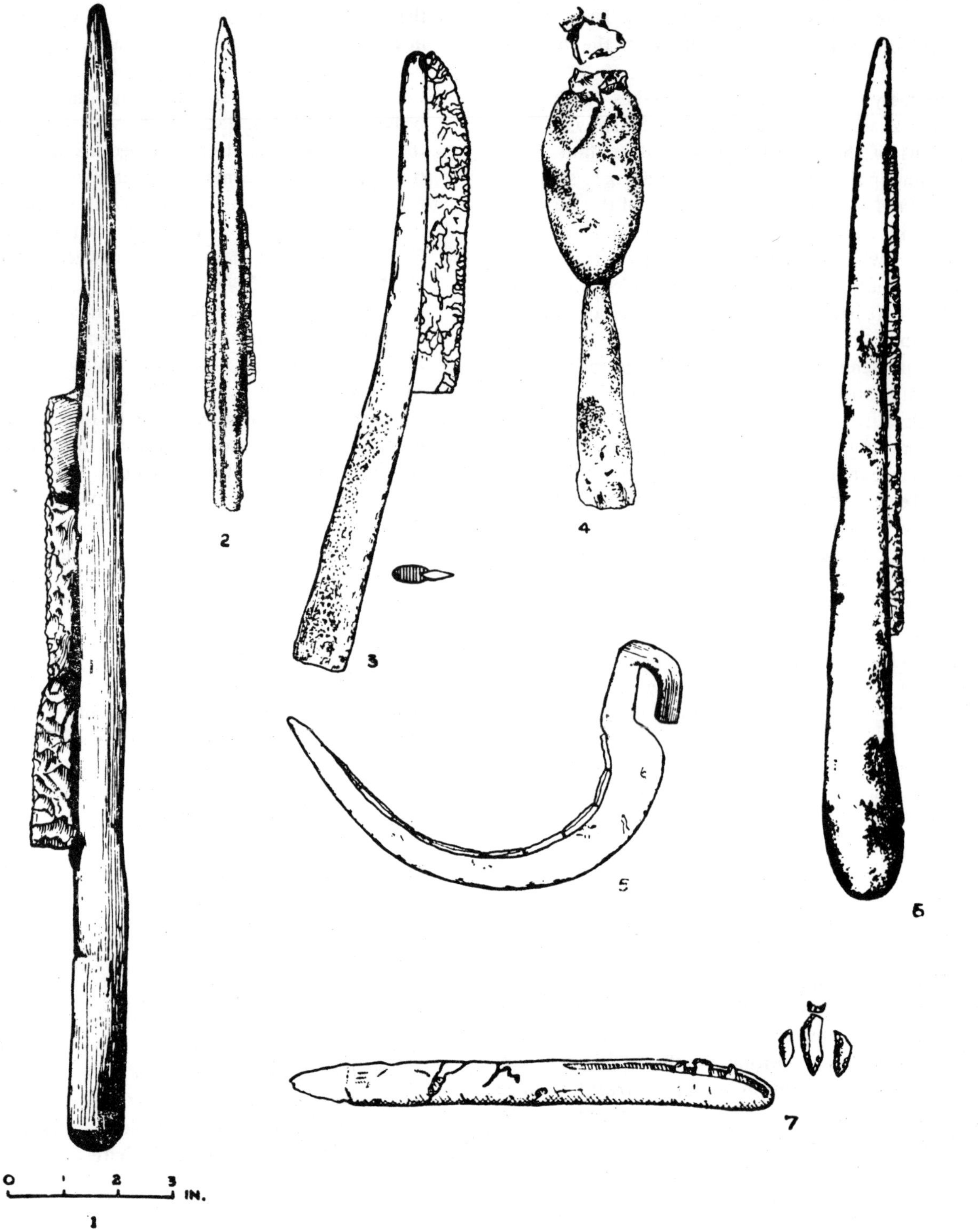

FIG. 2. *1, sickle with wooden haft from Fayum*; *2, spearhead from Isakovo, Eastern Siberia*; *3, side-bladed knife from Ponomarevo, Eastern Siberia*; *4, crescent adze-flake mounted on a rhino-horn handle from Plettenberg Bay, eastern Cape Province, Africa*; *5, flint-sickle with wooden haft from Saqqara, Egypt*; *6, dagger of Kitoi period from Rasputino mound, Eastern Siberia*; *7, sickle with microliths set in a bone shaft from Colummata, Africa*

Mugharet el-Kebarah.[1] The complete specimens have lengths of 38 and 23 cm respectively. The head of the handle is decorated by a carving of an animal head which, in the case of the bigger specimen, appears to be a goat (FIG.1,*6*). Towards the tip on the side opposite to groove is a semicircular knob, the function of which is not clear. The blade has a deep groove on one edge from the base of the handle to the tip. It was intended to receive the flint insets. In both pieces, the blade is very slightly curved, the grooved edge being concave. Several fragments also bear this kind of projection. From this site there are also two other carved animal heads, representing respectively a bovine animal and a deer. These, as also a decorated fragment, and a fragment pierced near the centre, were, in the opinion of the excavator, handles of other hafts.

From Mugharet el-Wad, thirteen specimens were found, but all are incomplete, and some mere fragments.[2] The largest of these, measuring 15 cm in length, is flat on one face and slightly convex on the other. Unlike the el-Kebarah specimen, in this the grooved edge is markedly convex and the semicircular projection is reduced to a slight swelling. A smaller fragment has two flint blades remaining in place in the groove; both flints have rather irregular edges without any trace of lustre, and as far as can be seen the backs are not retouched. This specimen was found in very tough red earth, almost as hard as breccia, and the blades are kept in place by a calcareous concretion, all trace of the original sticking matter having disappeared.

Two other specimens represent a different type of sickle haft. In one of these the bone blade is much broader and flatter than in others. The groove runs nearly to the base which is bevelled and flattened. and is pierced by two holes. It is clear that it must have been inserted into a separate handle, possibly of wood, and held in place by lashing. In the second specimen there are four holes instead of two.

Many of the flint blades found at Natufian sites bear a lustre or sheen on their edges, which apparently results from the friction with the silica in the corn stalks. It is therefore believed that the Natufian sickles were used for harvesting wild cereal grasses though some archaeologists think they might have been used only to cut reeds.

Stone-bladed sickles are more common in Neolithic sites. Two specimens with wooden handles were found in silos in the Fayum, one complete, the other represented only by the handle.[3] The complete specimen consists of a slightly curved wooden shaft of oval cross section, 20·4 in in length, tapering to a blunt point. The bevelled butt measures 3 in in circumference. A centrally placed longitudinal groove is fitted with three serrated flint blades held in position by resin. This incision is 10·25 in long by about 0·25 in broad, and for ninety per cent of its length has a depth of approximately 0·4 in The three blades are of flint and, from the butt side, measure 3·1, 3·3 and 1·9 in in length. The tip of the flint is broken, but from the size of the groove its original length must have been about 3·4 in. All the three flints are serrated and worn in varying degrees. Two complete ones are pressure flaked on both faces while the broken specimen is worked only on one face. The three flints are carelessly fitted, the first one projecting farther than the other two, but all the three are effectively held firm by resin. The wood of the handle was identified to be *Tamarix sp.* (FIG. 2, *1*). The other specimen, without blades, is similar to the one described above, but it is smaller.

A slightly different type of sickle is known from Hassuna.[4] One specimen was found in Room 17 of Level II among many flint blades and nodules. The flakes were found to be held in the original bitumen. They were set overlapping, and upon the bitumen were traces of the wooden backing which gave strength to the implement. The flakes used were not serrated. An even better preserved example was found in Level III. It consisted of nine broad crescentic flakes which are held together by bitumen. No serration or other retouch is visible on them. The blade was slightly curved and was probably attached to a wooden handle, as suggested by the excavator (FIG. 3, *6*).

[1]F. Turville-Petre, 'Excavations in the Mugharet el-Kebarah' *Journal of the Royal Anthropological Institute of Great Britain and Ireland*, vol. LXII (1932), p. 272, pl. XXVII, figs. 1-3; and D.A.E. Garrod and D.M.A. Bate, *The Stone Age of Mount Carmel* (Oxford, 1937), vol. I, pp. 37-38.

[2]*Ibid.*, pp. 37-38, pls. XII and XIII.

[3]G. Caton-Thompson and E.W. Gardner, *The Desert Fayum* (London, 1934) (in two vols.), p. 45,pls. XXVIII and XXX and figs. 1-2.

[4]S. Lloyd and F. Safar, 'Tell Hassuna: Excavations by the Iraq Government Directorate General of Antiquities in 1943 and 1944', *Journal of Near Eastern Studies*, vol. IV, pt. 4 (1945), p. 269, fig. 37. Commenting on the Hassuna sickle-blades, Linda S. Braidwood (*Ibid.*, p. 269) says "The Hassuna sickle blades are made on irregularly shaped blade segments or on flakes. In this they differ from the sickle blades of other available early village assemblages (e.g., Judaidah, Mersin, Sialk), which have neat sickle blades made on small narrow blade sections".

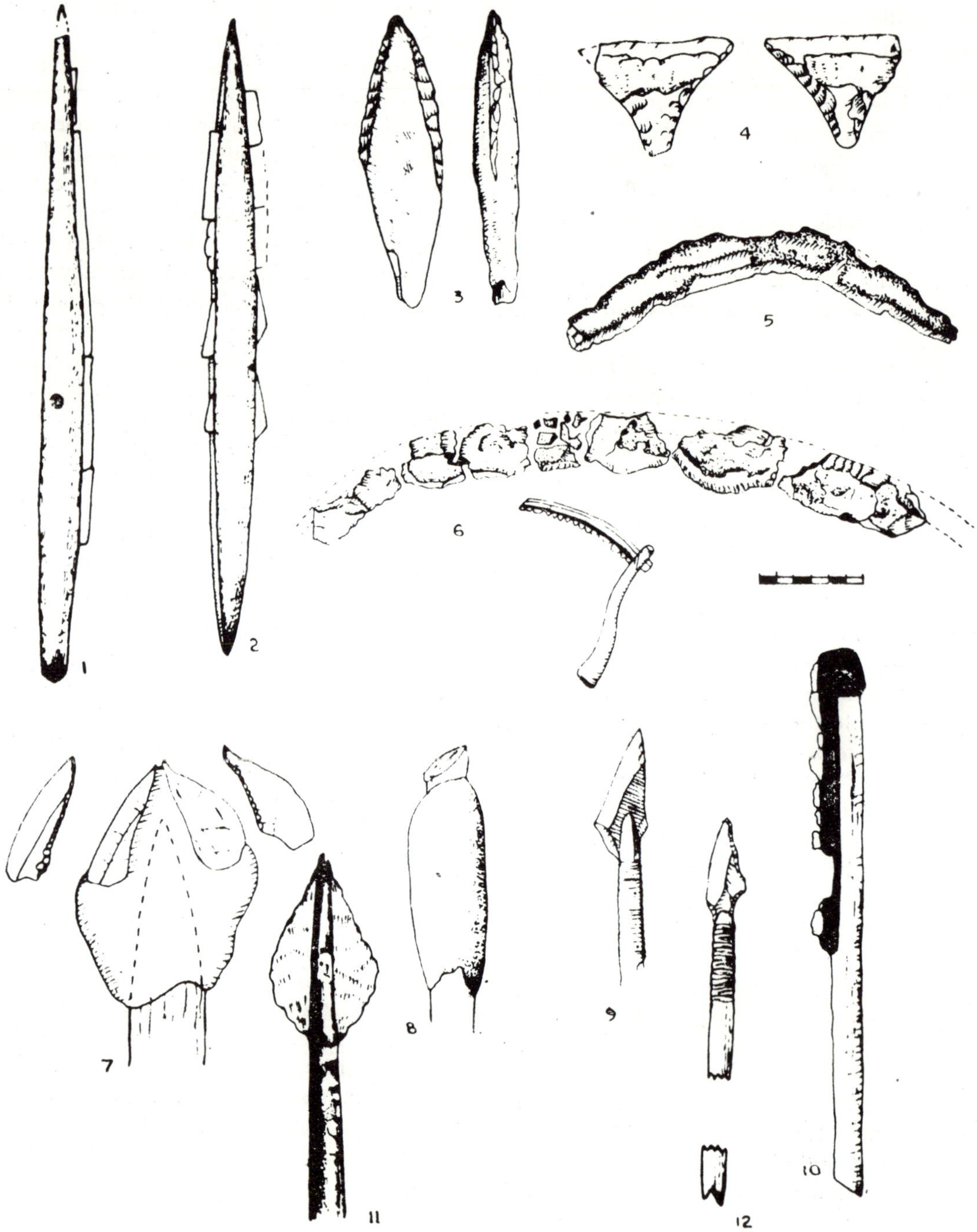

FIG. 3. *1-2, flint-bladed bone spear points from Poland; 3, flint arrowhead mounted with birch pitch covering from Zugesburg-Gasboden, Switzerland; 4, chisel-ended arrowhead mounted with birch pitch from Switzerland; 5, flint sickle mounted with bitumen from Jarmo, Iraq; 6, flintsickle mounted with bitumen from Hassuna, Iraq; 7, arrowheads with glass bladelet inserts from South Africa; 8, triangular microlith set in gum on a stick handle from Birdsville, Queensland, Australia; 9, oblique arrowhead of the Danish early coastal culture; 10, taap knife from Western Australia; 11, leaf-shaped arrowhead from Fyvil, Switzerland; 12, reconstruction of Ahrensburgian arrow from north Germany.*

A sickle with a curved blade is available from Jarmo (PL. IA).[1] It consists of parallel-sided blades set edge to edge and held together probably by bitumen. There was distinctive sheen on the inner cutting edge. Unfortunately the bitumen was too crumbly to retain the impressions of the haft's material. This sickle blade is more curved than that of the Hassuna specimen (FIG. 3, *5*). A curved 45 cm long sickle with wooden handle and flint teeth is also known from Saqqara, Egypt, in the deposits belonging to the First Dynasty.[2]

Four bone sickle hafts are known from the site of Sialk[3] in Iraq. The handles of all these are artistically decorated. The sickle-hafts were made by fitting, with the help of bitumen, a flint knife or a series of small pointed flints in a groove made in the length of an animal bone. The groove is always on the curved side of the bone to facilitate the fixing of equally curved flints. The thickest part of the flint was not grooved and served as the handle which was decorated with carving of an animal head.

One of the hafts[4] bears on the extremity of its handle the representation of the head of a hare with ears raised. Its length is 145 mm and could contain blades of 50 to 65 mm length. A light hollow at two-thirds length from the handle permitted the index finger to hold the tool better in the hand, the handle being of thin diameter. The holding of the tool is facilitated by the fact that the bone is lightly turned on its axis which permits the middle finger to rest on the tip below the carved head. Another similar haft[5] is preserved only up to the handle which is carved in the form of the head of a goat. The best example of this art is provided by the carved sickle haft.[6] The actual length of the tool is 128 mm, but must have originally been about 180 mm long. The haft represented a standing person with legs shown by a light modelling, and the feet, barely to be seen, forming a border limiting the groove for setting the flints. Another haft, larger than the three already described, is made from the side of a large animal. The groove for the flints is very large.

Finally, a sickle with bone shaft and flint insets is known from the Upper Capsian culture at Columnata in Africa.[7] Less than half the length of the bone shaft is grooved and contains three microliths set vertically. Two of these are diminutive triangles and the third an elongated lunate (FIG 2, *7*).

KNIVES

Use of long pressure-worked blades in making knives is known from the Isakovo Neolithic culture in Siberia.[8] The shaft which is of bone is slightly bent and flattened in cross-section. The grooving in the shaft is much deeper and wider. In differentiation from the spear points, the knife side blades are wider and retouched all over. The blades, with the exception of the distal end blade, have the shape of elongated rectangles. The distal blade usually comes to a point and thus has the appearance of a triangle with one long side convex and the inserted side straight. In cross-section, the blades usually have a lensoid shape and the inserted edge is always thinner than the cutting edge—although the inserted edge is not as finely retouched as the cutting edge. There is no space between the individual side-blades. A smooth junction was achieved by cutting the short ends of the blades in a chisel-edge manner so that when fitted together they overlapped (FIG. 2,*3*). These knives have their roots in the Upper Palaeolithic.

From Australia several types of knives are known. One of these is *Taap* saw knife.[9] This consists of up to a dozen irregular, unretouched stone chips of the type used in death spears and mounted on a wooden handle in gum cement. There is no groove and the chips are of quartz, quartzite or chert. This tool was used for cutting meat and is known from the south-western part of Western Australia (FIG. 3, *10*). The second type of knife is *Leilira* knife blade.[10] It is a long pointed blade with triangular section, or an elongated rectangular blade trapezoid in section. It was hafted in gum cement to provide a hand grip and sometimes a short piece of flat pointed wood was inserted in the gum grip. The length of these blades ranges from 9 to 22 cm (handle or grip included) and they rarely bear any retouch. The *Leilira* was used for cutting up animals, cutting cicatrice scars, circumcision and subincision on men and introcision on women. Similar blades were used as spear points

[1]R.J. Braidwood, *Prehistoric Men* (seventh ed., Glenview. 1967), fig. 119. m; and personal communication.

[2]H. Frankfort, *The Birth of Civilization in the Near East* (London, 1951), p. 11, pl. I and fig. IE.

[3]R. Ghirshman, *Fouilles de Sialk, près de Kashan*, 1933, 1934 1937 (Paris, 1938), vol. I, pp. 17-20.

[4]*Ibid.*, pl. VIII, fig. 2 and pl. LIV, fig. II.

[5]*Ibid.*, pl. VIII, fig. 3 and pl. LIV, fig. III.

[6]*Ibid.*, pls. VII and LIV, fig. I.

[7]Clark, *op. cit.* (1969), p. 156 and fig. 44, no. 7.

[8]Michael, *op. cit.* (1958), pp. 43-44.

[9]Mulvaney *op. cit.* (1969), p. 93; and McCarthy *op. cit.* (1967), pp. 34-35.

[10]McCarthy, *ibid.*, p. 32; and Mulvaney, *Ibid.*, pp. 69-70.

in Northern Territory and Central Australia and western Queensland and as heads of fighting picks in Northern Territory. A type somewhat related to *Leilira* blade is known as *Juan* knife but differs from the *Leilira* in that it is asymmetrical and has a thick back which is usually trimmed. It was provided with a fur grip and is recorded from central and western Queensland.[1]

DAGGERS

In Serovo and Kitoi cultures of Siberia, Neolithic pressure-worked rectangular stone blades were hafted in bone shafts to make unilateral as well as bilateral daggers.[2] These daggers are up to 45 cm long and have straight edges.

ADZES

From the Neolithic site of Isakovo in Siberia[3] composite adzes are also known. The flint "inserts" for these are comparatively narrow but massive and the groove in the holding shaft is very deep and wide. J. D. Clark[4] has illustrated a crescentic adze flake in chert, mounted in mastic at the end of a rhino horn handle, from a cave at Plettenberg Bay, eastern Cape Province, Africa (FIG. 2, *4*). A type of adze known as *Tula* adze is widely recorded from Australia, both ethnographically and archaeologically.[5] In its most common form, it is a broad D-shaped flake too with its undersurface a plain flake surface and the outer surface trimmed along the margins. It is hafted on the opposite end of a wooden spear-thrower and serves as a multipurpose tool. Among its many uses are "cutting and shaping bark, and wooden weapons, dishes and bowls (coolamons), ceremonial objects, disembowelling animals, and occasional digging". When its edge is worn out and becomes blunt, the *Tula* is taken out of the gum cement, re-chipped and re-mounted. Finally, the thick, narrow butt end of the flake is left which is discarded. This discarded slug has been called *Burren* slug. The main concentration of the *Tula* adzes is in Central Australia. *Tulas* are up to 10 cm long. Finally, we may mention the find of a hafted microlith from Australia which might have been used as a chisel or adze (FIG. 3, *8*). It is a triangular microlith which was hafted at the end of a wooden handle, with its sharp unretouched edge projecting outward. The find was made at Birdsville and is now preserved in the Queensland Museum.[6]

The above account is far from being exhaustive. There would doubtlessly be many more archaeologically and ethnographically recorded examples of hafted tools but the examples referred to above should suffice to illustrate the various uses to which microliths and blades and flakes associated with microlithic assemblages could be put to, as also the ways in which they can be hafted on bone and wooden handles.

[1]Mulvaney, *ibid.*, p. 112; and McCarthy, *Ibid.*, p. 32.
[2]Michael, *op. cit.* (1958), pp. 49 and 64-65.
[3]*Ibid.*, p. 44.
[4]Clark, *op. cit.* (1969), p. 157, fig. 45.
[5]Mulvaney, *op. cit.* (1969), pp. 70-73 and 113-16; and McCarthy, *op. cit.* (1967), pp. 27-28.
[6]McCarthy, *ibid.*, pp. 41-42.

A Techno-Typological Review of the Middle Palaeolithic Cultures of India[1]

Vidula Jayaswal

Banaras Hindu University, Varanasi

[*Received on 28 September, 1973*]

SINCE the initial recognition of the Middle Palaeolithic[2] phase at Nevasa[3], numerous Middle Palaeolithic sites have been located in different parts of the country. Its stratigraphical position is also well established belonging as it does to 'Gravel II', or the finer gravel which overlies 'Gravel I', consisting of Lower Palaeolithic tools.[4] As no stratigraphic division within Gravel II itself is possible, the tool-types recovered from this gravel cannot be further subdivided on a stratigraphic basis. It has, therefore, to be conceded that stratigraphic basis for the study of Middle Palaeolithic phase in the subcontinent is largely missing and stands no comparison to the situation in Europe, where changes in tool types can be studied in direct correlation with theirs tratigraphic position. A fruitful line of enquiry could be a techno-typological study of the palaeolithic tools, which might show variations, regional or evolutionary, if any, within the Middle Palaeolithic cultural complex.[5] The present paper aims at classifying some of the Middle Palaeolithic industries on techno-typological considerations. After selection of the representative industries, the material was grouped into two categories: the finished tool-types and blank-types.[6] Thereafter, a comparative study of the proportion of various tool-types and blank detaching techniques was made. Such an analysis might afford evidence for determining the effect of advanced tool-typology on technological development. It must be made clear that the present study is based on such collections as were made available to the author at the various institutions.[7] Some of

[1]The author is thankful to Dr. K. K. Sinha (Reader in Archaeology), and Shri P. C. Pant (Lecturer in Prehistory) Banaras Hindu University, for making necessary corrections in the manuscript.

[2]Though the term 'Middle Stone Age' was adopted in the meeting held at Delhi in 1961, the author prefers the term 'Middle Palaeolithic' instead as advocated by V. N. Misra, 'Problem of terminology in Indian Prehistory', *Eastern Anthropologist*, vol. XV (1962), pp. 113-24.

[3]H. D. Sankalia, *et al.*, *From History to Prehistory at Nevasa* (Poona, 1961).

[4]H. D. Sankalia, *Pre- and Protohistory of India and Pakistan* (Bombay, 1962).

[5]H. D. Sankalia, 'Middle Stone Age Cultures in India and Pakistan', *Science* (1965), pp. 365-75; and S. N. Roa, 'Regional variations in the Indian Middle Stone Age Cultures with special reference to Nalgonda in Andhra', *Puratattva*, no. 2 (1968).

[6]The term 'blank' has been adopted after Movius, which includes both flakes and blades. This has the advantage over the existing term 'flake' in having more objective sense; see, H. L. Movius *et al.*, 'The analysis of certain major classes of Upper Palaeolithic tools', *Harvard University Bulletin*, no. 26 (1968).

[7]The author is grateful to Prof. H. D. Sankalia and Dr. R. V. Joshi for giving her facilities to study the collections, preserved in the Deccan College, Pune, and Prehistory Branch of the Archaeological Survey of India, Nagpur, respectively. The number of tools made available may not always tally with the number mentioned in the previously published account of particular collections.

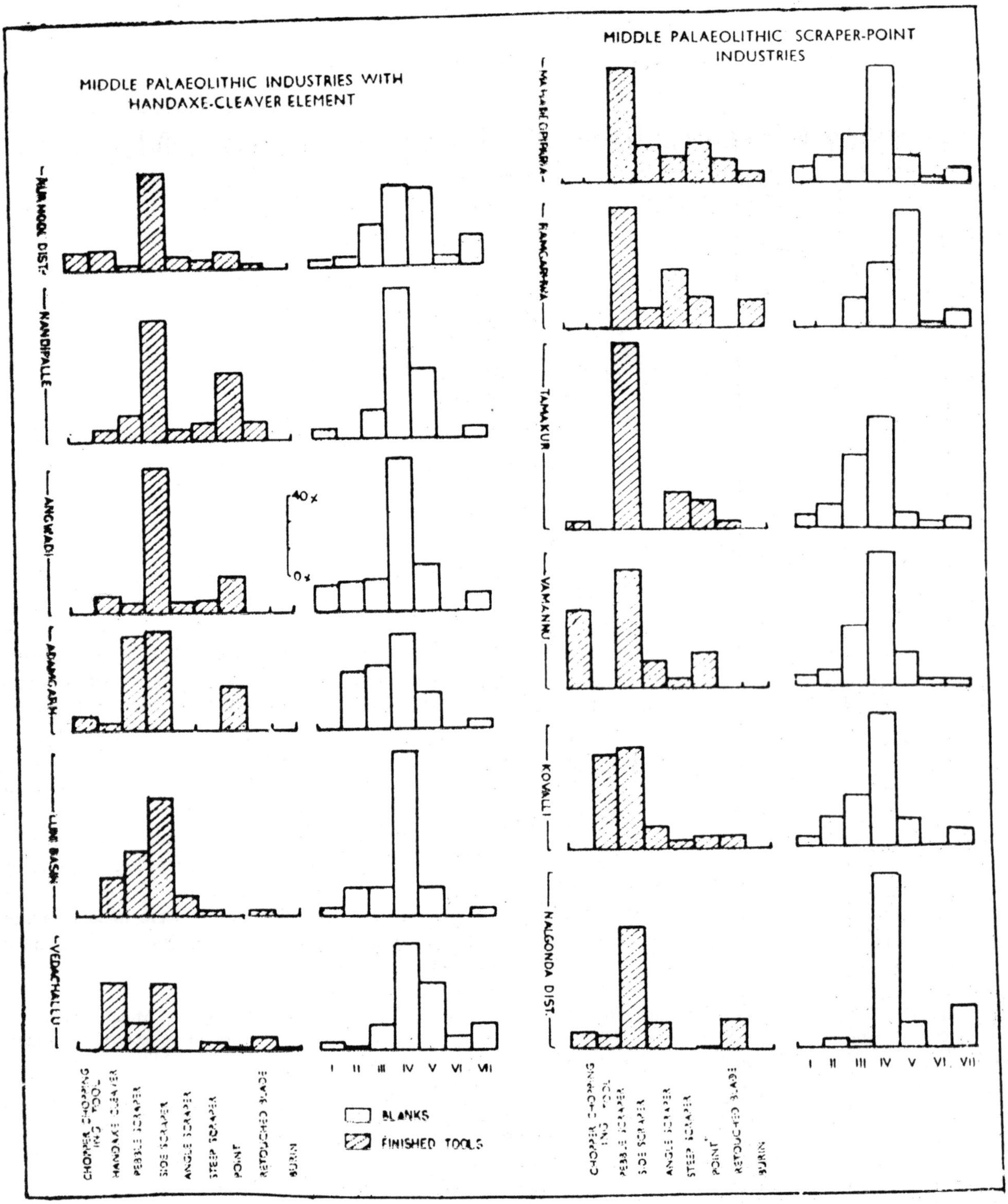
MIDDLE PALAEOLITHIC INDUSTRIES WITH HANDAXE-CLEAVER ELEMENT
MIDDLE PALAEOLITHIC SCRAPER-POINT INDUSTRIES
NANDIPALLE
ANGWADI
TAMAKUR
VAMANNU
KOVALLI
NALGONDA DIST.
VEDACHALLU
40%
0%
I II III IV V VI VII
BLANKS
FINISHED TOOLS

FIG. 1

the important collections like those from Potwar region,[1] Orissa,[2] Attirampakkam,[3] and Singhbhum,[4] have thus been left out as either they were not available,or if available were found to be so mixed as to make any scientific study almost impossible. In order to apply the statistical method it is desirable that artifacts should be available in good numbers. As such only twelve industries of Indian Middle Palaeolithic phase could be brought within the scope of this study.

In the Middle Palaeolithic assemblages, two broad groups can be easily recognized: the first consisting of those industries which show a presence of handaxe-cleaver element, while the other includes those industries which show a complete absence of handaxe-cleaver element. The other tool-types differ only marginally from one industry to the other. With the exception of Ramgarhwa industry, the technological features are also generally shared by all.

The frequency of the handaxe-cleaver element ranges from 4 to 25 per cent. The first group which shows a frequency of 4 to 25 per cent of the handaxe-cleaver element has been identified in the following regions of the sub-continent: Kurnool District,[5] Rajputana,[6] Potwar region,[7] Narmada basin,[8] Bundelkhand,[9] Upper, Son basin,[10] Upper Krishna basin,[11] Chittoor District,[12] and a few other places in Andhra Pradesh. The following six of these have been selected for detailed analysis :Kurnool District;[13] Luni basin;[14] Adamgarh;[15] Nandipalle;[16] Anagwadi[17] and Vedachalluvu.[18]

The statistical analysis of the frequency of each finished tool-type reveals that except the industries of Vedachalluvu and Luni basin, which respectively contain as much as 25 and 10 per cent 'handaxe-cleaver element', this group can only claim to have a nominal presence (4 to 8 per cent) of this feature. Adamgarh is the other industry of the group which deserves special mention owing to the predominance of pebble-scraper along witht he various types of side-scrapers.

The technological features are shared almost equally by all the six industries (FIG. 1). They are characterized by the predominance of the flakes detached from prepared cores and a small proportion of unprepared flakes and those with unprepared dorsal surface and prepared striking platform. However, the industries of Vedachalluvu, Nandipalle and the Kurnool District group show a higher percentage of Levallois flakes in comparison with the remaining ones of the group. A few blades have also been found in all the industries. In the histogram, the unprepared flakes have been numbered: (i) flakes with unprepared dorsal surface and prepared striking platform; (ii) flakes with partial preparation;[19] (iii) prepared flakes;[20] (iv), Levallois flakes;[21] (v) Leval-

[1]H. de Terra and T. T. Paterson, *Studies in the Ice Age and Associated Human Cultures* (Washington, 1939).

[2]G. C. Mohapatra, *The Stone Age Cultures of Orissa* (Poona, 1962).

[3]*Indian Archaeology* 1964-65—*A Review*.

[4]A. K. Ghosh, 'Palaeolithic Cultures of Singhbhum', *Transactions of the American Philosophical Society*, *New Series*, vol. 60 (1960).

[5]S. Issac, *The Stone Age Cultures of Kurnool*, Ph.D. Thesis, 1960 (unpublished), Deccan College Library, Poona.

[6]V. N. Misra, *The Stone Age Cultures of Rajputana*, Ph.D. Thesis, 1961 (unpublished), Deccan College Library, Poona.

[7]T. T. Paterson and H. J. H. Drummond, *Soan, the Palaeolithic of Pakistan* (Karachi, 1962).

[8]R. V. Joshi, 'Acheulian succession in Central India', *Asian Perspectives*, vol. VIII no. 1, (1964).

[9]R. Singh, *Palaeolithic Industries of Northern Bundelkhand*, Ph.D. Thesis, 1965 (unpublished), Deccan College Library, Poona.

[10]N. Ahmed, *The Stone Age Cultures of the Upper Son Valley*, Ph.D. Thesis, 1966 (unpublished), Deccan College Library, Poona.

[11]R. S. Pappu, *Pleistocene Studies in the Upper Krishna Basin*, Ph.D. Thesis, 1966 (unpublished) Deccan College Library, Poona.

[12]M.L.K. Murty, 'Blade and burin industries near Renigunta on the south-east coast of India', *Proceedings of the Prehistoric Society for* 1968, vol XXXIV, no. 2.

[13]Issac, *op. cit.*

[14]Misra (1961), *op.cit.*

[15]Joshi, *op. cit.*

[16]K. T. Reddy, *Prehistory of Cuddapah*, Ph. D. Thesis, 1968 (unpublished), Deccan College Library, Poona.

[17]R. S. Pappu, *Pleistocene Studies in the Upper Krishna Basin*, Ph.D. Thesis, 1966 (unpublished), Deccan College Library, Poona.

[18]Murty, *op. cit.*

[19]This group of flakes seems to be prepared by a few scars on the dorsal surface, approximately half of which retains the cortex. The flakes of this group may or may not have prepared striking platforms.

[20]Prepared flake group should not be confused with Levallois flake group, for, though the former has fully prepared dorsal surface, it does not follow the conventional pattern of centrally directed scars. Thus it could not be placed in Levallois flake group. Both the prepared and unprepared striking platforms are found in this group of flakes.

[21]We prefer the term Levallois technique instead of facetted platform' or 'prepared core technique'. The first, being well defined by Bordes is now almost universally in use and also avoids many such confusions which arise in the use of the latter two; see, F. Bordes, *Typologie du Paleolithique, Ancien et Moyen*, Institute of Prehistory of the University of Bordeaux, Memoire 1 (1961).

lois points; (vi) and blades (vii).

The other group which also consists of industries from Nalgonda,[1] Kovalli,[2] Vammanu,[3] Tamakur,[4] Ramgarhwa Pahar,[5] and Mahadeopiparia,[6] differs from the previous one in being devoid of handaxes and cleavers.

A typological analysis of these industries would show that in these assemblages various types of side-scrapers predominate, while the other tools like point, angle-scraper, end-scraper and pebble-tools occur less frequently. Coming within the same general pattern, the industries of Kovalli and Vammauu deserve special mention because of the presence of certain distinguishing features. Kovalli has a high proportion of pebble-scrapers while Vammanu shows a distincitive preference for chopper-chopping tools. It may be mentioned that Vammanu seems to be the only Middle Palaeolithic industry of the subcontinent which contains such a high percentage of chopper-chopping tools. Adamgarh and Kovalli share identical features except for the fact that Adamarh has a handaxe-cleaver element which is absent in Kovalli.

Technologically, all the industries of this group are characterized by an overwhelming preference for prepared flakes. Ramgarhwa has to be regarded as an exception both because of the presence of Levallois blanks to the extent of 48 per cent and a small proportion of other important types.

If all the twelve industries of the two groups are taken together for technological considerations, they could broadly be classified under three heads: (i) industries with high percentage of Levallois blanks and comparatively lower proportion or total absence of other types; (ii) industries dominated by prepared flakes and followed by Levallois and other types; and (iii) industries showing an overwhelming preference for prepared flakes and low to very low percentage of other types including Levallois. The first group is represented by Ramgarhwa only, while the industries of Vedachalluvu and Kurnool district, with 25 and 28 per cent of Levallois blanks respectively, fall under second category, and the remaining industries under the third. The industries of the first two categories may be regarded as technological variation.

A typological comparison between the above mentioned two groups clearly indicates that the only point of difference is the occurrence or absence of handaxe-cleaver element in them. Theother types are almost equally distributed among the various industries with a few exceptions formed by those of Vedachalluvu, Kovalli, Adamgarh and Vammanu. These exceptions are in fact the typological variations within the Middle Palaeolithic culture-complex of peninsular India. As pointed out earlier, the percentage of handaxes and cleavers is low to very low in all the industries of the first group except of course Vedachalluvu. This phenomenon gives rise to certain fundamental queries—how far the occurrence of the handaxe-cleaver element along with the normal Middle Palaeolithic assemblage has to be regarded with any degree of certainty? Could it be suggested that there were two techno-typological traditions (or cultures) in the Middle Palaeolithic phase of peninsular India, having more or less the same chronological horizons? The evidence at hand is unfortunately insufficient to support any hypothesis. Nor does it seem possible at present to explain the variations as regional.

[1]S. N. Rao, *The Stone Age Cultures of Nalgonda District*, Ph.D. Thesis, 1966 (unpublished), Deccan College Library, Poona.

[2]Pappu, *op. cit.*

[3]Reddy, *op. cit.*

[4]K. Paddaya, *Pre- and Protohistoric investigations in the Shorapur Doab*, Ph.D. Thesis, 1968 (unpublished), Deccan College Library, Poona.

[5]This factory-site in the vicinity of the river Belan, a tributary of the Tons, is in District Allahabad, and was examined by the author with Shri P. C. Pant.

[6]S. G. Supekar, *Pleistocene Stratigraphy and Prehistoric Archaeology of Central Narmada Basin*, Ph.D. Thesis, 1968 (unpublished), Deccan College Library, Poona.

Recent Archaeological Discoveries in North-Eastern India*

T.C. Sharma
Gauhati University, Gauhati

[*Received on 10 October 1973*]

INTRODUCTION

THE triangular landmass lying to the east of the plains of Bangladesh forms the north-eastern part of India, previously known as Assam. In the post-Independence period, however, the province has been broken up into a number of small states such as Nagaland, Meghalaya, Manipur, Mizoram, Arunachal and Assam. With a view to keeping the current political set up of the region in mind, the term north-eastern India seems to be more appropriate, for it enables us to keep the previous studies in their true geographical perspective.

North-eastern India is archaeologically one of the least explored regions of India. The reasons are not far to seek. Owing to the unfavourable climatic conditions of this region, with its torrential rain, and impenetrable jungles, an extensive ground survey of the area is very difficult. Almost every part of the area is covered with thick vegetation. Although T. Bloch[1] in 1902 and 1906 and T.N. Ramachandran [2] in 1936 made some attempts to open up the area for the archaeologists, practically nothing worthy of note as compared to other parts of India was done in north-eastern India, with the result that an imbalance in the knowledge of Indian archaeology has been created.

ARCHAEOLOGICAL RESEARCH IN N.E. INDIA

The beginning of archaeological research in north-eastern India, was made sometime in 1866, only three years after the discovery of a true palaeolith from Pallavaram, near Madras by Bruce Foote: the first report of archaeological discovery in Assam appeared in *Athenaeum* of London as early as 1866.[3] The report was accredited to Sir John Lubbock. Similarly, the beginning of the study of Pleistocene geology and environment was made as early as 1875 by Godwin Austen[4] who observed evidence of post-glacial action in the Naga hills. This important work has so far failed to attract the attention of geologists and archaeologists.

Besides, several British anthropologists and civil servants like J. H. Hutton, J. P. Mills, G. D. Walkar, C. R. Pawsey and J. H. Grace made large collections of ground and polished stone tools from different parts of north-eastern India. Only a small part of this collection is now available in this country, the

*The author is grateful to Prof. M. C. Goswami of Gauhati University for his kind help and guidance in this work. The author is also thankful to Dr. H. C. Sharma for his kind help.

[1] T. Bloch, 'Conservation in Assam', *Annual Report of the Archaeological Survey of India* (hereafter *ARASI*). 1906-7, pp. 17-28.

[2] T. N. Ramachandran, 'Explorations in Assam', *ARASI*, 1936-37, pp. 17-28.

[3] Sir John Lubbock, 'The Stone Age—Stone tools in Upper Assam', *Athenaeum*, June 22, 1867, p. 822.

[4] H. H. Godwin Austen, 'Evidence of past glacial action in the Naga hills', *Journal of the Asiatic Society of Bengal*, vol. XLIX, pt. 3, pp. 209-13.

bulk being exhibited in the Pitt Rivers Museum at Oxford. A very valuable collection of neolithic material, found in the north bank of the Brahmaputra river in central Assam, was deposited in the Indian Museum at Calcutta. This collection has been catalogued by Coggin Brown.[1]

Almost all the material referred to above consists of surface collections made by the tribal people.

After the Second World War and with the opening of Anthropology Department in the Gauhati University in 1948, the problem of prehistoric archaeology in north-eastern India attracted the attention of Professor M. C. Goswami. Soon, he and the present writer[2] were able to locate a stratified neolithic site at Daojali Hading in the hilly region of south-central Assam. The small-scale excavations conducted by us at the site in 1961 and in 1963 resulted in uncovering some stratified neolithic material consisting of ground and polished stone axes and adzes including square cut shouldered and quadrangular adzes, corn grinders, mullers and pottery with cord-impressed designs. This work had the merit of attracting the attention of other archaeologists in India and abroad.

Thereafter, we extended our field investigations to the Garo Hills. Within the course of the last six years we could explore only a limited area of the Rongram and the Simsang river valleys and were successful in locating some Stone Age sites in the area: Rongram Alagiri, Chitra Abri, Selbalgiri, Michmagiri, Watri Abri, Waramgiri, Chibragiri and Rombhagiri. Excepting the last-named site which is in the Simsang valley, all the remaining sites are in the Rongram valley. Almost all the sites were found to be very rich in their lithic contents.

The sites are located in an undulating hilly area having altitudes varying between 1500 to 2500 ft (457·2 m to 761 m). The entire area is covered with a thick natural vegetation. The sites are exposed when the river terraces are cleared off their natural vegetation by the local tribal people for shifting cultivation. The site at Waramgiri was exposed at the time of construction of a road. As a result of erosion, after the removal of vegetative cover, the cultural materials are exposed on the surface of some sites. At Selbalgiri and Waramgiri there are still some undisturbed cultural layers where artifacts are found to occur in their proper contexts.

So far we have not been able to do detailed stratigraphical study of the sites. At the same time it may be mentioned that we have been able to locate well stratified gravels and silt at Rongram Alagiri and Chibragiri in the Rongram valley, and at Rombhagiri in the Simsang valley. The cemented gravel at Alagiri has yielded pebble tools and choppers. A cleaver was also found at this site near the section on loose gravel in the river bed. At Rombhagiri, two handaxes were dug out from the cemented gravel.

SITES AND TOOL TYPES

SELBALGIRI.—The site is located on the terrace of the Rongram river. The southern side of the terrace is cut by a nullah while its top is seriously eroded, as a result of which stone tools were found exposed on the surface. On the northern face of the terrace, where erosion is less severe, a trial trench was dug which yielded ground and polished stone axes and pottery in the upper 60 cm deposit, below which only microliths were found to occur till the natural soil was reached.

Typologically, the Selbalgiri stone tool assemblage consists of four distinct industries: (i) a flake and blade industry; (ii) a microlithic industry; (iii) a chipped stone axe industry; and (iv) a ground and polished stone industry occurring in association with a crude handmade pottery. In addition to these there are some roughly flaked discoid tools and stone axes showing Lower Palaeolithic tool traditions.

WARAMGIRI.—The site is located on the terrace of a hilly stream. At this site there are some well exposed dolerite dykes. These dykes are the sources of raw material for stone tools in the Garo Hills. This rock has been used in the Garo Hills for fabricating stone tools from Lower Palaeolithic period up to the end of the Neolithic. The occurrence of a large number of cores and waste flakes found at the site might indicate a workshop. Further, the tool assemblage of the site suggests that the site supplied raw material for stone tools of several cultural periods. Many tools are exposed on the eroded surface of the site, while a large number of tools are found in mint condition in a layer of yellowish silt. The tools dug out from the silt layer consist of a few handaxes and a large number of scrapers and points showing Mousterian character. The tools exposed

[1]J. Coggin Brown, *Catalogue of Prehistoric Antiquities in the Indian Museum* (Calcutta, 1917), pp. 131-33.

[2]M. C. Goswami and T. C. Sharma, 'Further report on the investigations into the prehistoric archaeology of North Cachar hills, Assam', *Journal of the Gauhati University*, vol. XIV, no. 2, 1963 pp. 45-47; T. C. Sharma, 'A note on the neolithic pottery of Assam', *Man* (New Series), vol. II (1967), no. 1, pp. 126-28.

on the surface mainly consist of small flake tools, blades, points, microliths and arrowheads. It may be mentioned that no ground and polished stone axes and pottery have been found at the site.

MICHMAGIRI AND WATRI ABRI.—At Michmagiri, the terrace sequence is well developed. There are four well formed terraces of which the second terrace yielded a rich lithic industry of fine flake tools and blades. Other terraces are yet to be explored as these are covered with a thick evergreen vegetation.

The site at Watri Abri is situated at a distance of about 3 km to the south of Michmagiri. It is located on a steeply sloped terrace of a small tributary river which has cut deep gorges at this place. The entire area is covered with a thick forest. A large number of stone tools, which have evidently been washed down the slope of the terrace, are found to have been deposited on a foot-track stretching along the river bank. The site has yielded a rich flake-and-blade industry where the frequency of blade flakes is found to be higher than in any other site of this area.

GARO HILLS LITHIC INDUSTRIES

The salient features of these industries show both pebble tool and chopper element in association with the handaxe facies (PL. IB). There are crudely flaked Abbevillian as well as late Acheulian types. The flake tool industry based on the Levalloiso-Mousterian traditions is also well developed. Among the flake tools, besides the usual types of scrapers and points (PL. IIA), there are some peculiar tools such as tanged point of Aterian type and Mousterian type of flakes with thick blunt back. The series also includes a large number of awls and borers PL. IIB). The blade industry is also well developed. There are well prepared blade cores in our collection; The microlithic industry is however not so well developed. The reason may be attributed to the use of dolerite as raw material which is not suitable for the preparation of microliths. The industry is mainly based on the production of tiny flakes, scrapers, points and arrow-heads. The characteristic geometric types are not so well defined. The technique of the production of microlithic blades or bladelets is well testified by the presence of small blade flakes with strong mid-ridge. In the Garo Hills there is also evidence of the presence of a stone axe industry which is based on the production of unifacially flaked axes from flattish oval pebbles—a characteristic tradition of the Hoabinhian culture of South-east Asia (FIG. 1).

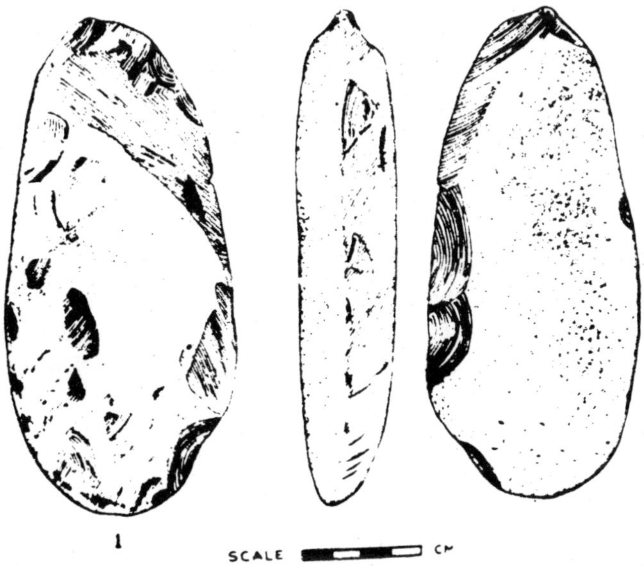

FIG. 1. *Hoabinhian type of stone axe from the Garo Hills*

Some Aspects of the Archaeological Evidence Relating to the Indus Script*

B. B. Lal

Jiwaji University, Gwalior

[*Received on 24 August 1973*]

INTRODUCTION

WITH the discovery of Harappa and Mohenjo-daro in the early twenties of this century an altogether unknown civilization was brought to light in the Indo-Pakistan subcontinent. Subsequent excavations at these two sites and at Chanhu-daro and the more recent work at Amri, Damb Sadaat, Gumla, Jalilpur, Kalibangan, Kot Diji, Lothal, Sarai Khola and Surkotada have added new dimensions to our knowledge of this civilization, called variously as the Indus Civilization or the Harappa Culture. Available evidence indicates that the Indus Civilization may have come into its own in the first half of the third millennium B.C., and may have continued till about the beginning of the next millennium.**

Like all other contemporary civilizations, the Indus Civilization also had a script of its own. Unfortunately, however, it has not been deciphered so far : all claims made in this respect have got to be treated with the utmost caution. In the present paper it is proposed to place before scholars some noteworthy aspects of the archaeological evidence regarding this script.

ORIGIN OF THE SCRIPT

For quite some time it was believed that the Indus Civilization was an import from western Asia. Researches, however, have not upheld this view. On the contrary, we now have evidence that by the beginning of the third millennium B.C. practically the entire Indus plain was already teeming with settlements which were fairly advanced in town-planning and knew metallurgy. The fortified sites of Kot Diji and Kalibangan may be cited as examples. It is, thus, probable that the Indus Civilization as such emerged in the Indus valley itself. The exact ancestry, however, has yet to be identified.

Like the Indus Civilization, the Indus script too seems to have originated on the Indus plains. Amri, for example, has long been known to have both pre-Harappan and Harappan settlements. Recent work[1] at the site has made the position still clearer: levels IA to ID are pre-Harappan, IIA and II B, intermediary and III A to III C, Harappan. The pre-Harappan levels have yielded potsherds which bear graffiti (FIG.1),[2] many of which are similar to those occurring on the pottery in subsequent levels which are intermediary (FIG.2, top row)[3] and Harappan (FIG.2, middle and lower rows).[4]

*Summary of the paper read at the Royal Asiatic Society Sesquicentenary Symposium on 'The Undeciphered Languages', held in London from 25th to 27th July 1973 and published here with the permission of the Society.

**The time-brackets used in this paper are broad and take into account the MASCA calibration as well.

[1] J. M. Casal, *Fouilles d'Amri* (Paris, 1964).

[2] *Ibid.*, fig. 46, nos. 63-67, fig. 53, nos. 132-136, fig. 61, nos. 194-198 and fig. 66, nos. 248 and 249.

[3] *Ibid.*, fig. 68, nos. 268-270 and fig. 72, nos. 305 and 306.

[4] *Ibid.*, fig. 81, no. 371 and fig. 90, nos. 463-467.

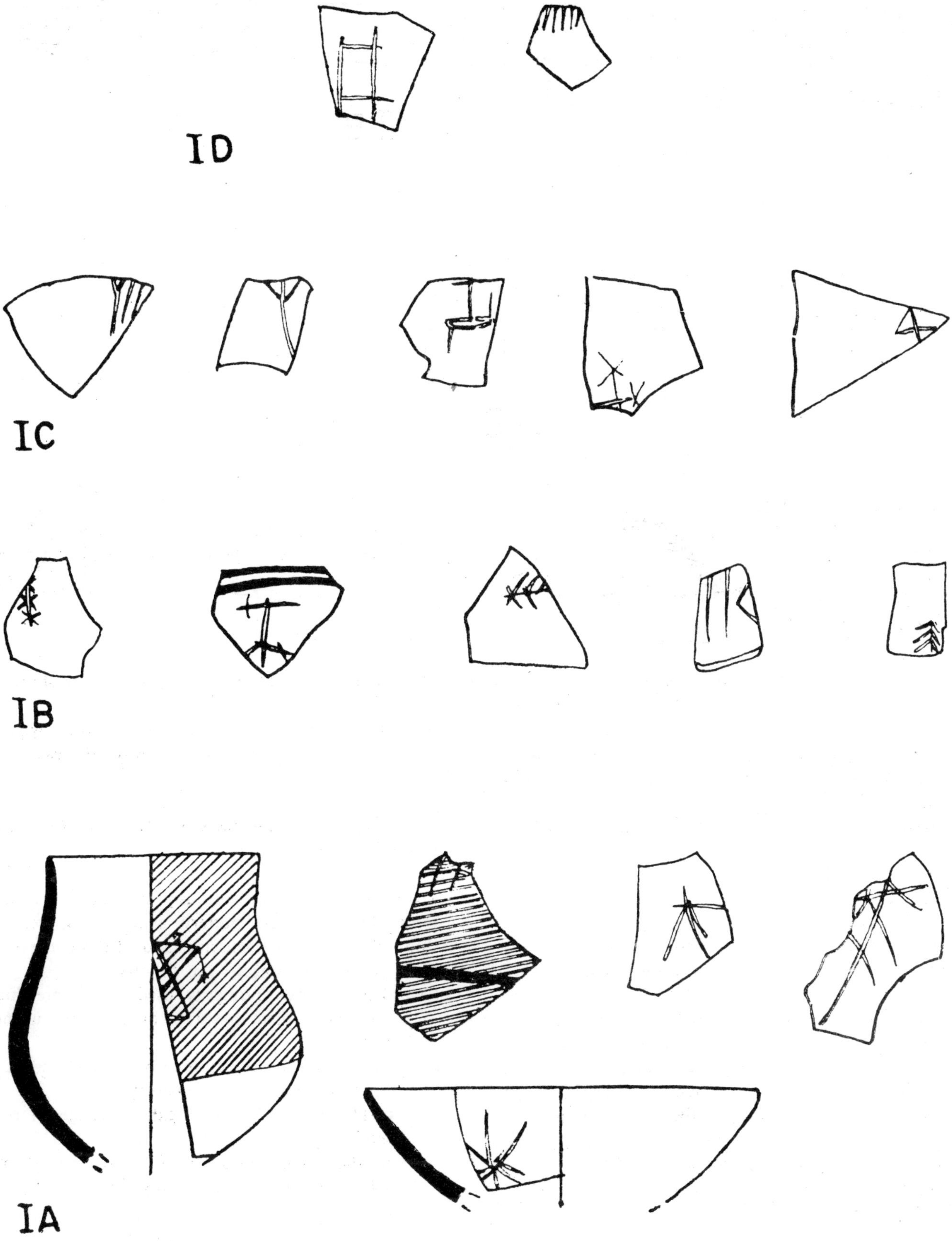

FIG. 1. *Graffiti on pottery from pre-Harappan (IA to ID) levels of Amri*

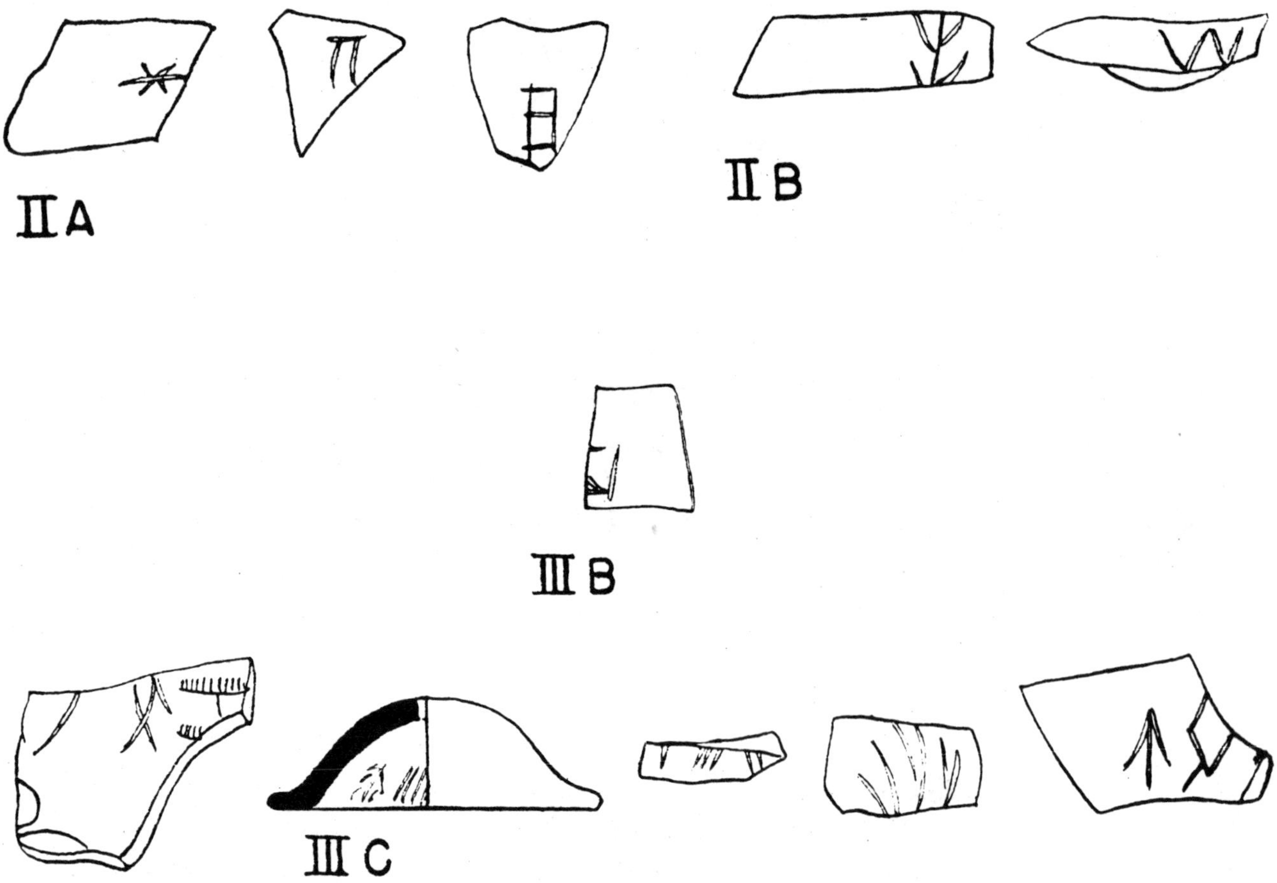

FIG. 2. *Graffiti on pottery from intermediary (IIA and IIB) and Harappan (IIIB and IIIC) levels of Amri*

These graffiti also form a part and parcel of the signary available on the Harappan seals. Thus, there is a posibility that the Harappan script originated in the pre-Harappan times. A similar indication is given by the evidence from Damb Sadaat (PL. III).[1]

DIRECTION OF WRITING

Amongst the inscribed potsherds found at Kalibangan there are two, the signs on which show overlaps. In one case (PL. VI A), the sign on the extreme left overrides the one next to it on the right and that, in turn, overrides the one further to the right. In the other case too, the same story is repeated, though the inscription is more fragmentary. The evidence thus shows that the sign on the extreme right was inscribed first and then came the ones successively to the left. This clearly establishes that the direction of writing in the Harappan script was from right to left. The second line, however, was boustrophedon though this was not necessarily always the case.

SOME OBSERVATIONS ON THE USE OF THE INDUS SEALS

The inscriptions occur variously on seals, sealings, copper/bronze objects, pottery, ivory sticks, etc. A study of the objects themselves and of the context of their occurrence suggests the following:

(i) The seals were primarily used for impressing, and hence their positives alone were meant to be read.

(ii) The sealings are essentially of clay and fall broadly under three categories.
(a)Those which actually sealed packages of one kind or another. This hypothesis is based on the physical evidence of the sealings themselves, as they bear impressions of seals

[1]W. A. Fairservis Jr., *Excavations in the Quetta Valley, West Pakistan* (New York, 1956), pl 14.

on the obverse and of reeds and cord on the reverse (PL. IV A). The hypothesis is also supported by the context of occurrence. For example, amidst the ruins of the warehouse at Lothal as many as seventy-one sealings were found. A further interesting observation in respect of the sealings recovered from the warehouse is that many of them bear identical inscriptions: in one case (PL. V D) there are as many as twelve examples with the same impression.

(b) Those bearing repetitive (votive ?) inscriptions. For example, at Kalibangan, as many as seven sealings bearing the same legend (PL. V A) have been found in the citadel area, the southern part of which has platforms on which are located 'fire-altars', wells, bathing pavements, etc., suggestive of rituals. The sealings are in the form of long strips of baked clay and do not have on the reverse any impression of packing material such as cloth, reed, thread, etc.

(c)Probable 'tokens'. Circular plano-convex pieces of clay, mostly unbaked, have been found to bear on the flat side a legend and/or an animal, there being no indication of the clay having come in contact with any packing material (PL. VI C). Such specimens may perhaps be regarded as 'tokens', say of X carried by Y to Z.

(iii) Categories (a) and (c) above would suggest that by and large it may be the names of individuals that are involved in the seals and sealings. A similar inference may perhaps be drawn from the inscriptions occurring on bronze/copper axes, chisels and tablets and on ivory sticks, Pottery, etc. Since the inscriptions are often divisible into 'blocks', it is just possible that the names consist of such parts as the place of origin of the family, the individual's personal name, his/her father's name, surname, etc.

SOME FURTHER OBSERVATIONS ON THE OCCURRENCE OF THE SEALS

A detailed study of the seals, sealings, inscribed pottery and other material excavated at Kalibangan is under way. Preliminary observations, however, are of some interest:

(i) A cylinder seal, bearing an inscription and depicting along with some human figures, a composite animal-*cum*-human figure (PL.V B), and a square seal, bearing an almost similar inscription and the same animal-*cum*-human figure (PL.V C), come from within a short distance of each other. Since cylinder seals are exotic to the Indus Civilization but were a common type in contemporary western Asia, could it be that in the concerned area there stayed a 'foreigner' who was using the seals for sealing goods he was sending out to his home country? In this context may also be recalled the occurrence of a 'Persian Gulf' seal at the port-town of Lothal.

(ii) The above-mentioned fact that two seals bearing an almost identical inscription and inter-connected motif come from the same area emphasizes the need for further examining a house-wise distribution of seals found at Harappa, Mohenjo-daro, etc. Perhaps something useful might turn up in the process.

THE V-LIKE SIGN: ITS PROBABLE GENESIS

Amongst the Indus signs is one which resembles the English letter V, with two slightly oblique strokes emerging from each of the upper ends of the arms. This sign occurs usually at the end of the inscriptions and has been taken to be a suffix by some of the decipherers. One of them[1] derives its shape from that of the boat, somehow (?) compressed up vertically. On this basis he assigns to it the phonetic value of '*ōṭa*', a word for boat in the Dravidian group of languages which he has chosen to read in the inscriptions. Using the principle of homophony, he equates the sign with *oṭa*,*-ōṭu* a comitative suffix in Tamil.

A study of the graffiti occurring on the potsherds at Kalibangan shows that the V-like symbol is a conventionalized form derivable most probably from the shape of a tall vase with a slightly concavo-convex profile and narrow base (cf. PL. VI B). Thus, one is afraid, the theory of equating it with the shape of a boat and consequently giving it the phonetic value of *oṭa*, *ōṭu* may not stand. Indeed, if the principle of shape-leading-to-sound, followed by that of homophony, must be applied, any suggested phonetic value for this sign has got to be nearer the sound for the word for a vase or pot than anything else.

[1]Asko Parpola, Seppo Koskenniemi, Simo Parpola and Pentti Aalto, *Decipherment of the Proto-Dravidian Inscriptions of the Indus Civilization: A First Announcement*, The Scandinavian Institute of Asian Studies, Special Publications, no. 1 (Copenhagen, 1969), pp. 21-22.

SURVIVAL OF THE INDUS SCRIPT

Did the Indus Civilization come to a sudden end through some catastrophe or did it decline gradually? Did it leave any vestiges behind? If so, what? These are some of the questions regarding the Indus Civilization to which no satisfactory answers are forthcoming. However, one thing seems to be most interesting and it is this. Most of the graffiti occurring on the pottery of the chalcolithic cultures of central India, Gujarat and northern Deccan, which are all post-Harappan in date (second millennium B.C.), and on the megalithic pottery of south India (PL. IV B), which is still later (first millennium B.C.), are the same as those on the Harappan Ware. Some of the graffiti on the 'Ochre Colour Ware' at Lal Qila, a site recently excavated in Uttar Pradesh, are also reminiscent of the Harappan ones. The Ochre Colour Ware falls broadly in the second millennium B.C. It is thus clear that at least some of the signs comprising the Indus script continued through time and space. What exactly is the significance of this observation cannot be stated in the present stage of our studies but the fact, such as it is should not be lost sight of by anyone attempting a decipherment of the script.

On the Origin of the Harappan Sign 

B.M. Pande

Archaeological Survey of India, New Delhi

[*Received on 3 September 1973*]

INTRODUCTORY

FOR the decipherment of the Harappan script, various kinds of analyses have been carried out by scholars, particularly in regard to the relative frequency and juxtaposition of signs, formation of blocks and contextual occurrence.[1] A study of the morphology of each Harappan sign and its analysis *per se*, however, does not seem to have been attempted by any scholar excepting Hunter.[2]

In the present paper we propose to analyze the the Harappan sign  (also rendered as ), and its variants  ,  ,  ,  ,  ,  , etc. The analysis is based on the data from Mohenjo-daro,[3] Harappa,[4] Chanhu-daro,[5] Lothal,[6] and Desalpur.[7] In the accompanying text-figures, we have included only a single example of a seal/sealing whereof more than one identical specimen have been found from the same site. It may also be pointed out at the outset that despite its desirability, corroboration by stratigraphical evidence has not been attempted due to obvious limitations.

APPROACH

The entire range of signs belonging to the  group of signs have been divided into three (broad) categories. These are:

(a) the basic sign  (FIG. 3) in which there are only two short vertical strokes drawn at right angles to the two parallel horizontal lines:

(b) the variants of the basic sign  in

[1]For references see, B.M. Pande and K. S. Ramachandran, *Bibliography of the Harappan Culture*, Field Research Projects (Miami, 1971). The more recent works are: *Proto-Indica : 1972* (Moscow, 1972) and the section on the Harappan script in (eds.), D.P. Agrawal and A.Ghosh, *Radiocarbon and Indian Archaeology*, Tata Institute of Fundamental Research (Bombay, 1973).

[2] G. R. Hunter, *The Scripts of Harappa and Mohenjodaro and their Connection with Other Scripts* (London, 1934).

[3]Sir John Marshall, *Mohenjo-daro and the Indus Civilization* (London, 1931); E.J.H. Mackay, *Further Excavations at Mohenjo-daro* (Delhi, 1938).

[4]Madho Sarup Vats, *Excavations at Harappa* (Delhi, 1940).

[5]Earnest J.H. Mackay, *Chanhu-daro Excavations 1935-36* (New Haven, 1943).

[6]*Indian Archaeology 1957-58—A Review*, pl. XIX B, bottom row.

[7]*Indian Archaeology 1963-64—A Review*, pl. VIII B, pp. 10-12.

which, instead of two, there are either three, four or five short vertical strokes drawn below. In this category are also included the examples wherein there is either no vertical stroke or only a single stroke; and

(c) the variants of the basic sign to which have been added strokes above and also those in which the blank space in between the two horizontal lines has been filled by oblique strokes, or the two short vertical strokes have been drawn but have not been joined to the lower horizontal line. It is very likely that in these cases different signs have been added to the main sign .

ANALYSIS

The available data have shown that the relative position of the sign in the inscriptions is not fixed and occupies the initial (FIG. 2, *2* and *11*), medial (FIG. 2, *3-10*, *13* and *14*) and terminal (FIG 2, *12*) positions. Barring an example from Harappa (FIG. 3, *6*), the sign does not recur in a single inscription. In this case, the sign occupies the initial and the sixth positions in the inscription. However, the sign in the initial position has been rendered as and in the second case, is followea by , a common sign occurring after the sign in most cases.

A second feature is the juxtaposition of the sign or , in a majority of cases, after the sign as can be seen in FIG. 2, *1-9*; FIG. 3, *1*, *5-8*, *10*, *14* and *15*. In FIG. 2, *10* and *11*, however, the sign is followed by the sign and . In nine cases, out of the tot... examples, the combined sign is followed by or its variants and, in other cases, by the signs , , , and . In the circular seal from Harappa (FIG. 2, *13*), in which the inscription seems to have been thus: ? , the sign is followed by the fish sign occurring twice. Thus, it becomes clear that the sign was used as an independent sign; however, the possibility of its connexion with the sign is not ruled out.

The position of the sign, *vis-a-vis* the same signs as the preceding or the succeeding ones, can be further seen in FIG. 3 where the sign has either none or one to five smaller vertical strokes in between the two outer ones, or where the sign occurs as , In these cases, again, the sign precedes, in a majority of cases, the sign or . In most of the rectangular steatite seals, the sign occurs as the initial one and is followed by the sign or its variant . The other combinations of the sign are with and where it occurs, alongwith , it is followed by , , , or . In FIG. 3, *9*, the sign is followed by . It may be mentioned that, in this case the space between the two horizontal lines joining the two outer lines has been filled in with oblique lines.

To the same class of signs belong the signs , , , , and as shown in the inscriptions in IG. 1, *7-10*, wherein the sign does not not occur as a simple sign, and has additional strokes, which perhaps represent its ligaturing with different signs.

The position of the sign in these examples varies: It appears singly (FIG 1, *10*) or at the first or the medial positions. In two cases, it is followed by the sign , or and, in one case by

PROBABLE ORIGIN OF THE SIGN

In a number of seals and sealings bearing three to six signs, the figure of a quadruped (dog?) forming part of the inscription can be seen. Out of the six examples (FIG. 1, *1-6*), the quadruped appears initially in four cases and, as the second sign in two cases. That the animal figure in each case is a stylized one seems to be more likely; its close similarity with the sign indicates the generic relationship between them, the quadruped figure being the original form of the sign .[1]

The identification of the animal figure as the likely original form of the sign is no doubt beset with certain difficulties, the chief among them being the lack of corroborative stratigraphical evidence to show the stylization in a sequential order. Besides, barring the seal nos. 2 and 4 in FIG. 1, the sign following the animal sign is not the same as in those inscriptions which contain the sign in its evolved form. The animal also, in nos. 5 and 6 in FIG. 1, perhaps faces left, whereas in the other cases the animal is shown facing right.

In the context of the process of stylization as envisaged by us in regard to the picture of a quadruped evolving into the sign we would like to cite the instance of a similar process of stylization of the gharial.[2] We would, however, hasten to add here the fact that perhaps the gharial does not form a part of the Harappan signary, unless we envisage the figure itself as forming a part of the inscription. This guess seems to be not unfounded since the gharial in some of these inscriptions has been shown alongwith the fish sign which is a common Harappan sign.

Mention may also be made here of another instance of the derivation of the common Harappan sign which seems to have evolved out of the bird figure. In this case, the original picture of the bird appears in the inscriptions alongwith other signs developing into the form and other variants, and, ultimately leading to the sign .[3]

[1] Hunter, *op. cit.*, pp. 111-12 and p. 175 containing Tables LVI and LVII. Hunter had also visualized the sign as representing the quadruped.

[2] Marshall, *op. cit.*, vol III, pl. CXVI, 20; Mackay, *op. cit.*, vol. II, pl. LXXXV, 133: R.E.M., Wheeler 'Harappa, 1946; the defences and cemetery R-37', *Ancient India*, no. 3 (1947), pl. LIIB, no. 1: for a similar example from Kalibangan, see, *Indian Archaeology 1961-62 - A Reveiw* pl. LXIX A, top right.

[3] A study of the origin of this sign is being published elsewhere.

KEY TO FIG. 1

Serial No.	Site/Locus	Object	Reference
1.	MOHENJO-DARO DK Area Bl. 9A House V Rm. 67 —15·7 ft.	Type B* SEAL (Silver) (Impression)	Mackay, *Mohenjo-daro*, pl. XCVI, no. 527 (DK 8406)
2.	MOHENJO-DARO DK Area Bl. 7 House IX Rm. 33 —10·4 ft	Type B SEAL (Steatite) (Impression)	Mackay, *Mohenjo-daro*, pl. LXXXVIII, no. 305 (DK 8041)
3.	MOHENJO-DARO DK Area Between Bls. 7 & 8 —10·3 ft.	Type B SEAL (Steatite) (Impression)	Mackay, *Mohenjo-daro*, pl. LXXXVIII, no. 313 (DK 3522)
4.	MOHENJO-DARO DK Area Bl. 9 House X Rm. 88 —8·4 ft.	Type B SEAL (Steatite) (Impression)	Mackay, *Mohenjo-daro*, pl. LXXXVII, no. 219 (DK 12182)
5.	MOHENJO-DARO —4′ 00″	Type B SEAL (Steatite) (Impression)	Marshall, *Mohenjo-daro*, pl. CXV, no. 544 (DK 3018)
6.	MOHENJO-DARO —1′ 4″	Type B SEAL (Steatite) (Impression)	Marshall, *Mohenjo-daro*, pl. CVIII, no. 150 (C 3155)
7.	MOHENJO-DARO DK Area Bl. 3 House V Rm. 8 —5·9 ft.	Type F SEAL (Steatite) (Impression)	Mackay, *Mohenjo-daro*. pl. LXXXIV, no. 92 (DK 3987)
8.	MOHENJO-DARO DK Area Bl. 1 House IV Rm. 30 —15·3 ft.	Type F SEAL (Steatite) (Impression)	Mackay, *Mohenjo-daro*, pl. XCVI, no. 515 (DK 5413)
9.	MOHENJO-DARO	Copper tablet	Hunter, pl. IV, no. 57
10.	MOHENJO-DARO	Copper tablet	Hunter, pl. III, no. 31

* The typological classification referred to in these tables is the same as given in the original reports of the excavators.

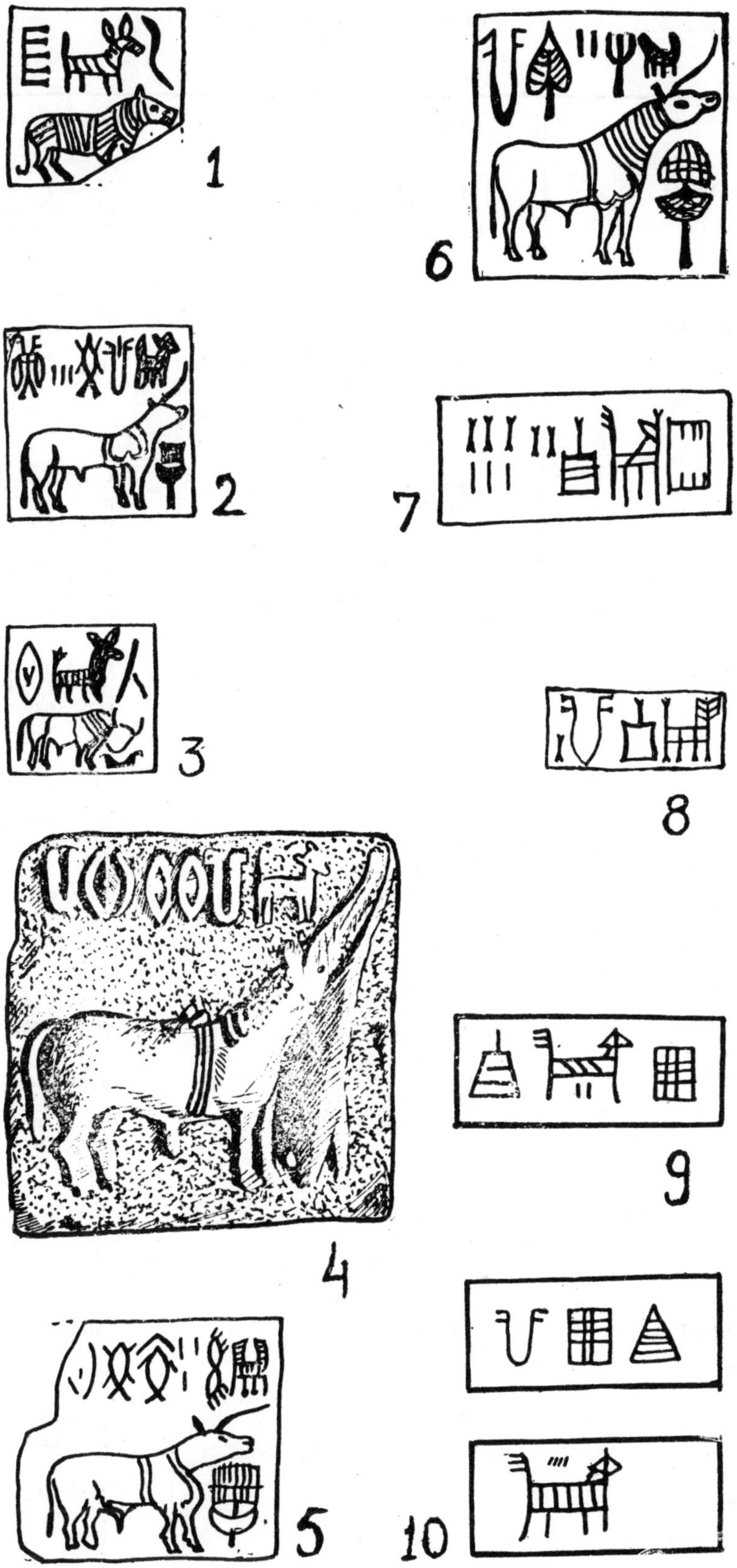

FIG. 1

KEY TO FIGURE 2

Serial No.	Site/Locus	Object	Reference
1.	MOHENJO-DARO DK Area Bl. 18 House— Rm. 17 —7·1 ft.	Type B SEAL (Steatite) (Impression)	Mackay, *Mohenjo-daro*, pl. LXXXV, no. 144 (DK 11026)
2	MOHENJO-DARO DK Area Bl. 1 House I Rm. 17 —18·0 ft.	Type F SEAL (Steatite)	Mackay, *Mohenjo-daro*, pl. XCVIII, no. 599 (DK 7288)
3.	HARAPPA Mound F —5′ 2″	Type h (Faience)	Vats, *Harappa*, pl. C, no. 661 (field no. 11467)
4.	HARAPPA Mound F —4′ 10″	Type a SEAL (Steatite) (Impression)	Vats, *Harappa*, pl. LXXXVII, no. 76, (field no. 1697)
5.	MOHENJO-DARO DK Area Bl. 17 House III Rm. 29 —4·0 ft.	Type B SEAL (Steatite) (Impression)	Mackay, *Mohenjo-daro*, pl. LXXXIII, no. 29 (DK 10895)
6.	DESALPUR Pd. I	SEAL (Impression)	*IAR*, 1963-64, pl. VIII B
7.	MOHENJO-DARO E Section 2′ 0″	Type B SEAL (Steatite) (Impression)	Marshall, *Mohenjo-daro*, pl. CVIII, no. 176 (E 96)
8.	MOHENJO-DARO HR Area 4′ 0″	Type B SEAL (Steatite) (Impression)	Marshall, *Mohenjo-daro*, pl. CVIII, no. 161 (HR 5630)
9.	HARAPPA Mound F 6′ 9″	Type ae SEALING (Terracotta)	Vats, *Harappa*, pl. XCIV, no. 334 (field no. 4532). Two more examples from 4′ 0″ and 6′ 9″
10.	HARAPPA Mound F 13′ to 14′ b.s.	Type o SEAL (Steatite) (Impression)	Vats, *Harappa*, pl. XCVII, no. 573 (field no. 11854)
11.	MOHENJO-DARO 3′ 0″	Type B SEAL (Impression)	Marshall, *Mohenjo-daro*, pl. CXI, no. 329 (HR 4348)
12.	LOTHAL	SEALING (Terracotta)	*IAR*, 1957-58, pl. XIX B bottom row
13.	HARAPPA Mound F —10′ 3″	Type ai SEAL (Faience) (Impression)	Vats, *Harappa*, pl. XCV, no. 371, (field no. 12538)
14.	MOHENJO-DARO DK Area 1′ 6″	Type B SEAL (Steatite) (Impression)	Marshall, *Mohenjo-daro*, pl. CVII, no. 142 (DK 3054)

FIG. 2

KEY TO FIG. 3

Serial No.	Site/Locus	Object	Reference
1.	CHANHU-DARO +9·2 ft.	SEAL (Steatite) (Impression)	Mackay, *Chanhu-daro*, pl. LII, no. 30
2.	—	—	Hunter, p. 175, Table LVI'2
3.	MOHENJO-DARO DK Area		Hunter, pl. XVII, no. 341. The inscription is in two lines, the last two signs being in second rowDK 1522.
4.	MOHENJO-DARO VS Area		Hunter, pl. XXIV, no. 456 (VS 456)
5.	HARAPPA Mound F 8′ 6″ b.s.	Type a SEAL (Steatite) (Impression)	Vats, *Harappa*, pl. LXXXIX, no. 119 (Field. no. 2281)
6.	HARAPPA Mound F 4′ 0″ b.s.	Type a SEAL (Steatite) (Impression)	Vats, *Harappa*, pl. LXXXVI, no. 23 (Field no. 180)
7.	MOHENJO-DARO DK Area	Copper Tablet	Marshall, *Mohenjo-daro*, pl. CXVII, no. 5 Another example, not included, pl. CXVII, no. 6
8.	MOHENJO-DARO DK Area Bl. 9A House V Rm. 75 —15·7 ft.	Type D Silver	Mackay, *Mohenjo-daro*, pl. XCVI, no. 528 (DK 6698)
9.	MOHENJO-DARO DK Area Between Bls. I (V) and —13·0 ft.	Type F SEAL (Steatite) (Impression)	Mackay, *Mohenjo-daro*, pl. XCIV no. 428 (DK 5820)
10.	MOHENJO-DARO DK Area Bl. 1 House I Rm. 15 —13·9 ft.	Type F SEAL (Steatite) (Impression)	Mackay, *Mohenjo-daro*, pl. XCV, no. 470 (DK 5708)
11.	MOHENJO-DARO DK Area First Street (10) – 15·1 ft.	Type D SEAL (Steatite) (Impression)	Mackay, *Mohenjo-daro*, pl. XCVI, no. 508 (DK 8089)
12.	MOHENJO-DARO Bet. Bls. 10A & 11 —11·1 ft.	Type D SEAL (Steatite) (Impression)	Mackay, *Mohenjo-daro*, pl. LXXXIX, no. 339 (DK 5663)
13.	MOHENJO-DARO E Section 2′ 0″	Type D SEAL (Steatite) (Impression)	Marshall, *Mohenjo-daro*, pl. CXIII, no. 413 (E 2039)
14.	MOHENJO-DARO DK Area Bl. 1 House I Rm. 12 —10·3 ft.	Type F SEAL (Steatite) (Impression)	Mackay, *Mohenjo-daro*, pl. LXXXVIII, no. 308 (DK 5429)
15.	MOHENJO-DARO DK Area BL. 7 House VI Rm. 76 —9·9 ft.	Type B SEAL (Steatite) (Impression)	Mackay, *Mohenjo-daro*, pl. LXXXVIII, no. 296 (DK 7200)
16.	MOHENJO-DARO DK Area Bl. 9 House VII Rm. 47 —8·3 ft.	Type D SEAL (Steatite) (Impression)	Mackay, *Mohenjo-daro*, pl. LXXXVII, no. 220 (DK 5748)

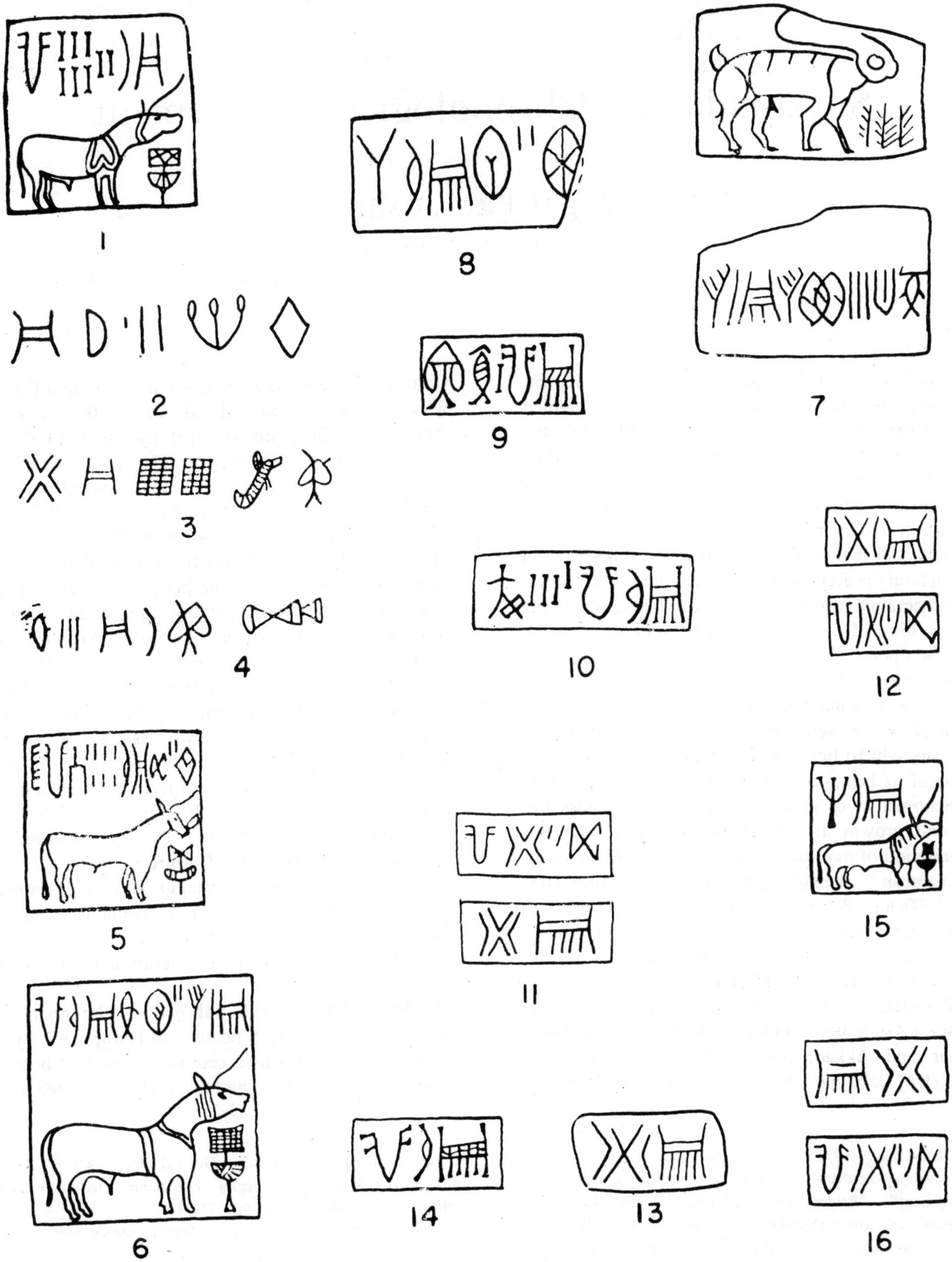

FIG. 3

Surkotada: A Chronological Assessment

Jagat Pati Joshi

Archaeological Survey of India New Delhi

[*Received on 18 February 1974*]

At Surkotada, a Harappan settlement in Kutch, Gujarat, the entire habitational deposit is divided into three Sub-periods called IA, IB and IC. These sub-divisions are based largely on ceramic evidence. The only common factor in the pottery of all the Sub-periods is the Harappan red ware, which though decreases in percentage in the later two Sub-periods, still remained an important ceramic tradition throughout the occupation. Another noteworthy feature of the ceramic evidence is the occurrence, in all the Sub-periods, of some other ceramic traditions which may be a pointer to different ethnic or cultural groups living with the Harappans in complete co-existence. Besides, a large number of crudely-shaped bone tools, some of which were probably used for agriculture, were brought to light for the first time. The site, by virtue of its being in continuous occupation, presents a phenomenon of permanent settlement, besides the inherent growth and development[1] along with the assimilation of new ideas and people, which has given a dynamism to the culture-development between 2100 and 1700 B.C. Before a detailed discussion on the chronology of the various Sub-periods is attempted, it will be worth while to sum up the chronology of the Harappa Culture as it stands today.

Wheeler, in 1947, basing his comparative study on the West Asian finds, more particularly those from Sumer and Akkad, postulated an inclusive time-bracket of 2500 B.C. to 1500 B.C. for the Harappa Culture with a strong focus on the Sargonid Period which is now closely dated to 2370-2284 B.C.[2] Agrawal in 1964, 'emboldened by the C-14 determinations obtained from some Harappan sites,' and strongly refuting the relative archaeological chronology of the Harappa Culture provided by Wheeler, Mode and Langdon, proposed a shorter time-bracket of *circa* 2300-1750 B.C. for the metropolitan centres and 2200-1700 B.C. for the peripheral sites.[3] Ever since then the shorter chronology, proposed by Agrawal, is being accepted by scholars. Allchin[4] also feels that the Indus Civilization should have endured for not more than four to five centuries. We are, however, inclined to accept this time-bracket with some reservations of unknown variables. [See also MASCA corrections]. Recently, Mandal, 'on the basis of emergent indications' has proposed a time span of 2500 to 1700 B.C. with every possibility of an extension on the earlier side. This span however is for the Central Harappa Culture.[5]

Keeping in view this background of Harappan chronology and the general traits available at Surkotada, we have to consider the period of occupation of this site. A period-wise consideration of the entire evidence is as below.

Sub-Period IA: In this Sub-period, Harappan red ware is 93%, the rest being non-Harappan. Most of the Harappan forms excepting the pointed bottom goblet are available. The typical Harappan red ware

[1]Allchin has rightly pointed out that "at almost every site of Harappan period there is at least some evidence of internal development"; Bridget and Raymond Allchin, *The Birth of Indian Civilization* (Harmmondsworth, 1969), p. 142; also Gregory Possehl, 'The Mohenjo-daro floods: a reply', *American Anthropologist*, vol. 69, no. 1 (Feb. 1967) pp. 33-34.

[2]R.E.M. Wheeler, 'Harappa 1946: The Defences and Cemetery R 37', *Ancient India*, No. 3 (Delhi, 1947), pp. 78-83; also, Sir Mortimer Wheeler *The Indus Civilization* (3rd edition, Cambridge, 1968), pp. 110-126.

[3]D. P. Agrawal, *The Copper Bronze Age in India* (Delhi, 1971), pp. 71-78.

[4]Allchin, *op. cit.* (1968), p. 140.

[5]D. Mandal, *Radio Carbon Dates and Indian Archaeology* (Allahabad, 1972), pp. 57 and 77.

shapes are comparable to Mohenjo-daro, Chanhu-daro, Harappa, Lothal, Rangpur IIA, Kalibangan (Harappan), Amri IIIa, b, c and Mundigak III and Kotdiji. The design repertoire is also comparable to these sites. Geometric and vegetal designs are also similar to classical Harappan, while landscape scenes are also available.

In the Harappan red ware some forms have similarities with pre-Harappan Kot Diji, Kalibangan and Amri, e.g., (i) low-necked jars with a broad band at the neck in black or tan slip, (ii) basins with or without cord impression, (iii) bowls, (iv) jars, (v) bowls on stand, (vi) squat dish on stand, (vii) flat dish-on-stand with cylindrical stem, and (viii) storage jars. The aforesaid comparative material certainly shows some affinities in the pre-Harappan sub-stratum of Sind and Baluchistan. A polytone cream-slipped red ware (PL. VIII A) has low necked jars, medium-sized convex bowls, and a few bowls on cylindrical stands. The designs are mostly geometric excepting a bird or fish. Though the cream-slipped red ware (PL. VIII B) is available from Amri, Bampur, Siah II levels of Kalat, and southern Turkemenia, the Surkotada material Sahr-i-Sokhta does not offer exact comparisons. However, similarities of a general nature are indicated. It shows a local adaptation of widespread ceramic tradition in the third and early second millennium B.C. in the areas of eastern Iran, Baluchistan and Sind. The polychrome red ware, wherein the usual black or brown, besides the white colour has been used in paintings, consists of low-necked round-bodied jars in varying sizes and few bowls. The design repertoire comprises geometric patterns and wavy lines, etc. This ware is broadly comparable with such pre-Harappan wares like Kechibeg white or dark reddish slip, the Jangal polychrome Fabric A of pre-Harappan Kalibangan and Saraikhola, Period II. It must be stated that this ware has only a superficial resemblance, there are many divergencies indicating a local adaptation of a widespread pre-Harappan tradition. The Reserved Slip Ware found at Surkotada is (PL. VII) represented by many fragments and also some forms which are not reported from elsewhere e.g., hole-mouthed oil bottles, concave necked jars with rounded body and a shallow basin. Reserved Slip Ware is reported from a large number of sites in Kutch, Lothal A (Phase IIB), pre-Prabhas deposits of Somnath, Sargonid levels of Brak, in the Khabur valley, Akkad and Nineveh in west Asia. This evidence furnishes a well-dated horizon of the Sargonid levels i.e., 2371-2316 B.C., for Surkotada and as such is of considerable significance. The deep red burnt amber slipped red ware with a waxy feel does not show any parallels with known ceramics of this period.

A study of the ceramic-content of Sub-period IA shows that the Harappan Culture of the mature type was associated with certain pottery traditions of earlier vintage which constitute broadly a widespread basal tradition prevaling in third millennium B.C. in the area, and it applies to Surkotada in Kutch as well. So far as the antiquities of Period IA are concerned they are typically Harappan and include seals, sherds painted with pictographic script, terracotta cakes, painted and unpainted bangles, wheels, cart-frames, sling stones, saddle querns, copper bangles, rings and spearhead, long ribbon flakes of chert and lapis-lazuli, carnelian, faience and terracotta beads. Saw-edged and sickle type blades, reported from Amri, Siah-damb, Sahr-i-Sokhta, Surab in Kalat and available at Surkotada Period IA, have a very early date Similarly, tanged blade and shouldered blades are also of early horizon.[1] Besides this there is complete absence of bulls and Mother Goddess so commonly known in the Indus Culture.

A large number of crudely made bone tools consisting of scrapers, piercers and points, mostly from split shaft, shows an earlier bone tool tradition. Some such bone tools are available at earlier dated sites like Sahr-i-Sokhta, Damb-Sadaat I, II and III, Kile Ghul Mohammed I-IV, Anjira and Siah-damb in Kalat and lastly at Periano Ghundai.

Even the tradition of pot burials with charred bones kept in pots has earlier parallels.[2] A pot in one of the burials with horizontally drawn grooves have Kot-dijian affinity. In the field of architecture

[1]"Stone blades of the Early Harappan period are marked by serrated edges as found at Amri IA and IC"; M. R. Mughal, *The Early-Harappan Period in the Greater Indus Valley and Northern Baluchistan* (Ph. D. dissertation, University of Pennsylvania, 1970), p. 142,; also see, Jean-Marie Casal, *Fouiles d' Amri* (Paris, 1964), fig. 115, nos. 5 and 10A; Beatrice de Cardi, 'Excavation and Reconnaissance in Kalat, West Pakistan', *Pakistan Archaeology*, no. 2 (1965), pp. 93-123; and Maurizio Tosi, 'Excavation at Shahr-i-Sokhta, a Chalcolithic settlement in the Iranian Seistan, Preliminary Report on the First Campaign October-December 1967', *East and West*, vol. XVIII (1968), p. 63.

[2]Post Cremation burials are met with at Periano Ghundai (*circa* 2500 B.C.), Mehi (*circa* 2000 B.C.), Shahi-Tump (*circa* 1800 B.C.) and Sutkagendor (*circa* 2200-1900 B.C.), S.P. Gupta, *Disposal of the Dead and Physical Types in Ancient India* (Delhi, 1972), pp. 33-35; M.R. Mughal, *Present State of Research on the Indus Valley Civilization* (Karachi, 1973), pp. 7-15.

the raising of the ground level, the building of fortification around the citadel and the residential annexe, bath-rooms and drains, street drains and the use of standard size of bricks (ratio 1: 2: 4) is amature Harappan tradition. The feature of fortification is available at Harappa, Kalibangan, Alimurad, Sutkagendor, Sotka Khoh, Desalpur and Lothal. However the tradition of the use of stone and mud bricks and lumps in construction has an 'Early Indus' tradition. The rampart of Period IA bears testimony to this. Taking the entire relative evidence into account one cannot but feel that the material remains of Period IA indicate an early 'Indus Horizon' of third and early second millennium B.C.

Let us now examine the absolute dates provided by C-14 determination, measured by the Tata Institute of Fundamental Research, Bombay, based on the radiocarbon half-life value of 5730 years. For B.C./A.D. scale, 1950 has been taken as a reference year. There are three C-14 dates for period IA.

TF-1305. 3890 ± 95 (4005 ± 100) (2055 B.C.) Charcoal; trench ZA1, qd 2, Citadel area; layer 19, depth 7·25 m. below surface; earliest level of Sub-period IA.

TF-1310. 2810±95 (3920±100) 1970 B.C.) Charcoal; trench ZA1, qd 2, centre of Citadel area; Layer 11; depth 4·6 m below surface; latest level of Sub-period IA.

TF-1304 and 1309. 3645±90 (3755 ± 90) (1805 B.C.) Charcoal; trench ZA1, qd 2, centre of citadel area; layers 18A and 20; depth 6·6 to 7·15 m. below surface. Since the sample is mixed it is not taken into consideration due to its inconsistency.[1]

As per the C-14 date the Sub-period IA of Surkotada is to be dated between 2055 B.C. to 1970 B.C. or if we take the earliest date of Period IB, 1940 B.C. (TF-1295 to be discussed later). These dates are in conformity with more or less similar dates from Mohenjo-daro, Kotdiji, Lothal, Kalibangan and do indicate an earlier to mature phases of the Harappa Culture. Of course, the absolute dating has to be taken with caution for Period IA and we cannot ignore the mingling of the pre-Harappan elements and the availability of Reserved slip ware, dating to 2371-2316 B.C. It appears that the movement of Harappans to Kutch took place at an early stage by *circa* 2300 B.C. when Surkotada was established; the waning pre-Harappans or early Harappan folks of Sind region, of course, in a small number with Harappans came and colonized, Kutch. The Kalibangan evidence, particularly in KLB-2, wherein the pre-Harappans continued upto mid-levels and then vanished away does not preclude such a possibility. Similar position is available at Kotdiji and Amri.[2] Thapar has rightly said: "It would appear that the Indus Civilization could be a natural evolution through diffusion or interaction from some industries of the substratum but the evolution seems to be complete when the distinctive culture came to the sub-continent in the form we see it at Mohenjo-daro, Kalibangan. . . may be the result of an expansive movement of village communities sharing between themselves basic elements but evolving their patterns in each region. This would perhaps explain the various ramifications within this sub-stratum." Keeping in view the above, the chronological horizon of Period IA has to be seen[3]

Sub-period IB : During this period the Harappan ceramics included a larger amount of buff ware sherds. The footed Indus goblet, absent in Period IA, was also found.

The coarse red ware (35-70%), which is the main ceramic ware of this Sub-period has Harappan adaptation on shapes in it. The non-Harappan forms include deep basins with incurved rim and channel handled bowls. The channel handled bowl is not available in Saurashtra but its profusion in IB of Desalpur is significant. Generally speaking, the coarse red ware itself marks a later date in the Harappan assemblage in Saurashtra and Sind. The predominance of this ware is significant and marks the arrival of a new folk of this ware on the site.

The sporadic occurrence of exotic wares like polychrome red ware, polytone ware and the Reserved Slip Ware shows a trickling of an early tradition and nothing more. So far as the antiquities are concerned all the Harappan antiquities are available. In the upper levels of the Sub-period, however a blade industry on chalcedony appears. Terracotta cakes and a heavy celt of copper and other copper objects are some significant finds besides crudely made bone tools of the type found in the earlier Sub-period.

There is not much change in architecture. As a matter of fact the same area of Harappans was continued. The size of the mud bricks continued to

[1]Earlier it was reported to belong to Sub-period IB; See Jagat Pati Joshi, 'Exploration in Kutch and Excavation at Surkotada and New Light on Harappan Migration', *Journal of the Oriental Institute, Baroda*, vol. XXII, nos. 1-2 (Sept.-Dec., 1972), p. 137.

[2]Walter A. Fairservis Jr., *The Roots of Ancient India*, (London, 1971), p. 183.

[3]Comments by B. K. Thapar on A. Ghosh, 'The Indus Civilization. It origins, Authors, Extent and Chronology', in (eds.), M. S. Mate and V. N. Mishra, *Indian Prehistory* : 1964 (Poona, 1965), p.137.

be $10 \times 20 \times 40$ cms (ratio 1:2:4).

An assessment of the cultural equipment of this Sub-period shows that besides the presence of coarse red ware in a substantial quantity there does not seem to be any material change in life. The deposit of 1.60 m. belonging to Sub-period IB does not indicate a very long span of habitational activity.

The entire evidence shows an assimilation of new trends into the Harappan Culture and its continuance, of course with a decrease, at the site.

One carbon-14 date is available for this Sub-period. TF-1295. 3635±95 (3770±95) (1940 B.C.) Carbon; Trench G1,qd 3, residential annexe; layer 8, depth 2 m below surface, early level of Sub-period IB.[1]

A C-14 date for the earliest levels of the latter Sub-period indicates *circa* 1800 B.C. as the end of Sub-period IB. The end of Period IB is evidenced by a huge fire at the site but the succeeding Sub-period IC does not show a culture break.

In Sub-Period IC the Harappan red ware continues; rather it gets a fresh lease of life showing some new influx of more Harappans. Some deterioration in forms and contents could be discerned. The Indus goblet increases and a mortar funnel of Jhukar levels of Sind appears. For the first time, flat-based, bulbous bodied bowls, jars, with a bottle neck and a hole mouth became common. The pottery lacks naturalistic patterns, and compares with late Harappan assemblages. The coarse red ware continues in this Sub-period with lowered frequency and the new shapes in this ware are (1) large dish with an internally clubbed rim, (2) perforated long handled bowls, (3) perforated double long handled bowls with incised concentric circles and shallow punches, and (4) short stud handled bowls. The appearance of short stud handled bowls in IC is very interesting as it occurs in Rangpur IIA and at Lothal from the earliest levels.

The forms in the coarse ware are almost similar to the types of ware associated with the black-and-red ware of Ahar. In black-and-red ware, the high necked jars, bowls and bases are akin to Ahar and Lothal, in addition to the short stud handled bowl of Lothal, The design repertoire shows a poor affinity. While on the onehand black-and-red ware connects it with Lothal and Ahar but there appears to be a chronological gap so far Lothal is concerned suggesting a movement of black-and-red ware people during Period IC from Saurashtra to Surkotada and Ahar to west.

The antiquities are typically Harappan, including terracotta cakes and copper objects e.g., chisels, a drill and arrow head. The short blade industry is quite prolific. The mid levels of Sub-period IC have yielded considerable quantity of carnelian beads including two hoards. The rampart of dressed stones, bastions and an elaborate gateway complex have Harappan influences. The building of houses very close to the rampart even in this Period is an early tradition of Kotdiji which in turn is comparable to Anatolian and west Asian sites as suggested by Clarke and Piggott.[2] However, the streets are not straight. Drains are also available. Mud bricks have scarcely been used and has the same size of $10 \times 20 \times 40$ cm. Use of baked bricks of the size of $8 \times 16 \times 32$ cm. is also in evidence on the top of one of the bastions. A large community oven is a significant find. A terracotta seal without animal representation is also available from this Sub-period.

An overall picture of the cultural equipment of Sub-period IC shows Harappan influences of no mean importance especially the contacts with the contemporary black-and-red cultures of Saurashtra and Ahar.

While the white-painted black-and-red ware is available at Lothal from the earliest levels along with the Harappan Culture and also at Rangpur where it continues throughout, this Ware is available only in Period IC at Surkotada. At Desalpar too, this ware occurs only in Period IB. The question arises why such a chronological gap exists between Surkotada and Lothal. The possible explanation available at present seems to be that at Lothal along with the Harappans the white-painted black-and-red ware remained in a subservient form but by *circa* 1700 B.C. with the decay of Harappan culture in Saurashtra it got a fresh lease of life and started moving to Kutch. It is also possible that at the same time with its remote connections with the Banas Valley, the white-painted black-and-red ware culture got a fresh impetus in movement and expansion. It may indicate the coming to power of a people represented by the white-painted black-and-red ware who remained in a subjugated state during the hey days of the Harappans and started a mass expansion by *circa* 1700 B.C. in western India. Change over to complete stone

[1]On correlation of strata, it is now found that TF-1295 belongs to the earliest level of Sub-period IB and not to the top levels of Sub-period IA as reported earlier, Joshi, *op. cit.* (1972). p. 137.

[2]M. S. Mate, 'Harappan Fortifications—a Study', ***Studies in Indian Archaeology***, Professor H. D. Sankalia Felicitation Volume (Bombay, 1970), p. 79.

architecture, short blade industry may tend to support this view.

Now let us examine the four C-14 dates for this Sub period.

TF-1297. 3635±95 (3740±95) (1790 B.C.)
Charcoal; trench Cl, qd. 4, centre of Citadel area; pit sealed by layer 3; depth 2·1 m below surface; mid level of Sub-period IC.

TF-1311. 3625±90 (3720±90) (1780 B.C.)
Charcoal; trench ZA1 1, qd. 2, centre of the Citadel area; Layer 4; depth 2·4 m below surface; an early level of Sub-period IC.

TF-1294. 3620±95 (3730±100) (1780 B.C.)
Charcoal; trench XCl, qd. 3; Citadel area; Layer 3; depth 2·7 m. below surface; late level of Sub-period IC.

TF-1307. 3510±105 (3610±100) (1660 B.C.)
Charcoal; trench XA1, qd. 1; Layer 5; depth 1·6 m. below surface, citadel area; late level of Sub-period IC. Thus the entire span of Period IC is from 1790 B.C. to 1660 B.C.

These carbon dates are more or less in conformity with the late phase of the Harappa Culture as evidenced at Mohenjo-daro, Rojdi and Lothal and also from Ahar IA and IB.

The emergent picture after an evaluation of relative chronology and absolute dating suggests that the entire culture range at Surkotada is well within 2300[1] B.C. to 1750 B.C. with likelihood of a later end of the bracket. The earlier date for the beginning could be postulated due to the presence of early Indus elements in Sub-period IA and close proximity of Kutch which is only about 400 km. away from the sites in Sind. This could be possible due to the early migration along the land routes. The Harappan influences at Ahar, discerned by Sankalia[2] and the availability of black-and-red ware at Surkotada and more recently in north Gujarat does suggest a contact with Rajasthan during movements of such cultures at a late stage of the Harappan Culture, which is obvious in the changing broad matrix of culture in *circa* 1800 B.C. to 1700 B.C. in western India without giving any clue to Aryan expansion as envisaged by Agrawal basing his evidence on White-Painted Black-and-red Ware of Banas culture.[3]

[1]This has now been confirmed by a recent C-14 date of a charcoal sample from early levels of period IA: **PRL-85.** 4140±133 (4265±135) (2315 B.C.).

[2]H. D. Sankalia, S. B. Deo and Z.D. Ansari, *Excavations at Ahar (Tambavati)* (Poona, 1969), pp. 221-22.

[3]D.P. Agrawal, 'C-14 dates, Banas Culture and the Aryans', *Current Science*, vol. 35, no. 5 (March, 5, 1968), pp. 114-17; also see, B. K. Thapar, 'The Aryans: A Reapraisal of the Problem', *India's Contribution to World Thought and Culture*, Vivekananda Commemoration Volume (Madras, 1970), p. 153.

Subsistence Pattern of an Early Farming Community of Western India

M. K. Dhavalikar and Gregory L. Possehl

Deccan College, Pune, and the University Museum, Pennsylvania

(*Received on 23 September 1973*)

INTRODUCTION

CULTURAL remains of early farming communities in western India were first discovered in the late forties. Systematic explorations during the last two decades have shown that these early farming settlements are distributed in the semi-arid black cotton soil zone of central and western India and the Deccan, the actual location being on or near the rivers. The cultures represented by these settlements are characterized by a fine wheel-made black-on-red painted pottery associated with a coarse red/grey handmade ware. These people had a specialized blade-flake industry of chalcedony and other siliceous material, but also used copper, though on a restricted scale. Their houses, either rectangular or circular on plan, were constructed of dwarf mud walls and wattle-and-daub. They cultivated grains like wheat, rice, and probably also *jowar*. They domesticated cattle, sheep and goat. These cultures can be dated, on the basis of radiocarbon determinations, to the latter half of second millennium B.C.[1]

Almost all the excavations conducted in this region during the last two decade were small-scale digs with the defined objective of building up a cultural sequence. However, large-scale excavations have recently been planned by Professor H.D. Sankalia at Inamgaon, a small village about 85 km east of Pune (Maharashtra) on the right bank of the river Ghod. The site was found to be a single-culture one and as such afforded possibilities of exposing the material remains of the settlement.[2]

The occupation at Inamgaon can be divided into the following three cultural periods with an appreciable overlap in between each.

Period I (*c*.1600-1300 B.C.)—Malwa Culture
Period IIA (*c*.1300-1000 B.C.)—Early Jorwe Culture
Period IIB (*c*.1000-700 B.C.)—Late Jorwe Culture

The excavations have laid bare large structural remains, including one house belonging to the Malwa period and a number of houses of the Early Jorwe and the Late Jorwe periods. The houses of the Early Jorwe people were quite large (5·50×3 m.) and were rectangular on plan (PL. IX). They were constructed by dwarf mud-walls and wattle-and-daub supported by strong wooden posts. The floor of the house was repaired quite frequently. Inside the house were found remains of the hearth and other cultural material of the occupants. A noteworthy feature of this period is the burial inside the house. The adults were buried in large pits while children were buried in two urns, placed horizontally mouth to mouth, usually in the north-south direction.

The houses of the Late Jorwe period were circular on plan (diameter: 2-2·50 m), in sharp contrast to those of the Early Jorwe Period. They had walls of reed screen plastered with mud on both sides. The houses were built so close to each other that they hardly left a small passage in-between the two. The burials, both extended and urn, continued in this period.

The pottery of all the three periods is quite dis-

[1] M. K. Dhavalikar, 'Daimabad—a rediscovery', *Puratattva*, no. 3 (1968-69), pp. 34-43; also see, 'A prehistoric deity of western India', *Man*, vol. V, no.1 (1970), p. 131 ff.

[2] The work, is being executed by Dr. M. K. Dhavalikar and Dr. Z. D. Ansari of the Deccan College Postgraduate and Research Institute, Pune.

tinctive. The Malwa Ware is characterized by a creamish slip over which designs are painted in black. The Jorwe Ware has a red wash over which geometrical patterns are painted in black. The most characteristic shapes in this Ware are a spouted jar and a carinated bowl. This pottery continues to occur in the Late Jorwe Period when it becomes extremely coarse in fabric. Some new shapes such as the channel-spouted bowl came into vogue during this Period. Associated with this is a hand-made red/grey ware represented by large urns and the black-and-red ware which possibly was an import from the south. Evidence regarding the religion of the people was also brought to light. The people worshipped a mother-goddess[1] and occasionally a male god,[2] terracotta figurines of which have been recovered.

Besides, the excavations also revealed the late phase of the Jorwe Culture which has not so far been found at any other site, and which can be dated to *circa* 1000-700 B.C.

SUBSISTENCE

In an effort to measure the impact which these cultures made on their environment we have attempted to quantify some of the data on subsistence. Our method has been to take population sizes which are felt to be the outside reasonable limits for Inamgaon, the largest site of the Jorwe Culture. From here a diet has been suggested. This rest on archaeological data for most of the items within it, but the proportions are obviously our own. From these two pieces of information and crop yields it has been possible to estimate the amount of farm land and the number of cattle which a settlement such as that at Inamgaon required for the subsistence of its people. Each stage in this process of reasoning has its pitfalls and assumptions. But, if reasonable limits are establised, and if some thought is given to the requirements, we feel an adequate picture can emerge. This will be a gross image to be sure, and resolution will not be fine, but it will still have its value.

The food producing villages of the second millennium in western India have a considerable range in size. Many of them are very small, only a few hundred square metres in size. But, some of them measure several hectares. Prakash, Daimabad and Inamgaon are all in this class. To compute an absolute population directly from the measured size of an archaeological site is difficult to establish. With varying influences of natural forces such as erosion, deposition, movement by water and gravity, and the possibility of different community structures in terms of house size and placement within a settlement, any general area population proportion is probably going to have exceptions. With this qualification we have used two estimates which appear to have had utility in other parts of Asia. The first of these was developed for south-west Asia and is a population of 200 persons per hectare;[3] The second was developed by Fairservis[4] in his work on the Harappan Civilization and is 800 square feet (75 square metres) per individual or 133 per hectare.[5] Each of these figures takes into account open space, roads, public architecture and other non-habitational features. By applying these estimates to Inamgaon, populations of approximately 1000 and 650 persons respectively can be computed for the settlement.[6] Certainly neither of these figures seems out of line for a site of five hectares. This brings us to the dietary habits of the inhabitants.

A variety of cultivars has been found in several excavated sites relevant to this discussion. Wheat, barley, rice, jowar, lentil, grass pea, two types of gram, linseed and fruits are all fully documented.[7] Of these, *jowar*, wheat barley and rice must be considered the staple food. In addition, several domesticated animals were kept. Cattle, sheep and goats are the most

[1]H. D. Sankalia, Z. D. Ansari and M.K. Dhavalikar, 'Central India 3000 years ago', *Illustrated London News*, August 1971, pp. 41-43.

[2]Dhavalikar, *op. cit.* (1970).

[3]R. McC. Adams, *Land Behind Baghdad* (Chicago, 1965), pp. 23-25 and 123-25.

[4]W. A. Fairservis Jr., 'The origin, character and decline of an early civilization,' *American Museum Nogitates*, no. 2302, American Museum of Natural History (New York, 1967).

[5]Neither of these population estimates can be said to come from our data. Work on their refinement is a part of the Inamgaon research strategy and they will undoubtedly be revised later. For the moment, inadequate as they may be, they are still the best figures available. It should be noted however, that they are in agreement with Hole's estimates of 60 to 80 persons per acre or 150 to 200 persons per hectare for early village communities of wester Iran: see Frank Hole, 'Evidence of social organization from Western Iran, 8000-4000 B.C.', in Binford and Binford (eds.), *New Perspectives in Archaeology* (Chicago, 1968), p. 268.

[6]Area estimates for each of its there periods are as follows; Malwa, 50,000 square metres, Early Jorwe, 50,000 sq. m Late Jorwe, 20,000 sq. m. These populations have been computed for the Malwa and Early Jorwe Periods.

[7]Vishnu-Mittre, 'Plant economy in ancient Navda-toli Maheshwar', *Technical Report on Archaeological Remains* (Poona, 1961).

common. Hunting and fishing are also attested.

It is reasonable to suggest that early villages such as these had a diet dominated by carbohydrates. Certainly it is unlikely that the domestic animals were kept primarily for their meat. Not only are these animals a part of the labour force, but they produce milk, fibres and others of their kind as well. Some young male animals and possibly carrion were consumed, but little else is probable. Hunting and fishing can supplement the supply of meat; however, it is time consuming. Moreover, the best hunting season in this part of India coincides with a period of considerable agricultural activity. Thus, it too must have made a limited contribution to any long term view of the subsistence of a large population. With these considerations in mind, an allowance for meat has been made. The other foods, vegetables, fruits, eggs, milk and such have been estimated using a similar process of thought.

Minimum requirements for long term survival are about 1700 calories per day taken within a reasonably balanced diet. Good health can be achieved with about 600 calories more. Based on this fact, and the ethnographic record of somewhat comparable modern cultures, the estimate presented here is of 2000 calories. This figure has the advantages of being a mean estimate so that if it misses the mark the resulting distortion would be minimized. These 2000 calories have been distributed as follows:[1]

all grains	1350 calories
vegetables	100 ,,
fruits and sweets	50 ,,
meat (eggs, fish, poultry)	200 ,,
dairy products	300 ,,
	2000 calories

If these two estimates, of the population and the food they ate, are close to actual fact the computation of an area of agricultural land is reasonably easy and secure.

FOOD GRAINS

The grains and vegetables are the two features of this diet which require significant amounts of farm land. For the three grains which are evidenced in the archaeological record (*jowar*, wheat and rice), yields were computed for the years 1909-10 to 1918-19 from the *Season and Crop Report of the Bombay Presidency*. These were averaged, combined and weighed for the final figure of 225 kg per acre. Weighing was necessary since it seemed unlikely that all of the grains were consumed in equal proportions. Rice is never likely to have played a great role in the subsistence pattern in upland western India. Lack of reliable water supplies over large areas is the reason for this. Even today only a small amount of rice is grown in very small, carefully tended plots. The grain itself is consumed chiefly on festive occasions. Wheat is only slightly more important because of the rainfall and temperature pattern in this part of the country. This crop is usually planted in large amounts only when a late monsoon has seriously threatened the earlier *jowar* sowing. In addition, some late rain is required for a successful wheat crop under these conditions. The weighing used here was 10 per cent rice, 20 per cent wheat and 70 per cent *jowar*. This gave a weighted yield of 225 kg per acre. Changing this weighing to 10 per cent rice, 40 per cent wheat and 50 per cent *jowar* changed the yield to 237 kg per acre. This change is not considered serious enough to modify the conclusions reached in the present study.

The content of a kilogram of grain is approximately 3350 calories. Within the diet presented here this would feed 2·5 people for one day. By dividing this into the population estimates for the large settlements such as Inamgaon, daily grain requirements are 260 kg for 650 people and 400 kg for 1000 people. Multiplying each of these figures by 365 gives yearly requirements of approximately 100,000 and 150,000 kg.

The area required for cultivation can now be calculated from the yield per acre and the total grain consumption. For 650 persons it comes to 444 acres and for 1000 persons to 667 acres. Something must be added for seed, spillage, spoil, loss to rodents and disease, and loss in processing. Vegetable crops will take additional land. A figure of 0·67 acres per person will satisfy the consumption requirement. If 15 per cent of this figure is added for a vegetable crop (0·1 acres) and another 15 per cent for loss (0·1 acres) and 10 per cent for seed (0·07 acres) the total reaches 0·94 acres per person. This has been rounded to an even one acre per person for the purposes of this discussion.

This is a conservative estimate. Leshnik[2] in a study of modern cultivation in central India reached

[1]This estimte is in agreement with the recent one calculated by P. V. Sakhatme, *Feeding India's Growing Millions* (Bombay, 1965), Table 3.2.1.

[2]Lawrence S. Leshnik, 'The system of dry farming in the West Nimar District of central India', *Year-book of the South Asia Institute, Heidelberg University*, 1966 (Wiesbaden, 1967), pp. 56-74.

a figure of approximately 2 acres per person. His statement in this regard is worth quoting:

'In a dietary study undertaken in this community it was determined that about one pound of sorghum (*jowar*) is the regular daily grains consumption of an individual (excluding feasts). This may be reduced to three-quarter pounds in the poorer families, or rise to one and one-quarter pounds or more in the wealthier ones. This grain, eaten in the form of unleavened bread (*rotli*), is the mainstay of the diet, besides which only a small quantity of pulses and/or vegetables are consumed daily. (To this may be added each third or fourth day a small quantity of meat or fish.) An average family of five will then need at least 2000 pounds of sorghum yearly, that is the fruit of six acres if the yield is taken at 350 pounds per acre. Another one and one-half acres may be used to meet the family's pulse requirements. But in order to be assured of this annual minimum of 2300 pounds of grain and pulse, the total acreage will have to be increased by nearly one-half. At least ten per cent of the crop will be lost due to disease and rodents, and the possibility of a partial crop failure resulting from a shortage or surfeit of rainfall must be considered. There are labourers to be paid, cattle to be fed and seed has to be put aside for the next sowing. Ten acres per family, or two acres per person are about the *minimum* at which grain self-sufficiency can be sustained. In a good year, with a bumper crop, the family may have excess grain to sell for cash, but with an average harvest, ten acres will hardly support more than its minimum needs'.[1]

By using Leshnik's figures as the upper limit for land requirement and our figure as the lower limit, we can conclude that a site of the size of Inamgaon required somewhere between 650 and 2000 acres. Expressed as a radius of agricultural land around a settlement these figures are translated to approximately 0·55 miles and 1 mile respectively.

Fallow periods present another problem. If land is left dormant every other year it doubles the area required for cultivation. In this case the radius increases to about 1·4 miles for a population of 1000, requiring 2 acres per person. Even with a two year fallow this radius is only 1·8 miles for the same population. In modern villages it is not uncommon for the fields of some families to be three to three and half miles from their home. Judged against this scale our figures are then well within reason for the land requirement.

FARMING

On the basis of the study of the houses of different cultures and the total area covered by them at the site, we have estimated that the population of Inamgaon during the Malwa and the Early Jorwe Periods may have been ranging from 650 souls to 1000 whereas the number decreased to about 400 during the Late Jorwe Phase of occupation. Our computation shows that the Malwa and the Early Jorwe people would have required about 650 to 2000 acres of cultivable land. There seems to be a general opinion that the authors of the chalcolithic cultures which flourished in the black soil zone were not able to cultivate the hard, clayey soil of the region in the absence of iron tools[2] and that the cultivation was therefore confined, of necessity, to the alluvial strips on the river bank, in close proximity to the habitation. Agrawal[3] thinks that the chalcolithic people with their poor copper technology could never cultivate the sticky, black cotton soils'.

It is of interest to note here that there are nc alluvial strips worth the name in many of the river valleys of central India and the Deccan. Pannikar rightly observes:[4]

> 'The question that poses itself as to why is it that inspite of the existence of large rivers like the Mahanadi, the Godavari, the Krishna, the Narmada and the Tapti which flow across India, population should be sparse and the economic development limited in these areas? The reason is simple. These rivers flow throughu plands, and not valleys and do not, therefore, spread their fertilizing waters on the country side till they reach the delta areas.'

These rivers are well entrenched, and have been flowing since the end of the Early Pleistocene. Sometime late in the Holocene, possibly during the period under discussion, there was a period of silty aggradation within the banks of this entrenchment. That it does not extend over wide areas can be inferred from the fact that the black cotton soil is not covered by this alluvium, even close to the river banks.[5] In the area near Inamgaon the Ghod river entrench-

[1] *Ibid.*, pp. 73-74.

[2] D. D. Kosambi, 'The beginnings of Iron Age in India', *Journal of the Economic and Social History of the Orient*, vol. VI (1963), p. 316.

[3] D. P. Agrawal, *The Copper Bronze Age in India* (New Delhi, 1971), p. 228.

[4] K. M. Pannikar, *Geographical Factors in Indian History* (Bombay, 1959), p. 37.

[5] S. N. Rajguru, personal communiction, 1971.

ment is quite narrow for many kilometres Itswidth probably averages no more than 152 m. feet. With allowance for the river course itself, a strip of cultiv-

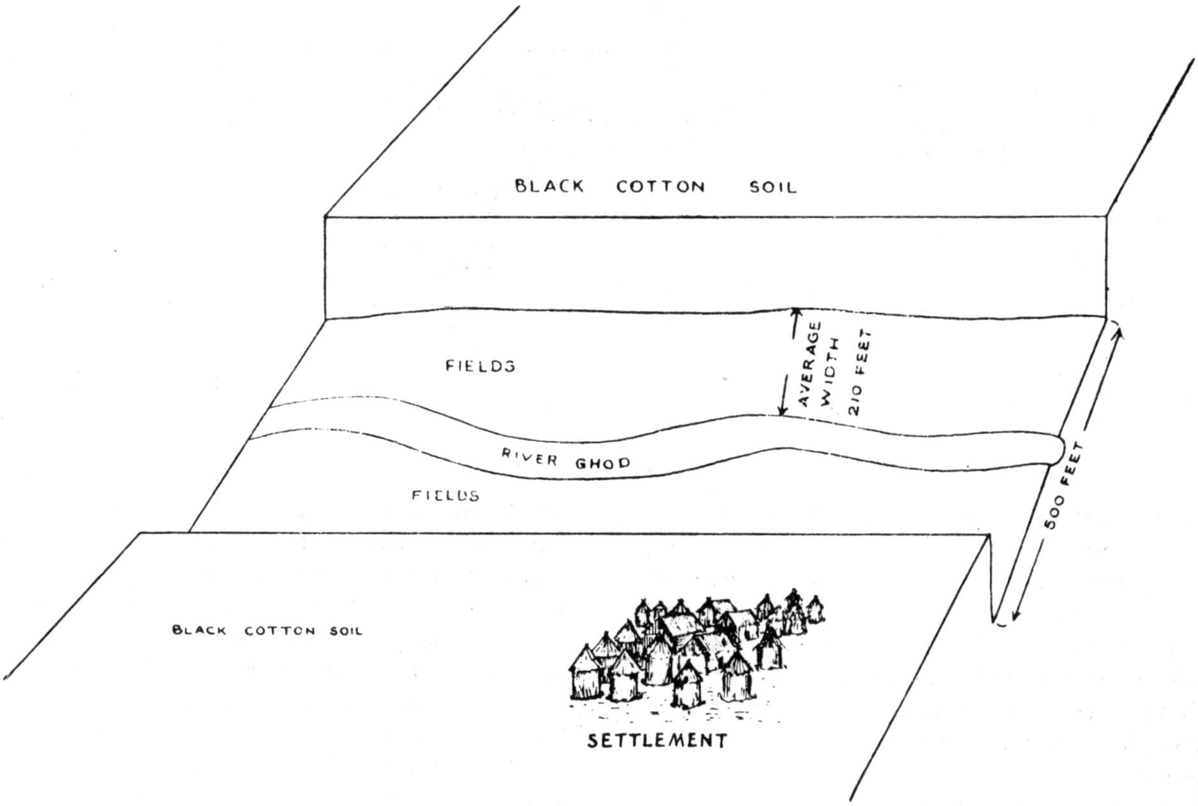

FIG. 1

able land between 200 and 225 feet wide may have been available on each side of the river (FIG. 1).

Using estimates made earlier for required agricultural land, the distance to the fields located farthest from the settlement can be computed. Take the lowest figure of 650 acres as an example. Land may have been available on each side of the river, both upstream and downstream from the settlement. Dividing the required acreage by four gives the area, available on one side of the river in one direction of the settlement. This gives a strip of 65 hectares squares, (FIG. 2). The length of the strip comes to about 9 km. Similar computations for the estimate of 808 hectarers yield a strip slightly less than 32 km length. Neither of these distances seems satisfactory. Even the minimum figure of six miles is considered in too far for man to walk on a daily basis for the performance of his agricultural chores. Certainly, it would be reasonable to suggest that before such a distance was reached some portion of the settlement would split-off and a new community more conveniently located for agricultural purposes would be established.[1] This is especially true since factors such as defence, water, resource concentration or patterns or incipient urbanization which would place a premium on nuclearization do not seem to be present. The alternative to this is of course to suggest that the black cotton soil was farmed, at least in the area adjacent to Inamgaon. Some alluvial strips may have been utilized for it would have been difficult to fully meet the needs of the entire settlement.

[1] The chalcolithic site nearest to Inamgaon is Walki which is approximately 40 km due west. It is, however, very small and seems to have remained under occupation for a shorter time.

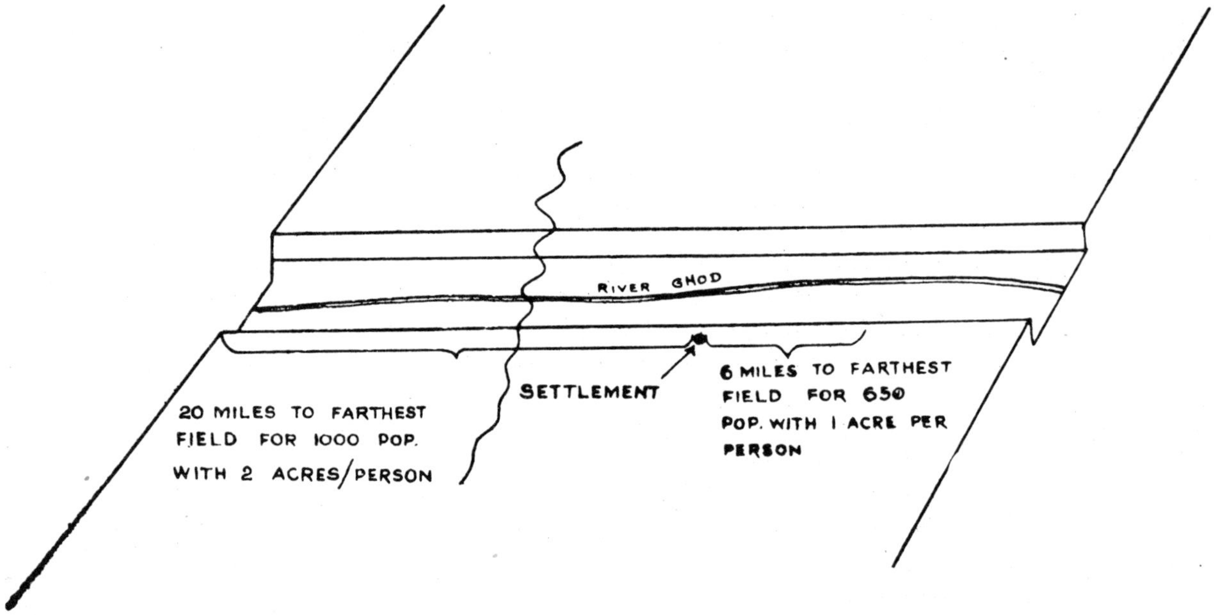

FIG. 2

Black cotton soil is credited with an extraordinary degree of fertility. It is in some cases known to have supported agriculture for centuries without manuring or being left fallow, and with no apparent sign of exhaustion or impoverishment. Although it is hard, compact and sticky, it could have been cultivated even in the absence of sharp iron tools. Strangely enough, it does not require as much water as ordinary soils do.

The black cotton soil was being effectively ploughed by a simple hoe and not by the large iron ploughs with up to twelve bullocks as done now. In some parts of central India wooden ploughs, without the attachment of any metal ploughshare let alone iron, are used. The plough is made of *khair* (*Acacia catechu*) which is very hard and lasting. We can, therefore, reasonably conclude that the black cotton soil could have been effectively cultivated in the absence of iron tools. The excavations at Inamgaon have yielded polished stone tools, a majority of which are axes. Hoes, which were quite common in the southern Deccan, are absent at Inamgaon. The only tool found at Inamgaon which would have been of great help, is the so called digging stick with ring stones which could have been used for cultivation.

ANIMAL REQUIREMENTS

The excavations have also yielded a large number of animal bones, predominantly of cattle. It will, therefore, be necessary to compute the number of cattle as also the quantities of milk and dairy products which the chalcolithic inhabitants of Inamgaon required. It has been estimated that the average requirement for cultivation was about one bullock for eight acres. On the basis of the range for agricultural land given above, the draft animals should have numbered between 80 and 250. Additional animals, would have been required for milk and an estimate must be made for young and milkless cows. Assuming for the moment that all animals were bovids, the milk requirement can be estimated from average yields and the caloric content of the diet presented here. This computes to 100 to 150 cows. Adding these two figures, total animals required for the community of 650 persons would be about 180 and for the human population of 100 the requirement adds to 400. An allowance of one-half of these figures is a standard added value for milkless cows and young animals. Total figures for cows and bullocks work up to 270 to 600.

Several assumptions must be made to estimate the amount of pasture utilized by this number of animals. First, pitifully little is known about the local environmental conditions pertaining to Deccan in prehistoric times. Thus, only the crudest estimates can be made for the amount of grass which was available. Secondly, there are several possible patterns for the use of pastures. A simple dichotomy between intensive and extensive patterns is common; however, this has a failing common to many typologies. It is a known fact that there are many gradations in seasonal shifts from one to the other. Based on the studies of the carrying capacity of pasture land near Pune[1] and the semi-arid woodland,[2] two acres per animal for the bovid population can be reasonably suggested. It should be stated, however, that variation of one or even two orders of magnitude are within the range of possibility. Using this estimate, the minimum estimated animal population would require approximately 218 hectares of pasture. For the larger occupation this estimate rises to 8.9 hectares acres. These two figures increase the radius of the required subsistence land to somewhere between 1 km. and 1·6 km.[3]

Of course all of the animals were not bovid; sheep and goat were also attested in the faunal remains. The bovine animals undoubtedly require more pasture per individual than either sheep or goat. Thus, we will leave the pasture estimate as it is in the hope that these differences will tend to cancel one another.

Such radii of activity are wholly in keeping with expectations, and at no time is a distance reached where daughter communities would necessarily be formed due to the scarcity of available pasture and farm land. Also of importance is the fact that competition between communities for land necessary for subsistence does not appear to be indicated by this data. In fact, the distances between adjacent communities are generally quite large and the sites quite small. The settlement pattern is rather an open one, even under the best conditions. This fact might suggest that the basic mode of subsistence was one which placed greater dependence on the extensive exploitation of pasture by herds of domesticated animals than on a more intensive agricultural pattern. Such a situation would, of course, require radical re-interpretation of much of the chalcolithic material from western India. It is one area where the diet presented here could be seriously in error. Food grains may not have played the dominant role in feeding this population. It could have been milk products. But this is trivial when we shift to considerations of social and cultural differences between fully settled agriculturists and nomadic or semi-nomadic pastoralists. Each of these has its own way of life with its own distinctive form of organization and pattern of seasonal activity.

An important fact to remember in this matter is that during the dry season, which comes to a peak in April and May, there is every little pasture available in the Deccan. Whether or not it is sufficient to support the human and animal populations presented here cannot yet be accurately estimated. On the other hand it can be reasonably stated that for the truly successful manipulation of even relatively small numbers of animals, seasonal transhuman movement is necessary during this season. In fact, the zone in which Inamgaon is locatedhas pasture resources for only three to four months of the year: during and just following the monsoon. In other seasons pasture is available across the Western Ghats on the Konkan coast. Today such a pattern of movement is practiced by a population numbering hundreds of thousands and animals in the millions. If this pattern can be shown to be present in the second millennium B.C. it would mean that parts or the entire population of some sites, possibly Inamgaon, were occupied only seasonally, that is during the monsoon and post-monsoon growing seasons. Other times of the year the same people may be moving first into the Ghats, then across the western coast where dry season pasture is available.

The foregoing is essentially a hypothesis at this time, and no more evidence can be marshalled to its side. As already mentioned, the settlement pattern suggests an extensive rather than intensive mode of subsistence. Also the houses which have been exposed at Inamgaon are rather insubstantial affairs, and do not appear to be anything more than might have been thrown-up for a few months of the year. Additional work at this and other sites in the region will hopefully throw further light on this thesis. Detailed exploration around the site aimed at the recovery of as complete a settlement as possible was planned. Selected small scale excavation at some of the chalcolithic sites should be directed toward recovery of house plans and a fair sampling of faunal and floral evidences. The latter material should yield an indication of both seasonality and the place of animals in the subsistence system. Caves and other very small sites should be investigated with the aim of locating at least one of the very emphemeral, transitory pastoral camps.

One positive aspect of this hypothesis of large-scale pastoral activity in prehistoric western India is that it goes far to explain the obvious inter-connections between the several archaeological cultures which have been defined. The inherent mobility of these people and their probable close relationships with more settled folk within their area of movement is an obvious explanatory mechanism. Their pro-

[1]R. O. Whyte, *The Grassland and Forest Resources of India* (New Delhi, 1964), p. 264.

[2]L. S. S. Kumar, 'Better utilization of forest grass lands in Bombay Province,' *Indian Forest*, vol. 72 (1946), pp. 162-64.

[3]Fairservis, *op cit.*, elaborates for these computations.

bable role in the movement of goods or their possession of specialized skills such as metal working, carpentry, trading or potting would place them securely within the social ecology as well as the natural balance. Those familiar with modern India will see a clear parallel with the present in this aspect of the suggested model. We hasten to add that no attempt is made to prove the hypothesis with the modern parallel. The latter has been a major source for the model's construction: but the hypothesis must stand or fall when it is tested against the archaeological record.[1]

It is not suggested that all these ancient settlements were seasonal encampments, or that the entire population was semi-nomadic. In many parts of the Deccan and Malwa, fully settled agriculture may have been the primary mode of subsistence. But even this has never been demonstrated, and questions of seasonality and pastoralism have never been addressed. Given the obviously complex and inter-related archaeological record during the second millennium B.C. so simple an answer should at least be held in doubt. It is too pat. It fails to capture the variegated richness and complexity of man's life as it has been observed elsewhere. The hypothesis offered here may be incorrect. But, it seems reasonable to begin an understanding of this material by investigating seasonality and the relative dependence of the population on their plant and animal resources.

EPILOGUE

The foregoing study of the subsistence pattern of the chalcolithic settlement at Inamgaon brings into sharp focus the need to excavate such sites on a large scale with a view to obtaining conclusive evidence regarding the prehistoric subsistence pattern and other aspects of life of the early farming communities. It may not be out of place to state that the present study is the first of its kind to be carried out for any site in India.

By way of summary we would like to emphasize several point. First, the details of interpretation included here are not intended to stand as a substantive contribution to our understanding of man's prehistoric way of life. Too many assumptions have been introduced. Every effort was made to illuminate as many of these as possible; however, each reader may have found others which might be considered important. Thus, variables such as the population of Inamgaon, the diet which was proposed, the yields per acre, the importance of hunting and fishing in the over-all exploitative pattern, and estimates of pasture resources may be in error. On the other hand, we hope to have presented a point of view; a way of looking at the archaeological record which goes beyond the almost exclusive concern for chronology in Indian archaeology.

L. R. Binford[2] has suggested that archaeology has three ultimate goals: 1) the reconstruction of culture history, 2) the reconstruction of past lifeways, and 3) the study of culture process. The present study is an attempt to reconstruct past lifeways. If it failed it did so not because of the nature of the archaeological record, but because of the way data has been gathered—the way sites have been excavated. In other words, we believe it potentially possible to completely and accurately deal with the ambitious topic undertaken here. But this can only be done when research strategies focus on topics such as population size, the definition of households (not houses), quantification of food resources (not lists of species), the place of seasonality in the system of exploitation, detailed environmental reconstruction and the like.

A single, but important, conclusion which we feel can be derived from this study is the substantial probability that these advanced village farming communities cultivated the black cotton soil in the absence of iron tools. We, therefore, reject the earlier hypothesis that these settlements depended solely upon what have been termed 'alluvial strips' as their source of agricultural land.

[1]L. R. Binford, 'The smudge pits and hide smoking: the role of analogy in archaeological research', *American Antiquity*, vol. 32, no. 1 (1967), pp. 1–12.

[2]*New Perspectives in Archaeology* (Chicago, 1968), pp. 5-10.

Functional Significance of the O.C.P. and P. G. W. Shapes and Associated Objects

H.D. Sankalia

Deccan College Postgraduate and Research Institute, Pune

(*Received on 18 September 1973*)

OCHRE COLOUR POTTERY

IT is inconceivable that during the second half of the third millennium B.C. and the first half of the second, when the whole of western and north-western India was passing through the Indus Civilization, the country to the east of this large land mass was either still under the Stone Age or was culturally blank. Already as early as 1930, traces of a culture known as Cemetery-H had been found at Harappa. Unfortunately, however, no steps were taken to follow up this discovery in Punjab, Sind, or Baluchistan which at that time formed parts of undivided India. During the last twenty-five years a few organized attempts, including many sporadic ones, have been made to search for (i) what are known as sites of the Ochre Colour Pottery (OCP) and Copper Hoards, and (ii) sites of the degenerate Harappan Ware. The OCP was first found in the lowest layers at Hastinapura, then at Ahichchhatra and Atranjikhera. At the first two sites, only a few shapes could be recognized. Later, similar pottery was collected from a large number of sites in western U.P. Its area of distribution, roughly 1,35,000 sq. kms, extended from Bahadarabad near Hardwar to Noh in District Bharatpur on the north-south axis and from Katapalon near Jullundar to Ahichchhatra on the east-west axis.

Then the excavations at Ambakheri,[1] District Saharanpur, gave definite evidence of the extension of the Harappan— be it Late or degenerate—in this and other western districts of U.P., whereas the work at Lal Qila[2] and Saipai[3] showed that the OCP did not always have a powdery surface, and that it was not all plian, but was also treated with a red slip, and was sometimes decorated with incised and even painted designs.

Saipai also furnished the much awaited evidence of the association of one of the three most characteristic tools of the Copper Hoard, viz., a copper harpoon with the OCP.[4] Thus, at one stroke two, birds seem to have been killed. The three excavations, though on a small scale, definitely tell us that the OCP people were probably connected with the Copper Hoard people; that both of them were not nomads and hunters as was hastily and prematurely postulated by a few scholars.

The evidence from Mitathal,[5] though not so definitive, cannot be ignored. Here a copper harpoon,

[1]H. D. Sankalia, 'The Chalcolithic Cultures of India, in (ed.) S. B. Deo, *Archaeological Congress and Seminar Papers* (Nagpur, 1972), p. 168.

[2]R. C. Gaur, comments in 'Session on OCP', *Puratattva*, no. 5(1971-72), pp. 9-10, figs. 6 and 7. See also, R. C. Gaur in (ed.) B. P. Sinha, *Potteries in Ancient India* (Patna, 1969), pp. 95-101.

[3]B. K. Thapar, 'Methodology in Archaeology: A critique of the methods and nature of archaeological discipline, in Deo, op. cit p. 202; L. M. Wahal comments in 'Session on OCP', *op. cit.* (1971-72), p. 12; also see, B. B. Lal, 'A note on the excavation at Saipai', *ibid.*, p. 46, and 'The Copper Hoard Culture of the Ganga Valley', *Antiquity*, vol. XLVI (1972), pp. 282-87.

[4]Lal, *op. cit.* (1971-72), fig. 2 and pl. XLII.

[5]Suraj Bhan, 'Excavations at Mitathal (Hissar) 1968', *Journal of Haryana Studies*, vol. 4 (1969), pp. 1-15.

almost identical with that from Saipai, was found from the surface, besides a flat celt, ring and a *parasu*. The latter had similarities with finds at Bargaon, Khurdi, Daimabad and Inamgaon.

Ecology—the environment, vegetation, plains and rivers—and the natural fauna of the Ganga-Yamuna *doab*, has changed considerably only recently. And the change is largely quantitative and not qualitative, that is, the forests have decreased, and the agricultural area increased. But, it is in this environment that all the early historical and later urban and rural cultures developed, right up to the present time, until rapid industrialization during the last fifty years and more has completely altered the face of the country around Delhi, Mathura, Kanpur, and other towns. Hence a general ecological setting is of little use in understanding the character of a prehistoric culture like the OCP. What we need is more precise knowledge about the food-habits, vegetation and the fauna.

Meanwhile, a brief re-consideration of the types of copper objects, which was first attempted by Agrawal,[1] is necessary. Agrawal thought that the three diagnostic objects, viz. the anthropomorph, the sword with an antennae, and the harpoon were all weapons for hunting. The antennae sword, he suggested, was (might have been) used for killing or wounding big game by trapping the animals in the manner that "this sword can be fixed securely in narrow clefts made in heavy wooden logs. Such logs, with antennae swords projecting out, could be placed in the bottom of big pits. The pits could be camouflaged........". This conjectural usage is not supported by any current historical, or prehistoric practices. Granted that we have no explanation for the use of the antennae, still to conjecture, as Agrawal has done, that hunters would go to the length of producing such highly advanced (comparatively) weapon just for trapping big game is unimaginable.

The same may be said about the conjectural and highly ingenious explanation of the heavy anthropomorph, viz., that it might have been hurled against a flying bird. Granting again that it has sharp forearms, which could produce a cut to suggest that nomadic hunters would employ such a heavy and complicated weapon for bringing down birds is in every way uneconomical, and not expected from such unsophisticated folk. All over the world, and throughout the ages, much more simple methods have been employed which are still in use.

Of the two types of harpoons both having a mid rib, as in a spearhead with oblique or backward cutting barbs, one is technologically crude, made by cutting and hammering from a thick sheet, while the second shows a superb example of craftsmanship, employing the use of double mould, and close casting of pure copper. Anyone who has seen and handled these copper/bronze objects will have to admit that in size (and weight), shape and technique these three weapons from the Copper Hoards are much finer and better than those seen in the otherwise advanced Indus Civilization. On that ground alone, one should have thought twice before crediting them to nomads, hunters and intinerant coppersmiths. The objects might have been made by such roaming smiths, but they were made for a society or people who needed or had developed the art of making such well developed weapons, probably by using local resources.

These people were no nomads but lived in simple mud (as well as brick?) walled houses, and had an assemblage of pots and pans, showing varied features as definitely indicated by the excavations at Saipai and Atranjikhera. Scholars who have previously written on this subject, have merely listed, but offered little comment on the types.

Krishna Deva and R. C. Gaur's list includes eighteen types, the main group being: (i) vases; (ii) bowls; (iii) basins; (iv) dishes-on-stand; (v) vases with loop or strap handles; (vi) vessels with channel or tubular spouts; and (vii) vessels with a ring-base. Even if we might omit some of those listed by Krishna Deva as not belonging to the OCP group, Gaur's list does contain all the main groups. This is further corroborated by Lal.

Now, simple globular vases, bowls and small or large storage jars and basins would form a part of any well-settled household, but dishes and bowls with stands, bowls and pots with a channel or tubular spouts and vessels—large or small—with strap or loop handles are a rarity in a Hindu house even today. In fact, handled vessels, such as teacups, and water or any kind of drink-servers that we find in some families today have become fashionable or common during the last fifty and twenty-five years respectively. Both these types of vessels can be traced to Western contacts. While we cannot recognize such an influence on the Copper Hoard people unless the full shapes are known, the existence of such spouted,

[1]D. P. Agrawal, *The Copper Bronze Age in India* (Delhi, 1971), pp. 199-201.

handled and footed vessels does indicate a way of life which should be more sophisticated than the one found in prehistoric or historical cultures, and certainly not among nomads and hunters.

This is also suggested by other associated objects like stone balls, pounders, rubbers, querns and pellets of sandstone, and a chalcedony flake. Further, the occurrence, even if solitary, of a chert blade is very significant. If this blade on spectrographic examination turns out to be identical with the Harappan chert blades from Sukkur and Rohri, then a contact with or an extension of the Harappan Culture into central U.P. might be inferred.

That the Copper Hoard people had domesticated the ox should have been expected; and probably it was used as a draft animal in a two-wheeled cart as well, besides ploughing.

Much more about the houses and settlement pattern of this people might be learnt if the excavations at Saipai, Lal Qila and such other promising sites, are carried out *horizontally*. The layers from which the harpoon and potsherds at Saipai and Lal Qila were found should be examined by a sedimentologist, as has been done at some sites in the Upper Ganga valley, and if after such an examination, it is established that the OCP sites were abandoned and present evidence of long exposure to a dry climate, then we shall have to reject the theories of sheet flood[1] or a deluge in the Ganga-Yamuna Valley after the seventeenth century B.C.,[2] the time-bracket of the OCP being determined by the thermoluniscence dating.

From the work done by the Universities of Punjab, Kurukshetra, Delhi, and Aligarh and by the Archaeological Departments of the Punjab and of Government of India, it is clear that so far the region now comprised under the various districts of western U.P., Haryana and the Punjab and drained by the Vedic rivers, Saraswati, Drishadavti, and the five rivers has not been systematically examined, from a prehistoric point of view. Siswal, Mitathal, and several other sites in the Hissar District show that here, a elsewhere, what we are seeking for is lying on the surface, or buried under the debris of historical periods. Unless a planned programme is chalked out (in which the electrical resistivity method might be tried whenever the sites like those of the OCP are shallow), jointly by the agenies named above we shall have to be content with a few vertical digs, and the resultant potsherds. These we can go on discussing *ad infinitum* without becoming wiser, as the seminar on the OCP shows.

PAINTED GREY WARE AND ASSOCIATED OBJECTS

For a time, it appeared that this blank or dark period, separating the Indus Civilization on the one hand and the Early Historical Period on the other would be filled up, or the darkness removed, by the discovery of the Painted Grey Ware Culture. Initially found at Ahichchhatra, and later at Hastinapura, its rapidly filled up distribution map appeared very significant. For the first time, the small and big places—towns and villages mentioned in the *Mahabharata* seemed to be truly living. Their antiquity was being established for the first time. But the archaeologists and the laymen were once again disappointed. The former because, after probing the depths of Hastinapura and Ahichchhatra, little was done to tell us about the sociological background of the people : their houses, layout of their settlement, habits, customs and manners, and disposal of the dead. It is more than twenty years since the first discoveries were made, but the knowledge we have of the Painted Grey Ware Culture can be told in a few sentences. The layman (and the scholar) were also disappointed, because, neither the original estimate based on depth of the deposits and relative dating, as also the subsequent Carbon-14 dates from Hastinapura and other sites, proved the culture to be older than seventh-eighth century B.C., at the most. Popular mind, even of the educated Indian, cannot imagine that the authors of the Painted Grey Ware Culture, whom the archaeologists associate with the Mahabharata heroes—the Pandavas, Kaurvas and Shri Krishna—should have lived only 2700 years ago, and not 5000 years ago. Disappointing in every way is the little knowledge that we have of this Culture, whom one author dubs the "Ganges Civilization". For except the wide distribution from the Punjab in the north, to Ujjain in the south, and Bahawalpur in the east in north Rajasthan and Sind border to Bihar in the east (covering the Indo-Gangetic plains, the Vedic and Upanishadic *Aryavarta, Brahmarshidesa*)—it has little to boast of by way of civilization. So far no evidence for the use of writing has been found, though material for doing so may be seen in the double-pointed bone points (styluses), though these might have been used alternatively for weaving or as

[1]B. B. Lal, 'A Deluge ? Which Deluge? Yet another facet of the problem of the Copper Hoard Culture?', *American Anthropologist*. vol. 70 (1968). pp, 857-63.

[2]Lal, *op. cit.* (1972), p. 286.

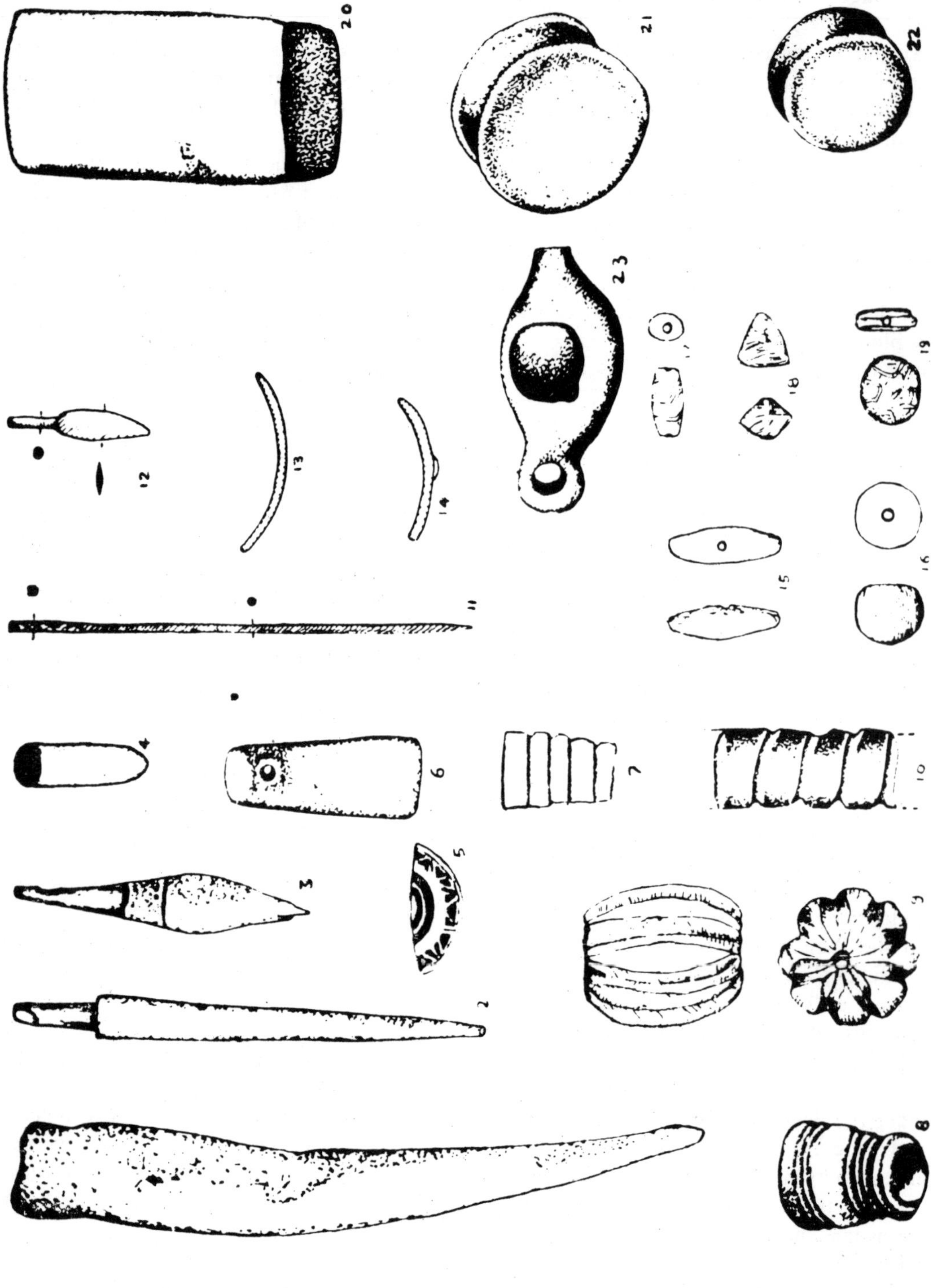

FIG. 1.

arrow-heads, nor monumental architecture. Even the size of a room of a modest house, whether made of mud or mud-bricks is not known. But structures of true bricks were probably known, as the occurrence of fragmentary piece from a pit indicates.

The inhabitants of such mud-plastered reed houses ate rice (and perhaps lentil), but supplemented it with beef, pork, mutton and venison and even horse's flesh. This is indicated by the occurrence of large quantities of bones of these animals, which bear cut-marks and are also charred. Naturally, as today, in communities depending upon agriculture and animal husbandry, the cow/ox, buffalo, pig, goat/sheep, horse were domesticated and used as draft animals and also for food (when useless). (In a future excavation this point can be cleared, if the bones found are proved to be of old animals only, and not young ones.)

Wheat should also have been eaten, as it is the staple diet of Haryana today and known from much earlier times in the Punjab, Sind, Madhya Pradesh and Maharashtra.

All this food—vegetarian and non-vegetarian—was eaten in bowls and dishes which were quite different from those hitherto known in India.

Though common, yet most distinctive, were bowls and dishes with ashy-grey surfaces, bearing painted designs like the *svastikas*, simple strokes in black or chocolate. The shapes lack variety, but the *thali* (dish) and *katora* (bowl) seem to have been found so useful, that all these two thousand five hundred years and more these two have continued to form an essential ingredient in any Indian kitchen.

The sixteen illustrated specimens from Hastinapura (*Ancient India,* nos. 10-11, 1954-55, fig. 6, p. 35) constitute only one type of bowl—a large bowl, about 8 to 20 cm in diameter, and about 8 to 15 cm in height with almost vertically straight sides. The other variety of the deep bowls would be useful for serving and for storing food, and eating therefrom, even putting it right on the lips, but not for *pouring* liquid, for they have no rim at all. Even for holding with the hand, it is a little inconvenient. The other variety of the bowl had a more rounded base. I have seen a Sadhu who held such a large bowl with the palms of both the hands. Only one has a lightly constricted waist (or sides), and expanding sides. The majority of the dishes have a broad flat base, and low slightly curved sides. This form of the *thali* has been found useful for dry as well as semiliquid food, but not only liquids.

In the other two varieties (*Ancient India*, nos. 10 and 11, fig. 9, *47*, *49* and *50*) the sides of the *thali* are straight and go out whereas in another, the sides are indented or have ledges and bear a punched decoration outside. These are indeed quite novel features. Probably these vessels with one or two corrugations outside were meant not for eating as much as for storing, and the ledges were probably meant for receiving a lid. So far, no *lotas*—small vessels for serving water for drinking and washing—are found in the Painted Grey Ware fabric from Hastinapura. But, these—only two types so far—as well as other medium-sized vessels in red ware occur in the deposits of this period.

A glance at these, as well as those from the Harappan or the Indus Civilization, as well as those from the Chalcolithic Cultures of central India, Maharashtra and Rajasthan would show (even to a layman), that the Painted Grey Ware Culture truly represents the ancestral form of life, seen today in the Hindus of northern India, particularly the Gangetic Valley. Its pottery—including the corase red, bright red and fine black wares does not contain any exotic form or forms like the dish-on-stand, pots with spouts of a peculiar nature, barring of course, a solitary specimen of a grooved grey ware stem and the small feeding cup.

Cooking was done on simple one-mouthed *chulah* with horse-shoe like sides. Unfortunately, none of these is illustrated. It is also strange that so many hearths should occur together. Since they were found in the upper levels, where iron ore and slag also was found, it is conceivable that some of them, as at Ahar, were meant for smelting iron.

The residents of these simple mud walled houses wore ornaments—necklaces, pendants, ear-ornaments and bangles, made of semi-precious stones, terracotta and glass. Spinning was done on one or two-holed terracotta discs. And the clothes (to judge from the scuiptural evidence of a slightly later period) must have consisted primarily of a *dhoti* as a lower garment for both men and women and made of cotton, and a covering for the head and the shoulder.

For weaving, double pointed bone pieces were used. Later, these were also made in kaolin, as the evidence from Nasik shows. Though these could also be used for writing, and if so, they would be regarded as styluses.

Not much can be said for other aspects of life. Iron was presumably unknown at the beginning of this period (c.800 B.C.) but later, not only known, but smelted as can be inferred from the occurrence of slags and ores not only at Hastinapura, but also at Atranjikhera and sites further afield, where though Painted Grey Ware has been found, no traces of habitation have been recorded.

Of copper objects, Hastinapura has yielded an arrowhead an antimony rod, a nail-parer and a borer. This is certainly a very modest, nay, very much incomplete, picture of a period which, apart from being called a civilization having a very wide extent, was at the threshold of a transition to the historical period proper.

While much can be said from the literacy evidence which can enliven this pucture, much of this material should be contemporary but unfortunately is not well dated, and has necessarily been here omitted. It is archaeology alone which can give fuller and more reliable picture of the life in Uttar Pradesh and Bihar but which unfortunately has not been properly tapped. However, the most important evidence provided by the excavation at Hastinapura is about the use (domestication) of the horse. Though the bones of a horse of an extinct type, and of the living type have been found from river gravels, nowhere had the bones of the domesticated horse (*Equus caballus*) been found.[1] These occur in the top layers of Period II at Hastinapura. So far only three cut pieces have been recorded. But these are enough to prove that the horse was known and even slaughtered for food. Unfortunately, this important clue has not been followed up, nor do we possess such a knowledge from sites like Atranjikhera, Kausambi and Ahichchhatra in Uttar Pradesh and Noh in Rajastan.

There is no item in the cultural equipment of the Painted Grey Ware deposit at Hastinapura which is indicative of a truly prehistoric phase in the evolution of the Indian Culture. There is nothing of a transitional phase either, except perhaps pottery, the shapes of which however became the hallmark in the historic period. The rest—the bone styluses or knitting pins, gadrooned beads, glass bangles, the copper arrowhead with a rounded body and large cylindrical weights or ear plugs—characterize the earliest historic deposits in the whole of northern India and elsewhere later. Hence it would be logical to think that the Painted Grey Ware Culture truly represents more the dawn of the historical period than the end of the prehistoric. Hence its lower dating as indicated by a series of Carbon-14 determinations from Ahichchhatra, Hastinapura, Noh is justified. The single date from Atranjikhera should be disregarded.

This conclusion would have an important bearing upon the view consistently held by our traditional accounts—the epics and the Puranas. All these have always maintained that the Bharata War saw the end of the Dvaparayuga and the beginning of the Kaliyuga. It might be recalled that this conclusion also supports one of the premises of Lal, viz., that the Painted Grey Ware sites seem to represent the sites mentioned in the *Mahabharata*, but contradicts his other hypothesis viz., that it also belongs to the Early Aryans. Traditionally, the Aryans lived at a much earlier period, about 3000 B.C., whereas according to some of the scholars they arrived in India in about 1200 B.C.

It is certain that we have still to fill up the gap in northern India—the Indo-Gangetic plains—between the disappearance of the Indus Civilization and the dawn of the earliest historical period. The Painted Grey Culture has narrowed the bracket by about three or four centuries (400—800 B.C.) but still the gap from 800 B.C. to 1500 B.C. remains to be filled. This may be done by planned, large scale excavations. One of the aims of these should be to expose a town or village site of the Painted Grey Ware Culture.

[1]Since this was written, bones of true horse have been reported from Surkotada, a Harappan site in Kutch and also from Hallur, District Dharwar and Navdatoll, For Surkotada, see Jagat Pati Joshi, 'Exploration in Kutch and excavation at Surkotada and new light on Harappan migration', *Journal of the Oriental Institute*, vol. XXII, nos. 1-2 (Sept.-Dec. 1972), pp. 98-144, But the statement of Shri A. K. Sharma is a little confusing, "The most important feature of the collection is the occurrence of *Equus caballus* Linn in the *later period* of occupation' (italics mine), And then "lot of Equus bones right from earlier to top levels have been recovered," How we differentiate between the Equus in the first and the second statement ?

Two Urbanizations in India : A Side Study in their Social Structure

S. P. Gupta

National Museum, New Delhi

(*Received on 22 October 1973*)

URBANIZATION may be defined as a process of effective change in the collective life of the people, brought about by progressive development in the existing agricultural and industrial technology of the peasantry or the folk (as the case may be). This change leads to the emergence of a new socio-economic order, reflected in a new planned pattern of habitation and new forms of art, craft and architecture, generally monumental and controlled and regulated by some form of an overall authority. It is basically a process, in some cases a long process, while in others a very short one indeed. The end product of this process is a city. In other words, even though a purely agricultural community, living in village-like settlements, has a highly-organized socio-political structure, still it will not be considered urbanized. However, in a sense, it may be called 'civilized', which means that the people are neither savage, nor barbarians, nor simple self-satisfied folk; they are sophisticated and have been able to create several items of higher culture. The example of the Later Vedic Aryans may be quoted in this regard,[1] since they had a definite socio-politico-economic structure and a vast literature. Egypt, before 4000 B.C. had developed writing, kingship, monumental palaces and temples but hardly any city as such[2] for the masses. The Mayans in Mesoamerica alsodid not have any city although they had art, literature, writing, astronomy, temples and palaces;[3] the masses lived in small hamlets around temples. All of them may, therefore, be called 'civilized' but not 'urbanized'. Similarly, a community with increased productivity in cereals and manufactured goods but without being organized by some effective super-authority for purposes of trade, civic amenities, defence, protection of trade, etc., may also not be called urbanized. In this connection the example of south Indian megalith builders[4] may be safely quoted. Thus, urbanized life is a well organized and corporate life, economic as well as

[1]R. C. Majumdar (ed.), *The Vedic Age*, The History and Culture of the Indian People, vol. I (London, 1957), pp. 333-401.

[2]J. A. Wilson, *The Burden of Egypt* (Chicago, 1951). As a' biological organism, Egypt was primitive. The arable land was packed tight with ... hundreds of agricultural and commercial villages within sight of one another. Yet the total organism did not develop a central nervous system .... successively the capital shifted from Memphis to Herakleopolis, to Thebes, to Lisht, to Avaris, to Ramses. There was no eternal city, no Rome which could exhibit such strong polarity that it became the inevitable centre of government, religion, commerce, art and science. The temporary capitals seem never to have gained any remarkable size. It is legitimate to say that for nearly three thousand years, until the founding of Alexandria, ancient Egypt was a major civilization without a single major city'.' See, John A. Wilson in (eds.), Carl H. Kraeling and Robert M. Adams, *City Invincible* (Chicago, 1960), pp. 135 and 164 for elaboration of this view. The same is true of the Maya civilization in Mesoamerica. She also 'offers a sequence of development toward civilization without cities *Ibid.*, p. 135.

[3]*Ibid.*, p. 158.

[4]S. P. Gupta, *Disposal of the Dead and Physical Types in Ancient India* (Delhi, 1972), pp. 259-60.

socio-political which, in some form or the other, must get reflected in the settlement pattern,[1] as also in antiquities. For the civilized life, on the other hand, neither a city nor developed technology is essential, although they are desirable. The archaeologists may find it possible to reconstruct all this from the available evidence. For example, on the basis of the structural evidence, they may reasonably visualize the social gradations like farmers, artisans, trading guilds, royal personages, priests, etc.

However, urbanization is a concept, an abstract idea about a socio-economic situation which unfortunately cannot be defined in exact terms, largely because in human society no two socio-economic situations have ever been the same. Seen historically, urbanizations in Western Asia, Egypt, India, China and Mesoamerica[2] show not only quantitative but also qualitative differences in the permutations and combinations of the items usually taken to constitute the phenomenon of urbanization.[3]

Historical writings often mention two major periods of urbanization in India—the Harappan (2500 1700 B.C.), and the Early Historical (600-500 B.C.-A.D. 100); the latter divided into two (a) Formative Stage (600-400 B.C.), and (b) Mature Stage (400 B.C.-A.D. 100), the intervening period of about one thousand years represents peasantry. The factors responsible for the emergence of this phenomenon have often been probed but they remain little understood, particularly those relating to social structure. It is often asked as to what are the factors which gave the achievements of the Early Historical Period the longest duration. In the same breath, it is also asked as to what was the social structure of the Harappans which made their urbanization phenomenal, and also why did it collapse? Why is it that the legacy of

[1]'Civilization' has also been a concept, defined variously by various people. Thus, Walter A. Fairservis Jr., *The Roots of Ancient India* (New York, 1971), p. 217, defines it as 'the most complex cultural level reached by man. Its symptom is the city'. Wheeler writes: 'In common usage 'civilization', is held to imply certain qualities... a systematic method of accounting, so that revenue and wages may be adequately registered and orderly government ensured... writing in some form or the other, is on this view a presupposition ; see, Sir Mortimer Wheeler, *The Civilizations of the Indus Valley and Beyond* (London, 1966), p. 10. Both these views are 'city' oriented, and archaeologists views, so to say, since they emphasize the elements which have got little to do with religion, philosophy, spirituality, art, literature and similar other things which have been universally acclaimed as the most powerful tools for changing the savage, barbarous, and simple village folks into polite, cooperative and thinking human beings. In them, mundane considerations predominate over extra-mundane considerations. Archaeological culture is material culture of tangible entities.

Culture-anthropologist's views are, however, slightly different. According to Kroeber, 'Civilization is multinational and multilingual ... (is) spontaneously participated in by a whole series of people... (who).... may frequently fight among themselves. Yet they share much the greater part of their civilization, and all the essentials. A civilization thus is something that has grown up of itself into a supernational product', A. L. Kroeber, *An Anthropologist Looks at History* (Berkley, 1963), pp. 17 and 20. According to this view, civilization is culture in a wider perspective, i.e., when a culture crosses its local or regional or national limits and, incorporates and absorbs in its own organic growth many foreign elements turning it into an almost supernational product, it becomes civilization as distinct from culture which is very closed and limited, and local in scope. For example the Hindu Culture is that which is typical of India but Hindu Civilization is that which is the product of Greater India, and incorporates into its iconography, etc., many local elements of Central Asia, China, Indonesia, and other countries of Asia where the culture had spread in time.

In fact, every social science looks at culture and civilization in its own frame of reference which is but partial. When one goes for the totality called civilization one finds an infinite variety—two civilizations are never the same, neither their towns, nor kingship, nor religion, nor art, nor writing, nor aspiration, nor ideal, nor social structure, nor economic pattern. Each civilization is a unique creation of its own genius and it is the sum-total of all the mundane achievements and extramundane attainments that its people gain in time and space. It is sharply distinct from the stage of primary concerns of sex and hunger, and its scope transcends the narrow limits of geography. It presupposes the existence of a corporate life in socio-politico-economic sphere—city or no city; the role of the city as a unifying force may be discharged in several ways, e.g., by a king (as in Egypt for a long time) or by a group of ruling families (as might have been in Harappan India or was the case in early Indian republics) or by a priest or a group of priests (as in pre-Columbian Mesoamerica) or by a combination of king and priest (as in early Mesopotamia) or by a king in consultation with priests (as in Vedic India) so on and so forth. Civilizations differ with each other in social structuring also, e.g. the caste system is peculiar to India. Civilizations also differ in their social and personal ethics; Hindu ideals of marriage, family, teacher-taught relationship, etc., are peculiar to the Hindus, resemblances with other civilizations are, by and large, always superficial.

[2]For details, please see the views of different scholars assembled in an international seminar embodied in Kraeling and Adams, *op. cit.*, chap. I and II.

[3]Dilip K. Chakrabarti, 'Concept of Urban Revolution and Indian Context', *Puratattva*, no. 6 (1972-73), pp. 26-36, and comments of several leading scholars.

urbanization through the intervening thousand years, and further, into the historical period, could not be carried forward? An attempt has been made here to answer these and other related questions. Our approach will be from known to unknown, i.e., from the historical period to the prehistoric period.

CASTE SYSTEM AND TWO URBANIZATIONS

A factor of great importance, from the point of view of historical urbanization, that occurred around 600-500 B.C. is the 'consolidation' of the society on the basis of '*dharma* concept' and the '*karma* concept' of the caste system. Renewed emphasis was thereafter given to the four different but complementary roles that the Sudras, Vaisyas, Kshatriyas and Brahmanas were called upon to play. Urbanization without economic growth is meaningless. Economic growth leading to urbanization without some form of regular trade and commerce is impossible to imagine. Literary, numismatic and architectural sources, which reflect the economic pattern of the country during sixth-fifth century B.C. clearly embody evidence of the beginning of increased trade and commerce and agriculture. As far as enhanced production of agricultural wealth is concerned, a few direct and indirect evidences may be considered.

None of the scriptural texts or the narrative stories, secular or religious, tells us about the general scarcity of food-grains in the country. On the other hand, the growth of monastic orders living exclusively on alms and donations, presupposes enough of agricultural produce. The establishment of sixteen *mahajanapadas*[1] (of them, at least Kosala, Vatsa, Magadha and Avanti were super *mahajanapadas*) along with their capital cities and standing armies were hardly possible if agricultural produce could not sustain non-agriculturists. The location of the capital towns of this period is also significant from the point of view of some surplus food production; they were in river valleys with broad flood-plains, as also on main trade routes. Trade was not restricted to industrial produce, some movement of food-grains is also attested, but it was never in bulk; it was probably restricted to the king's share, *bhaga* (probably 1/6th of the gross produce, which was reduced to 1/8th for Lumbini by Asoka, as mentioned in his Lumbini Pillar Inscription), a cess over *bhaga* (*bali*), a cess payable for survey and settlement (*rajju*), and a cess for police or chowkidar (*chorarajju*),[2] or to the limited quantity which the open market of the cities consumed (which could not have been very big in quantity considering the size of population in the limited number of early historical towns). There is hardly any evidence of large-scale inter-state movement of grains, or storage of grains, except probably during the time of famine and other natural calamities.[3] The archaeological evidence of greatly enhanced agricultural produce comes from a variety of iron implements, including ploughshare, sickle, hoe, chopper, etc., discovered at Ataranjikhera, Kotia, Kampti and other sites.[4]

The equilibrium of the Vedic society in which only the Brahmanas and the Kshatriyas played the major roles (the Vaisyas had a subordinate role to play) got badly disturbed due to the rise of a trading class whose strength emerged from the money earned from inside and outside the country.[5] Quickly the Brahmanas acted. The Vaisyas were enjoined only

[1] V. S. Agrawal, *India as known to Panini* (2nd ed. Varanasi, 1963), pp. 49-64 and 400-409. Also, Ratilal M. Mehta, *Pre-Buddhist India* (Bombay, 1939), pp. 61-71.

[2] U. N. Ghoshal, *Contribution to the History of the Hindu Revenue System*, (Calcutta, 1972), pp. 101-107; also, Agrawala, *op. cit.*, pp. 415-17.

[3] D. C. Sircar, *Select Inscriptions Bearing on Indian History and Civilization* (Calcutta, 1965), pp. 79-83. The inscriptions in question are 'Sohagaura Bronze Plate Inscription', and 'Mahasthan Fragmentary Stone Plaque Inscription', both dated to third-second century B.C.

[4] Gupta, *op. cit.*, pp. 194, 175-76 and 216-17.

[5] It is significant to remember that the merchant guilds were so powerful that no king before the second century B.C. could himself issue a coin; the Punch Marked coins were issued by guilds alone. R. K. Mookerji, in the *Age of Imperial Unity* (Bombay, 1960), Chapter XXIII, Economic Condition, pp. 599-606. The *Sreni* occurring repeatedly in the literature of this period means a guild of traders. It was usually headed by a *Jetthka* or *Pramukha*, i.e. an elderman or president. The *Arthasastra* is full of references showing the wealth and importance of these guilds for which, Kautilya mentions, separate quarters are reserved in an ideal planning of the town. It is extremely important to note that some of these guilds maintained a regular army, and it is included among the various classes of troops which the king might call upon to serve under him.

There were also merchant guilds organized under *Setthis*. Anathapindaka was a *mahasetthi*, the president of a commercial federation, with numerous *Anusetthis* under him. For further details on guilds see, R. C. Majumdar, *Corporate Life in Ancient India* (Calcutta, 1922), Chapter I.

To quote an instance, Anathapindaka purchased a whole mango grove from the king Ajatasatru for Buddha. The king wanted gold coins amounting to the number which would cover the whole land. The Setthi gave that. This Jataka story is fully illustrated in a medallion on a railing from Bodhagaya. This shows the enormous power of wealth that the Vaisyas had assumed during this period.

to look after the production and distribution of cereals and manufactured goods through the help of the Sudras. Although they formed guilds, issued coins,[1] exploited geological and human resources, and embarked upon long distance trade, they required different types of protection in all these ventures. The merceneries and Kshatriyas were the obvious choice but the former could never be a permanent arrangement although this arrangement was often made. The Kshatriyas, in any case, provided a better alternative, because usually from them came the rulers, the *rajanya* of Panini, who maintained permanent armies.[2] They received a part of the new wealth earned by the Vaisyas in return for the protection that they often gave to the trade as well as to the agriculture, and adjudicated in different financial and agricultural disputes between the Vaisyas and the Sudras or any other class and between them and the other states in which they traded their goods. With this, at least, from about the fourth century B.C. they built forts, palaces and other monumental structures, of which actual remains have been found in excavations, and maintained regular military and civil services. The rise in the wealth (accumulated through taxes and tributes, or also booty) of the *rajanyas* and the establishment of fortifications, etc., by them at a few capital towns, strategic for inter regional trade also, in the sixth-fifth century B.C., have been amply testified by archaeological sources, e.g., Ujjain and Kausambi have yielded fortifications dated by the excavators to the pre-NBPW, i.e., pre-500 B.C.[3] But this was considered hardly enough to give stability to new achievements. The social structure was to be fashioned in a way that at no stage an open conflict of interests between these three forces—the power of religion (priests), the power of capital (traders) and the power of palace (kings)—takes place. This was provided by the Brahmanas through the moralizing influence of the texts (containing, besides many things, myths and legends) in favour of the hereditary nature of the caste system, moral emphasis on *varnasrama dharma*, and the emphasis that they had put on such principles as 'the greatest dharma of a man lies in following the vocation of his own forefathers', not only that, 'man commits greatest sin when he leaves the vocation of his birth and adopts another's'.[4] Thus while the rise of historical urbanization in India may be attributed to the birth of a powerful 'Middle Class' which includes the intellectuals coming up in the wake of the new religious movements—the Buddhism and Jainism—and the traders, its stability may be attributed to the phenomenon of consolidation of the caste system in terms of *'karma'* and *'dharma'* and *'adharma'* con-

[1]S. P. Gupta, 'C-14 Dates determining the chronology of the N.B.P. Ware and Punch-Marked Coins', *Chronology of the Punch-Marked Coins*, Proceedings of the Seminar on Punch-Marked Coins, College of Indology, Banaras Hindu University (Varanasi, 1966), pp. 39-43.

[2]Panini uses the term 'Rajanya in *sutra* vi. 2.34 (*Rajanya-bahuvachana-dvande Andhaka-Vrishnishu*) in a new constitutional significance where *Kasika* defines *rajanya* as a member of such families in a Kshatriya tribe as were consecrated to rulership (*abhishikta-vamsya, kshatriya*)', Agrawal, *op. cit.*, p. 79. Also see Moti Chandra, *Sarthavaha* (Patna, 1953). For the most balanced views on these early fortifications, see, A. Ghosh, *The City in Early Historical India* (Simla, 1973), pp. 59-72.

[3]*Indian Archaeology—A Review*, 1957-58, p. 50; G. R. Sharma, *Excavations at Kausambi*, 1957-59 (Allahabad 1960).

[4]Brahmanas are prohibited to cultivate land since this is specifically the vocation of the Vaisyas: *Brahmanastu krshim krtva mahadoshamavapnuyat* .... (*Parasara* II, 12-13), i.e., 'the sin of ploughing the earth for a day with an iron tipped ploughshare is equal to that incurred by a lfisherman fishing for a year.' P. V. Kane has quoted a arge number of references of this category in his *History of Dharmasastra* (Poona, 1941), Vol., II, pt. I. Chapter III, pp. 123-33; *Gautama Dharmasutra* X, 5-6; *Narada* V, III; *Apastamba Dharmasutra*, I, 9.27.10; *Parasara* II, 12-13; *Manu* VIII, 102, etc. *Manusmrti*, X, 95, 96, 97 specifically forlids any one to try to adopt the vocations of the castes higher than his own:

na tveva jyayasim vrthim abhimanyet kahirchita

"One should under no circumstarces adopt the mode of life prescribed for the varna or varnas higher than his own.' Further, *Manu*, X. 97

varam svadharmo vigane na parakya svanushthitah para dharmena jivanhi sadhhah patati jatati

"It is better to discharge one's own dharma incomplete (or imperfectly) than to perform completely that of another,"

cepts[1] a system which successfully achieved the delicate balance that was required between the controlling hands which were effecting economic changes and the hands which were effecting socio-political changes in a society struggling for urbanization.

In the same context it may also be pointed out that much of the continuity of the material culture of the early historical period throughout the later history of India may be safely attributed primarily to the same phenomenon of caste system; of course, besides several other factors. This I say because of three very important implications of the caste system. Firstly, the technical know-how of things (both on production and distribution sides, as far as agriculture, industry and trade are concerned; and on polity as far as socio-political factors are concerned) smoothly passes from one generation to another. Secondly, acquired knowledge crosses all geographical boundaries since all members of a particular caste, both rich and poor, are socially equal, and are prohi-

[1]Here a very brief background may be given. Castes are mentioned in the *Rgveda*, although they do not seem to have been very rigid during the Early Vedic period. They are mentioned in the *Purusha Sukta*, which, according to some, chiefly Zimmer, is a later interpolation. But they are also mentioned in *RV*., 35, 16-18; I, 113, 16 along with their respective vocations. Hereditary nature of castes, however, may not have been there during this period. In *RV*, X, 39, 14 it is stated that of the descendants of the Brahmana *rishi* Bhrigu, some were reported to be experts in the art of making chariot. In *RV*, IX, 112, 113, a Brahmana sage says: "I am a poet, my father is aphysician my mother a grinder of corn . . . ." Marriages between Brahmanas and Kshatriyas are mentioned in *RV*, VIII, 134, *RV*, 1, 126, etc.

In the Later Vedic period, however, a certain amount of rigidity seems to have crept in. *Satapatha Brahmana*, I, 1, 4, 12; XIII, 8, 3, 11; II, 1, 3, 4; II, 1-4, 11; V, 3, 2, 11, prescribe different rituals, etc., for different castes, even in matters of funeral cakes (*pinda*). *Aitareya Brahmana* I, I, also toe the same line. So much so that the social priorities were given to these castes, one over the other; Vaisyas were the lowest in the three Vedic castes. In the *Atharva Veda*, 17, 9, a Brahmana youth is given priority over a Vaisya youth in marrying a Vaisya girl. Obviously, Vaisyas played a minor role in the social structure; mainly, they looked after agriculture, and although it is absolutely essential for subsistence, its practitioners never gained any high social status in the Vedic society. They achieved a higher status only when they turned their attention to trade and industry. This they started doing in some effective quantity only in the sixth-fifth century B.C.; the earliest dated levels from which the Punch Marked coins come are dated to this period, dates determined by C-14 method. However, it took some two to three hundred years to consolidate that power.

A few other points may also be made clear. According to our texts and present day state of affairs, castes (i.e. *varnas*) are only four, but sub-castes (i.e. *jati*) are several. During the time of Manu, there were 57 *jatis*. It means, in the time of Manu, there were 57 *jatis*. It means, the process of *jati* which is said to be a product of inter-*varna* marriages (*anuloma* and *pratiloma*), and also greater and greater specialization of trades, becomes more rigid in matters of marriage, occupation, etc., than a *varna*. I have a feeling, which, I wish, I could very well substantiate, that the *jati* system also started in sixth-fifth century B.C. since Panini mentions it but in a comprehensive sense "so as to include both *gotra* and *charana* indicative of natural and cultural lineage as implied in *sutra* II. 1.63 (*katara katamall jati-pariprasne*). Patanjali explains *jati* in this extended sense . . . Evidently, the *gotras* and *chranas* were fast developing their separate entity as *jatis*" (Agrawal, *op. cit.*, p. 77).

The rigidity in the caste system was not achieved in a day. There was a long period in which the society's mind was vacillating. The *Mahabharata*. represents that transitional phase. In it there are several instances to show that people did change the prescribed vocations of their *varnas*, e.g., Dronacharya, Asvathama, and Kripacharya, were Brahmanas but acted as commanders in Kaurava's army, a job primarily of the Kshatriyas; 'deeds' (*guna* and *karma*) and not 'birth' is proclaimed as the only valid basis of one's *varna* (*MB. Santiparva*, 188, 1-17). At another place, one's birth in a particular *varna* has been attributed to one's *karmas* (*MB. Vanaparva* 207, 2-3) of the previus birth (which cannot be changed). It has also been repeatedly mentioned that only by faithfully performing the vocations of one's *varna*, got by birth, one can hope to change one's *varna* for a better one in the next life (*MB. Vanaparva*, 207, 21, 22, 39), but only in the next birth'. Conversely, it has also been said that by not doing the duties of one's *varna* rightfully one degrades himself to the lower *varna* (*MB. Anusasanaparva*, 143, 1-47; 51; *Vanaparva*, 180, 25) even in this life, what to say of the next. Thus, by turn, 'birth' and 'deeds' has been taken as the basis of one's caste-- the ideal basis was 'deeds'; but 'birth' could not be overlooked since it is divine, it is the natural outcome of one's *karmas*, it has to be endured'. Think of the great difficulty which Visvamitra had to undergo in order to attain the Brahmana *varna* (*Ramayana, Bala Kanda*, VII, ff. and *MB. Adiparva*. 71, 79). In fact, to get degraded in a lower *varna* by adopting the vocations of that *varna* (as a punishment, of course) was much more common (the Brahmana Indra became Kshatriya; Naghaba, a Kshatriya, became a Vaisya) than to get upgraded (*MB. Salya*. 40: Devapi, Sindhudvipa and a few others did attain Brahmanahood but these are exceptions). I have not a single reference to quote in which a Vaisya could ever become a Kshatriya or Brahmana'. For a good detailed study, see P. Prabhu's *Hindu Social Organization* (Bombay, 1954), on which the above study is primarily based. See also, Agrawal, *op. cit.* pp. 77-28.

bited to marry outside caste boundaries (many technical know-hows travel from one place to another through the mechanics of marriage—in patriarchal societies children are often found staying with maternal relations and learning the tricks of the trades of the maternal relations; in many trades, e.g., pottery making, even the girls carry the technical know-how to the family of their husbands). Finally, members of different castes hardly encroach upon each others' profession, of course, *apad kale* (period of crisis endangering survival) apart.

Thus, professional and class rivalries were reduced to a minimum. Interests did not clash openly. Clearly, the socio-politico-economic structure was so nicely balanced in the early historical times, mainly due to the strong and stratified structure of the society, that the inherent tension amongst different pillars of social strength did not openly clash and the process of urbanization emerged in the sixth-fifth century B.C. and the legacy of each generation passed on to the other without getting lost (except those techniques which were either confined to a few, or where people willingly changed certain traits, for example, the fashion in pottery or clothing). By the fourth century B.C. a number of fortified towns with well established kingship and flourishing trade had come to stay.

But the caste system also imposed, unwittingly of course, certain unavoidable restrictions in the overall growth of our society—economic and intellectual both. The hereditary nature of the caste system and the overpowering sense of *dharma* and *adharma* attached to the allotted vocations led the people to become a closed community. Individual talents, which are inborn in human beings, do not admit any class or caste restrictions. A Brahmana or a Kshatriya, born with exceptional talents for trade and commerce (i.e., the vocation of the Vaisyas) was, exceptions apart,[1] strictly prohibited to use them (although this might have brought about the overall social good) since that would mean leaving one's allotted vocation, i.e., commiting *adharma*. In a society where the sense of *dharma* and *adharma* was supreme one would have preferred to die rather than use his or her talents in a way that might lead him or her to commit an act of *adharma*. But in how many cases vocational *adharma* was really commited, we do not know: it might not have been commited in very many cases. But the geniuses who really bring about phenomenal changes in any society at any particular time are always a few. Obviously, all this meant a social situation in which the entire burden of technological innovations and the resultant economic growth fell squarely on the shoulders of only 20 per cent or less of the people, the Sudras counted for 40 per cent of the totality. And out of this 20 per cent, hardly 50 per cent actually seems to have directly participated in any meaningful way, since they alone lived in cities and suburban towns. What could we expect from this state of affairs? Urbanization again remained confined to a handful of capital and trading cities in ancient India—Pataliputra, Vaisali, Kasi, Kausambi, Mathura, Ujjain, etc., a single state had hardly one or two 'cities' as such; the majority of the settlements in India have always been only villages, even today India has only 120 cities with a population of more than one lakh; many district headquarters are only big towns at best. This phenomenon is, of course, not surprising since it was not peculiar to India: throughout the ancient world the cities were few and far between, and in their composition village folk always formed a major portion; more towns and fewer villages is the by-product of heavy industrialization through which our country has as yet not passed.

Thus, the basic nature of the first and second urbanization remained the same—the growth of only the capital cities or trading centres under the political patronage of the ruler, given directly to the trading community to create wealth and thereby earn prestige to the ruling authority; the remaining part of the country stood at the level of peasantry and nomadism.

Now we may be in a better position to work out whether the Harappans and pre-Harappans had the social structure based on caste system or not. We may rather ask a more direct question: what could have been the social structure of the Harappanes I do not see any possibility of the caste system existing with them since I feel that had it been there the material culture of the Harappans would not have died out without leaving any legacy of urbanization since the technical know-how of things would have been smoothly passing through the ages. Of course, the forms and meaning might have been changing in the natural process of history, and this can alway be traced out, but the elements of urbanization woud not have been lost. The question then arises as to why

[1] H. Luders, 'Three Early Brahmi Inscriptions', *Epigraphia Indica*, vol. IX, (1970-08), Ins. no. 3, p. 239. It clearly mentions the two kshatriyas of Mathura doing a good business. to earn their livelihood

some writers, like Malik[1] feel that the caste system is likely to have existed among the Harappans? Obviously, because they think that the Harappan urbanization was the 'formative period' of the Indian Civilization as a whole and its success depended on a highly stratified society. According to this concept, the legacy of the Harappa culture passed on to the post-Harappan cultures in a continuous manner. I am afraid, archaeology does not stand by them. The patterns of houses, drains, roads, town planning, monumental structures (including fortification and granary), script, system of seals, etc., were simply non-existent in the period between the two well-known urbanizations; we had to start afresh in the historical times. The Harappan period can hardly be called the 'formative period of Indian Civilization' and the society may not at all have been as stratified as the prevalence of the caste system would imply. Societies with much less stratification have been found developing civilization and/or urbanization in the Middle East and Mesoamerica.[2]

SOCIAL STRUCTURE OF THE HARAPPANS

If the possibility of caste system is remote in the Harappan context, what else could have been the basis of the social structure of the Harappans? Before we try to visualize it, a few things, which are already known, may be recapitulated. Since the seals are still undeciphered, we are sure only of three things: first agricultural technology, including the 'double crop', i.e., two crops in a year, and the 'twin crop', i.e., single sowing of two types of cereals, one maturing a little earlier than the other,[3] was considerably improved and redistributional system of the agricultural produce within the city was, at least partially, controlled and regulated through State granaries;[4] secondly, industrial technology witnessed several innovations and, industrial produce and distributional system, i.e., trade and commerce, was highly organized through warehouses, navigation, exchanges,[5] etc., and, thirdly, there was a super authority in each city which, for its own use, erected citadel with admini-

[1] S. C. Malik, *Indian Civilization, the Formative Period* (Simla, 1968), p. 106. Here he maintains that 'caste' is not 'class' of the Western concept. Caste is unique to India.... because of its emphasis on the religious aspects, i.e., the ideological aspect of caste'. On p. 107 he takes the roots of this institution 'to the Harappan society' In short, he writes 'we see a very early beginning of one of the most important social institutions of later India that characterize the Indian style'. Lewis Mumford, however, uses the term 'caste' in the sense of stratified classes when he says 'The early city, as distinct from the village community, is a caste managed society, organized for the satisfaction of a dominant minority: no longer a community of humble families living by mutual aid'; see, Lewis Mumford, *The City in History* (London, 1961), p. 38.

[2] M.E.L. Mallowan, *Early Mesopotamia and Iran* (London, 1965), pp. 1 3-25. Also see, Sol Tax, R. Fernea, M. Singer, B. F. Hoselitz and R. M. Adams in Kraeling and Adams, *op. cit.* pp. 35-46. Hoselitz says, 'I would conclude that essentially unstratified societies also are capable of making very considerable adjustments in their livelihood patterns or technology'; p. 43. The same was true with the Maya civilization, *ibid.*, p. 45.

[3] B. B. Lal, 'Perhaps the earliest ploughed field so far excavated anywhere in the world, *Puratattva*, no. 4 (1970-71), pp. 1-3.

[4] R. E. M. Wheeler, *The Indus Civilization* (Cambridge, 1968), pp. 33, 43-45. Fairservis, *op. cit.*, p. 304, feels that 'one crop system, probably, needed the establishment of big granaries'. According to him, 'one crop system was the outcome, as in Egypt, of the fact that every year after the floods, the flood plain alone was cultivated .... Each flooding re-fertilized the land, and its extent led to a 'lean or 'prosperous year in terms of agricultural economy. .... (these factors) necessitated granaries. Against this 'danger of scarcity' theory, so to say, there are two arguments: first, as Lal has shown, from about 2400-2300 B.C the Harappan Zone knew fairly well about the 'twin crop' system; geomorphologists have already exploded the myth of the Nile and Tigris parallelism by clearly showing the difference in the original sources of the two rivers, the former arises from lakes while the latter form mountains-- a factor which effects the nature of flood, the water retaining power of the land, the type of agriculture in the two types of flood-zones, etc. These differences, if clearly worked out by scientists, will certainly apply to the Nile and the Indus. See, C. W. Thornwaite in Kareling and Adams, *op. cit.*, pp. 158-59; also, J. A. Wilson, in *ibid.*, pp. 127-28; W. F. Edgerton, in *ibid.*, on pp. 145-46. Allchins have further listed separate Rabi and Kharif crops showing the knowledge of the Harappans of two crops in a year; Bridget and Raymond Allchin, *The Birth of Indian Civilization* (Harmondsworth, 1968), p. 260.

Secondly, it appears that Fairservis has at the back of his mind the modern conditions of scarcity in agricultural wealth in Indo-Pakistan sub-continent where granaries are being established to store grain, both imported and locally purchased, to meet national emergencies, but probably it will be better to remember that the present cannot be imposed on the past; there was hardly any scope for the import of grains, there is no evidence to show that the population ratio with agricultural produce was as odd as it is at present. On the other hand, the division of labour, the growth of cities, the expansion of culture and the movement of people during the Harappan period could not be sustained under the Damocles sword of agricultural scarcity; in fact, they appear to go hand in hand with the pehnomenal growth in agricultural produce, phenomenal when seen vis-a-vis the pre-Harappans and the contemporaries in Baluchistan.

[5] S. R. Rao, 'Shipping in Ancient India', in *India's Contribution to World Thought and Culture*, A Vivekananda Commemoration Volume (Madras, 1970), pp. 83-107.

strative and ritualistic buildings, and other monumental public structures, and regulated all civic affairs. In complete absence of monumental structures of 'temples' as such (although Wheeler proposes one each on the citadel and the lower city of Mohenjo-daro),[1] we are hardly in a position to visualize the nature of religious authority[2] although mother goddesses, sculptures of the so called 'priests', several pictorial and narrative depictions on seals and tablets, fire altars, etc., do indicate the existence of some sort of magico-religious practices; it is likely that most of them were purely of folk origin. At Mohenjo-daro,[3] Kalibangan[4] and Surkotada,[5] there are definite clues that the citadels were composed of two units, one having structures which may be considered as basically religious, while the other which may have been primarily for political and administrative purposes. It appears to be a good case for the theory of Lewis Mumford which seeks the beginning of cities in coming together of the religious and political authorities.[6] 'Workmens' Quarters' and 'Industrial Sector' 'Market Place' are some of the other vocational divisions of the Harappan cities which we come across in archaeological writings.[7]

The entire picture of the social structure that emerges out of the above details admits one basis: 'vocational class system', which means that although the society was divided into certain professional classes, the membership of these classes was not strictly governed by heredity. It was a stratified society but not closed. But what appears to be there, which, of course, can hardly be proved at the present state of our knowledge, since Harappan inscriptions have still not been read, is the existence of a hereditary ruler, or a group of ruling families, i.e., some sort of an oligarchy, in each city. Why do I conceive the hereditary nature of the political rule, may be a very valid question. My feeling is based upon both internal and external evidences. Internal evidence is the continuance of one and the same citadel throughout the period of efflorescence of a city; the highly regimented nature of the citadel's plan; the imposing character of the citadel's architecture; the separateness of the citadel from the town, from the point of view of its placement in the overall plan of the city; the special features of the buildings on or adjacent the citadel, etc. External evidence is the 'absolute' nature of political authority in contemporary West Asian cities which too have imposing citadels with distinguishing structures, both religious and political (the *concept* of citadel in the Harappan matrix seems have come from West Asia, whether along with the hereditary nature of the ruler or not, we do not know). Since I favour the theory of regional autonomy and some sort of oligarchy as the basis of political structure of the Harappans, I derive the political authority of the Harappans both from the respect of the masses for 'tradition' and 'traditionally ruling families' as also from the religious predilection of the people, unlike Mesopotamia, militarism and heroism in war do not seem to be the source of political authority for the ruler. Our city-states do not seem to have waged wars against each other.

[1]Allchin, *op. cit.*, pp. 244 and 247.

[2]K.N. Shastri, *New Light on the Indus Civilization* (New Delhi, 1957), vol. I, pp. 15-55. Also see, Allchin, *op. cit.*, pp. 137-38; Fairservis, *op. cit.*, pp. 291-95; Sir Mortimer Wheeler, *Civilizations of the Indus Valley and Beyond* (London, 1966), p. 40.

[3]J., Marshall, *Mohenjo daro) and the Indus Civilization* (London, 1931), vol. III. Also see, Allchin, *op. cit.*, figs. 69 and 70; Wheeler, *op. cit.* (1966), fig. 23.

[4]B. B. Lal, and B. K. Thapar, 'Excavations at Kalibangan: New Light on the Indus Civilization,' *Cultural Forum*, vol. IX, no. 4. Also, B. K. Thapar, 'Synthesis of the multiple data as obtained from Kalibangan,' *Radiocarbon and Indian Archaeology* (Bombay, 1973).

[5]J.P. Joshi, 'Transformation of Harappa Culture in Kutch: examination of evidence from Surkotada, Paper read in VI Annual Conference of the Indian Archaeological Society held at Kurukshetra in 1972 (unpublished).

[6]Lewis Mumford in his presidential address in a Symposium on 'Urbanization and Cultural Development in the Ancient Near East', Kraeling and Adams, *op. cit.*, pp. 7-8. He says 'at some point in human development, somewhere perhaps between the establishment of the Egyptian solar calendar and the organisation of the Sumerian phalax. *there was a sudden fusion of sacred power and secular power*, which produced the nucleus of the city'. In the Harappan context, so long as the inscriptions remain unread, we can only guess this fusion although its form may not at all be similar to that of Egypt or Mesopotamia.

[7]Wheeler, *op. cit.* (1968), pp. 30-55.

Notes and News

Problems of the Neolithic Cultures in India: a Retrospect

The time-hallowed conventional term 'neolithic' continues to be used with qualifying phrases like stone-using agriculturists or the like. Although the term as a culture-label seems to have been established through usage, having wormed its way deeply into the literature,[1] it is now being increasingly realized that its application has to be confined to that stage of human development which is characterized by (a) the systematic exploitation of the natural resources in animals and plants and shifts in basic patterns more stimulating to man's creative and intellectual capacity, and (b) increasing tendency to settle more or less permanently in the open or to make seasonal migrations to potential areas. Against the background of this knowledge, relating to deterministic criteria, including terminology, we may review the problems of neolithic cultures in India. The objective of the present investigation is indeed less to present definitive results than to stimulate interest in the lines of enquiry. May be at this stage of research, questions will be found to be more valuable than answers.

In India, the first find of implements, proved by subsequent work to be associated with the neolithic assemblage, was made as early as 1842[2] in District Raichur (Mysore) and it was not until a century later that the tools of this category were placed in a proper archaeological perspective, both chronological and cultural. The excavation at Brahmagiri (Mysore) in 1942 by M. H. Krishna, and in 1947 by Sir Mortimer Wheeler for the first time put the neolithic culture of the region in a culture-sequence, besides a relative time-scale. Subsequent work in this region as also in others, carried out in the following two decades as a result of deliberate and informed strategy, made it possible to recognize the neolithic cultures in three principal regions,[3] labelled the northern, eastern and southern. Recent findings have, however, indicated that the former two regions have to be further subdivided respectively into northern and north-western and central-eastern and north-eastern.[4] Besides, one new region, viz. north Bihar has to be added to this list. In the Indo-Pak subcontinent, therefore, at the present moment, the existence of neolithic cultures has been established in six different geographical regions: (1) Northern, covering Kashmir (excavated site, Burzahom); (ii) North-western, covering Baluchistan, Swat and the contiguous areas of Upper Sind valley in West Pakistan (excavated sites, Kile Gul Mohammad, Ghaligai and Saraikhola);

[1] Derek Roe, *Prehistory, an Introduction* (London, 1970).

[2] F.R. Allchin, 'Ideas of history in Indian archaeological writing : a preliminary study', in (ed.) C.H. Philips, *Historians of India, Pakistan and Ceylon* (Oxford, 1964). The reported implements include a 'bagful of jasper, agate and chalcedony knives and arrow heads'. The first recognized notice of celts or stone hatchets, however, was made by H.P. Le Mesurier in 1860 from the Ton river region in Uttar Pradesh. Cf. *Proceedings of the Asiatic Society of Bengal* for February 1861 (Calcutta, 1862), pp. 81-85.

[3] B.K. Thapar, 'Neolithic problems in India', in (eds.) V.N. Mishra and M.S. Mate, *Indian Prehistory : 1964* (Poona 1964) ; also V.D. Krishnaswami, 'The Neolithic Pattern of India', *Ancient India*, no. 16 (New Delhi, 1962), pp. 25-64 and H.D. Sankalia, *Prehistory and Protohistory in India and Pakistan* (Bombay, 1962), pp. 152 ff.

[4] F.R. and Bridget Allchin, *The Birth of Indian Civilization* (Harmondsworth, 1968), p. 158.

(iii) Central-eastern, covering Chota Nagpur plateau with its peneplains in various Districts of Uttar Pradesh, Bihar, Orissa and West Bengal (excavated sites, Barudih and Kuchai); (iv) North-eastern, covering Assam, Chittagong and the sub-Himalayan regions including Darjeeling (excavated site, Daojali Hading); (v) north Bihar, covering District Saran (excavated site, Chirand); and (vi) Southern, covering peninsular India (excavated sites, Brahmagiri, Sanganakallu, Maski, Piklihal, Utnur, Nagarjunakonda, T. Narsipur, Hemmige, Paiyampalli, Tekkalakota, Terdal, Hallur, Palavoy, Kupgal and Kodekal). It must be emphasized, however, that the present group ing of the neolithic cultures is as tentative and subject to revision as the one suggested ten years back.[1] Its only merit or utility is that, being an up-to-date stock-taking of the evidence, it may provide a suitable framework for future research on the subject. Furthermore, the six areas referred to above seem to follow broad physiographic sub-divisions and as such may provide possibilities of studying the relationship between the cultures and the characterized environment. As regards nomenclature, it would be more expedient if geographical regions are used as adjectives to qualify the various neolithic cultures,[2] so that their spatial boundaries are well defined. Excepting the use of ground stone implements, each of these cultures differs from the other in material equipment, and to some extent, in the specific level of subsistence economy. Any attempt to consider these cultures as ramifications of one single development[3] may be regarded as premature. At the same time it may be remembered that while certain areas still remain unexplored, the main difficulty at the present moment lies in the varying intensity of archaeological fieldwork in these six areas.

We may now turn to the natural and human background including antecedents of these cultures. In the last two decades, there has been a growing realization of the importance of environment in human progress. With a view to obtaining a reasonably complete data on environmental history of the area under study, one has to depend on Quaternary research. Unfortunately, however, much less is known of the ecological transformations in India, with the result that we have to base our evidence on the generalized knowledge gathered from the subsistence mode of these early farming communities. Let it be admitted at the outset that in none of the areas have the details been worked out of the transition from the stage of food-gathering to that of food-producing and primary or settled village farming. The excavated sites reveal settlements which are later (excepting those at Sanganakallu[4] and Kuchai[5]) than would be pertinent to the transition itself. While at Sanganakallu, the neolithic settlement was preceded by an occupation characterized by the use of heavily patinated flakes of trap and sandstone and crude microliths of quartz, without pottery, at Kuchai, it overlay an occupation distinguished by the use of non-geometric microliths, also without pottery. At both these sites, there was no continuity in the succession of occupations. The occurrence of 'highly rolled potsherds in the top weathered granite murrum layer below the earliest neolithic occupation'[6] at the former site is less clearly understood at the present stage.

There is yet another set of sites where the use of pottery has been attested in an evolving sequence of Late Stone Age industries—from a non-geometric microlith series through a geometric one, both without pottery, to a geometric one with pottery. The sites are located in different geographical areas: Lekhahia, Morhana Pahar and Baghai Khor[7] in the Kaimur range, where a complete sequence of the industries was revealed; Adamgarh[8] and Pachmarhi[9] in the Mahadeo hills; Langhnaj[10] on the fossil sand dunes

[1]Thapar, *op. cit.* (1964). Already scholars feel that the Southern Neolithic Culture may not be treated as a homogenous entity. Cf.K. Paddayya, *Investigations into the Neolithic culture of the Shorapur Doab, South India* (Leiden, 1973), p. 87.

[2]B.K. Thapar, 'Methodology in Archaeology : a critique of the methods and nature of archaeological discipline', in (ed.) S.B. Deo, *Archaeological Congress and Seminar Papers* (Nagpur, 1972), p. 201.

[3]I.K. Sarma, 'South-east Asia, India and West Asia, a study on the beginnings of the food producing stage, in, (ed.) Deo, *op. cit.* (1972), pp. 95-112.

[4]B. Subbarao, *Stone Age Cultures of Bellary* (Poona, 1948).

[5]*Indian Archaeology 1961-62—A Review* (New Delhi, 1962).

[6]H.D. Sankalia, *Excavations at Langhnaj* 1944-63, pt. 1, Archaeology (Poona 1965), p 43.

[7]G.R. Sharma and R.K. Verma, in (eds.) Mishra and Mate, *op. cit.* (1964), pp. 73-79

[8]R.V. Joshi, 'Late Neolithic Culture in Central India', in *La Prehistoire Problems et Tendences* (Paris, 1968), pp. 245-54.

[9]G.R. Hunter, 'Interim and final reports on the excavation in the Mahadeo hills', *Nagpur University Journal*, 1935 and 1936 respectively ; also cf. D.H. Gordon, 'The stone industries of the Holocene in India and Pakistan, *Ancient India*, no. 6 (New Delhi, 1950), pp. 64-90 and *The Prehistoric Background of Indian Culture* (Bombay, 1956).

[10]Sankalia, *op. cit.*, (1965).

in the Sabarmati valley; and Bagor[1] in Rajasthan, where the deposits of the non-geometric microliths were not encountered. At Langhnaj, which was an open air settlement, besides a ground stone industry, represented by mace-heads, ringstones, small-sized wedge-shaped sandstone pieces (querns?) and axes, dentalium shell beads were also found. Pottery has also been reported to have been found along with microliths at Marve[2] (near Khandivli) and Jalahalli[3] (near Bangalore) but its stratigraphic association is not clearly established at either of the sites. At Yerangal, near Khandivli, ground stone mace-heads were also found along with microliths. The use of pottery (and of ground stone tools in case of Langhnaj) does not appear to have brought about any change in the basic economy of these communities which continued to remain largely in a hunting-gathering stage. The distinction between geometric and non-geometric as also between pottery and non-pottery microliths has not been properly worked up, and is at present not a sure basis for recognizing a transition from the food-gathering to food producing economy. At a factory-site, pottery, though in use, may not be found.

This brings us to the evidence relating to the domestication of animals[4] and plants[5] in these areas. Among the excavated neolithic sites, animal remains have been examined from Maski,[6] Piklihal,[7] Utnur,[8] Tekkalakota,[9] Hallur,[10] Kodekal[11] and Kile Gul Mohammad.[12] Of these, the last-mentioned one falls in the North-western region, and the remaining ones in the Southern. From the other regions, the relevant evidence is not so far available. At Adamgarh, bones of domestic animals have been found in association with a microlithic industry. This admittedly unsatisfactory state of our knowledge about domestication of animals would, it is hoped, stimulate renewed search for the recovery of such vital information for reconstructing the environment of the neolithic cultures. Coming to the available evidence we find that cattle (*Bos indicus*), sheep (*Ovis vignei Blyth*) and goat (*Capra hireus aegagreus Gmelin*) were commonly domesticated both at Kile Gul Mohammad and at the south Indian sites. Besides, in both the areas, bones of the horse tribe (*equidae*) were found. In the southern area, they are reported from the neolithic-chalcolithic deposits at Hallur and in the North-western, from the pre-pottery levels at Kile Gul Mohammad (where the identifiable fragments with good probability are those of *Equus hemionus* and not *Equus caballus*). The existence of the buffalo (*Bos bubalus bubalis*) is also attested at Maski[13] and Kodekal. Bones of the cattle, however, formed the large majority, indicating that animal husbandry became the chief source of their economy during that period. Among the cattle in south India, both the short-horned and the long-horned varieties of breed were known. Two more points merit our attention in this respect: (i) the occurrence of charred and split bones is indicative of the use of animal-flesh as an item of diet; and (ii) the anchylosis of the hock joint, as noticed by Alur, shows that the cattle were used for heavy draft or weight-lifting work. It may be recalled that horse belongs to the category of animals domesticated primarily for transport and labour.[14] The presence of ass has already been reported from Maski and Brahmagiri. This animal must have served as a beast of burden. The pastoral and agricultural character of the economy of these communities is thus clearly indicated. Whether all these animals were locally domesticated from the corresponding wild species in each area or were brought as ready-made breed, like perhaps the horse, has not been adequately investigated any more than the

[1]V.N. Mishra, 'Late Mesolithic settlements in Rajasthan—a brief review of investigations', *Journal of the University of Poona*, no. 35, pp 69-77

[2]K.R.U. Todd, 'Palaeolithic industries of Bombay', *Journal Royal Anthropological Institute*, vol LIX, pp 257-72; also, 'The microlithic industries of Bombay', *Ancient India*, no 6 (New Delhi, 1950), pp. 4-16.

[3]Gordon, *op. cit.* (1956), p. 17.

[4]F.R. Allchin, 'Early domestic animals in India and Pakistan', in (eds.), P.J. Ucko and W. Dimbleby, *The Domestication and Exploitation of Plants and Animals* (London, 1968), pp. 317-22.

[5]F.R. Allchin, 'Early cultivated plants in India and Pakistan', in (eds.) Ucko and Dimbleby, *op. cit.* (1968) and Vishnu Mittre, 'Palaeobotanical evidence for the history of plants', (in press).

[6]Bhola Nath on 'Animal Remains' in B.K. Thapar, 'Maski 1954 : a chalcolithic site of the southern Deccan', *Ancient India* no. 13 (New Delhi, 1957).

[7]P. Srinivasan on 'Animal Remains' in F.R. Allchin, *Piklihal Excavations* (Hyderabad, 1960), pp. 114-20.

[8]P. Srinivasan on 'Animal Remains' in F.R. Allchin, *Utnur Excavations* (Hyderabad, 1961) and *Neolithic Cattle Keepers of South India* (Cambridge, 1965).

[9]M.S. Nagaraja Rao and K.C. Malhotra, *Stone Age Hill Dwellers of Tekkalakota* (Poona, 1968), pp. 87-89.

[10]K.R. Alur, on 'Animal Remains' in M.S. Nagaraja Rao, *Protohistoric Cultures of the Tungabhadra Valley, a report on Hallur Excavation* (Dharwar, 1971), pp 104-24.

[11]D.R. Shah on' Animal Remains from the Kodekal Excation, in Paddayya, *op. cit.* (1973), pp. 92-95

[12]Walter A Fairservis Jr., *Excavations in the Quetta valley West Pakistan*, vol. 45, pt 2, Anthropological papers of the American Museum of Natural History (New York, 1956), pp. 382-85.

[13]Bhola Nath, 'Animals of Prehistoric India and their affinities with those of the Western Asiatic Countries', *Records of the Indian Museum*, 59(4), pp. 335-67.

[14]F.E. Zeuner, *A History of Domesticated Animals* (London, 1963), p. 64.

interplay of biological phenomena leading to the growth of such communities. A study of the fossil soils below the neolithic deposits at Kupgal[1] shows that during the time of the neolithic occupation, the region experienced wetter climate and had more vegetation with scrub forest and grassland.

At this point it would be appropriate to discuss the evidence relating to the plant-remains obtained from these neolithic sites. The evidence, it may be admitted, is appallingly inadequate, and is available only from the following sites: (i) Maski,[2] Utnur,[3] Hallur,[4] Tekkalakota[5] and Paiyampalli, all located in the Southern region; and Baidipur,[6] located in the Eastern . The knowledge of the cultivation of rice from the latter area and of millet (*Eleusine coracana* and *Eleusine indica*) and horse gram (*Dolichos biflorus*) from the former was attested. Thus, there is no doubt that both cereals and pulses were grown by the people. Besides, evidence for the existence of teak (*Tectona grandis*), date palm and *Acacia* Spp. (*Leguminosae: Mimosoidae*) were also recorded from the former area. It is significant to note that the millet, identified as *ragi* (*Eleusine coracana*) is considered to have been developed by selection from *Eleusine africana* and as such appears to have come from Africa.[7] For a full comprehension of this significance it may be recalled that the sample containing the millet came from the same phase of the Neolithic Period (viz. Neolithic-Chalcolithic) which yielded the bones of the horse; the mechanism of the diffusion of these component elements respectively from Africa and West Asia will have to be worked out, keeping in view the areas on the route and principles of transmission and acceptance.

For the palaeobotanical evidence, palynological studies have been made at four places: (i) Haigam Lake in Kashmir valley;[8] (ii) Quaternary deposits a round Calcutta;[9] (iii) Sambhar Lake in Rajasthan;[10] and (iv) Naukutchiya Tal (near Naini Tal) in Kumaon. Of these, the evidence relating to the Kashmir valley is of vital interest in the context of the present investigation. Pollen diagrams constructed from the Haigam Lake have furnished evidence for a three-stage disturbance of natural vegetation as shown by the decline and appearance of pine forest. The clearance of pine forest at one stage is thought to be related to the farming experiments of the neolithic settlers in the valley. The discovery of the seeds of *Lithospermiem arvensa, Medicago deniteulacta, Lotus corniculatus* and *Ipomoea Sp.* at Burzahom, implying thereby the cultivation of wheat and barley in the earlier centuries of the second millennium B.C., lends support to the above postulate. The pollen diagram from the Naukutchiya Tal also furnishes evidence for the disturbance of natural vegetation as revealed by the destruction of pine forest by fire. The charcoal in the sediments have, however, not been dated so far. In Rajasthan, cereal pollen were encountered in one of the stages dated to *circa* 6000 B.C. but it is not accompanied by any disturbance of natural vegetation. This evidence may have some bearing on the economy of the Late Stone Age settlements in the area, experimenting with colonisation or harvesting stages of agriculture as defined by Hawkes.[11] The excavated site of Bagor[12] in District Bhilwara, however, does not take the evidence of occupation as far back. Lastly, the superficial peat deposits of Bengal (dated in *circa* 3000 B.C.) yielded pollen of a cultivated variety associated with *Plantago* (a weed of wheat or barley). No archaeological evidence, has, however, been attested for such an early cultivation of wheat and barley in this area.

The foregoing account brings forth a body of significant evidence: on the one side are sites showing varying levels of productive (neolithic) economy, but without any preparatory processes, and on the other are those indicating largely a hunting and gathering economy, but elaborated at some stage of cultural evolution by the use of pottery and of ground stone implements, and occasionally attesting the presence of domestic animals. The apparent gap in the culture historical sequence, as revealed by the level of economy at these two sereis of sites, is due largely to our obsession to find sites with continuous succession of

[1]G.G. Mujumdar and S.N. Rajguru, *Ashmound Excavations at Kupgal* (Poona, 1966).

[2]S.S. Ghosh and K.A. Chowdhury on 'Plant-remains' in Thapar, *op. cit.* (1957), pp. 133-42.

[3]Allchin, *op. cit.* (1961),

[4]Vishnu Mittre on 'Ancient Plant Economy at Hallur' in Nagaraja Rao, *op. cit.* (1971), pp. 125-33.

[5]*Ibid.* p. 129.

[6]*Ibid.* p. 129.

[7]Sir Joseph B. Hutchinson, in *Ibid.* p. 131.

[8]Vishnu Mittre, 'Some aspects concerning pollen analytical investigations in the Kashmir Valley', *Palaeobotanist*, vol. 15 nos. 1 and 2, pp. 157-75 ; Vishnu Mittre and B.D. Sharma, 'Studies of post-glacial vegetational history from the Kashmir Valley, Haigam Lake', *Palaeobotanist*, vol. 15, nos. 1 and 2, pp. 185-212.

[9]S. Chanda and B.B. Mukherjee, 'Radiocarbon dating of two microfossiliferous Quaternary deposits in and around Calcutta', *Science and Culture*, vol. 35 ; pp. 275-76.

[10]Gurdeep Singh, 'A preliminary approach towards the resolution of some important problems in Rajasthan', *Indian Geohydrology*, vol. 3., no. 1, (1967), pp. 111-28

[11]J.G. Hawkes, 'The ecological background of plant domestication' in (eds.), Ucko, and Dimbleby ,*op. cit.* (1969), pp. 17-29.

[12]V.N. Misra, 'Bagor—a late mesolithic settlement in north-west India' *World Archaeology*, vol. 5, no. 1 (June 1973) pp. 92-110.

culture deposits. Nevertheless, the twain has got to meet This, however, is not said with a quasi philosophical speculation. Theoretically, evidence for the preliminary level of incipient food production should on *a priori* grounds be expected in same areas. The distribution of the wild animals and plants which became the basis for the new mode of subsistence food-producing pattern has got to be worked out.

In the Central-eastern region, more particularly in District Mirzapur, many factory sites of the Mesolithic Period have been located. At one of these,[1] a fragment of a neolithic axe was also found upon the flaking floor, indicating that the site was used by the neolithic people. Here, therefore, is a potential area for a multidisciplinary investigation of the problem. Similarly, in the Peninsula,[2] or in fact in any region, such areas should be taken up for intensive investigation which promise an evidence for the potential of food production. The potential may be in technology or in the pattern of migration from the plateau to the plain.

B. K. THAPAR

Archaeological Survey of India,
Janpath, New Delhi-110011

[1]Bridget Allchin, *The Stone-tipped Arrow* (London, 1966), pp. 83-84.

[2]We may not necessarily agree with the grouping of five variants in the Southern Neolithic Culture until we have in the nuclear area (Bellary and Raichur *doab*) recognized the transitional industries. (Cf Paddayya, *op. cit.* (1973), pp. 87-91 ; also, 'Radiocarbon dates and South Indian Neolithic Culture', *Antiquity*, XLV, no. 178 (June 1971), pp. 234-38.

Harappan Chronology: an Integrated Study

An attempt is made in this study to draw up an integrated chronology of the Harappan and the pre-Harappan cultures on the basis of *all* the available data.

A coefficient of correlation is also found for the conversion of the primary uncorrected radiocarbon dates so as to correspond with the historical or the calendrical dates.

CROSS-CONTACTS

The basic spadework in Harappan chronology was done by Sir John Marshall.[1] He found Harappan seals at Kish, Lagash, Umma, Ur, etc. On the basis of this comparative study, he (and also Gadd[2]) were of the opinion that the period of contact was largely Sargonid and pre-Sargonid. Marshall, therefore, proposed a span of 3250-2750 B.C., because Sargon of Akkad was then taken to have ruled in *c.* 2800 B.C. The date of Sargon has now been revised to 2371-2316 B.C., with the result that Marshall's chronology has accordingly to undergo changes; Marshall's revised chronology for the Harappan Period would be 2800-2200 B.C.

Recent work has shown that some of the seals were also found from the deposits of the Isin-Larsa Periods. The most important seal find is by Buchanan,[3] who found the impression of a Harappan seal on a dated cuneiform tablet of the tenth year of the king Gungunum of Larsa. As Gungunum ruled during 1932-1906 B.C., the seal must have belonged to 1922 B.C.

RADIOCARBON DATING

On the basis of C^{14} work, carried out almost exclusively at the Tata Institute of Fundamental Research (TIFR), date bracket of 2300-1750 B.C. has been proposed by Agrawal,[4] which Allchin has accepted.[5]

[1]Sir John Marshall, *Mohenjo-daro and the Indus Civilization*, 3 vols. (London, 1932); also see, *Indian Archaeology—A Review* (1960-61 to 1965-66) for Kalibangan excavations.

[2]C. J. Gadd, 'Seals of Ancient Indian styles found at Ur', *Proceedings of the British Academy*, 1932.

[3]B. Buchanan, 'A dated seal impression connecting Babylonia with Ancient India', *Archaeology*, vol. 22 (1967).

[4]D. P. Agrawal, 'Harappa Culture—new evidence for a shorter Chronology', *Science*, 143, 3609, pp. 950-52.

[5]Bridget and Raymond Allchin, *The Birth of Indian Civilization* (Harmondsworth, 1968).

Sir Mortimer Wheeler originally proposed a span of 2500-1500 B.C., and relied *inter alia* (but heavily) on the radiocarbon work.[1] He has now expressed serious doubts on the value of C^{14} chronology and is inclined for a drastic upward revision of the chronology.[2]

Recent work on the method of dendro-chronology has shown that the basic postulate of radiocarbon dating—absolute constancy of C^{14} in the atmosphere—is not justified, and, therefore an upward revision of the radiocarbon dates is imperative.[3] (The correction proposed is called MASCA corrections.)

In our opinion, a radiocarbon date is only a statistical estimate, and the archaeologists went wrong in treating the C^{14} date as if it was a chronometer reading. In spite of its faults, however, this technique does offer an objective method, and it is necessary to find out a coefficient of correlation which would re-align the objective radiocarbon dates with the historical dates i.e., with the calendar, if at all possible. Such a correction factor will be proposed on the basis of astronomical chronology.

ASTRONOMY, RIGVEDA AND THE PURANIC KING-LISTS

The king-lists of the Puranas have now been exmined in the light of the astronomical observations made by the known *rishis* and recorded by them in the *Rigveda*. It has been found that the relative chronology of the Puranic king-list is in perfect agreement with the astronomical events and the dates of the *rishis* who observed them.[4]

The astronomical chronology thus drawn up, has now been further verified by the evidence of cross-contacts as revealed in the dated cuneiform inscriptions of Ur, Elam and Larsa.

It has also been found that the battle of the ten kings (*R.V.* 7-18) which was the culmination of a long-drawn war between the Vedic Aryans and the Hariyupeans (i.e., the Harappans) was fought in *c.* 1930 B.C.[5]

It is, therefore, now possible to work out a correlation coefficient on the basis of these investigations. The correlation works out (*as a first order linear approximation*) to a factor of 1·095, when the half-life of C^{14} is taken to be 5568 ± 30 years.

For the present preliminary first order analysis, therefore, the coefficient of correlation (i.e., the correction factor to the radiocarbon dates) is taken to be x1·1. Further work with a second order equation ($T = bt + ct^2$) is in progress.

The revised Harappan chronology, viz., the C^{14} primary dates, as rectified by the above correlation factors, is now presented in the form of tables.

Whatever may be the ultimate result it is now fairly clear that the C^{14} dates are too low, and require correction. Till final agreement is reached, it is suggested that :

1. The C^{14} dates should not be compared with historical or astronomical dates, for the like should be compared to the like always.
2. Whatever method of dating be employed, it should be clearly explained and mentioned as follows :
   (i) D (Hist) = Historically determined date.
   (ii) D (5568) = C^{14} date with a half-life of 5568 ± 30 years.
   (iii) D (5730) = C^{14} date with a half-life of 5730 ± 40 years.
   (iv) D (MASCA) = Date corrected according to MASCA scale.
   (v) D (Sues) = Date after Suess correction (D-1·4 T—1100).
   (vi) D (Eclp) = Date according to eclipse (this being the most certain method).
   (vii) D (Ast) = Date according to the astronomical chronology in this book; and
   (viii) D (SBR) = A C^{14} date corrected by the factor × 1·1 now proposed.

SUMMARY

On the basis of this evidence, the data have been divided into two sections : Pre-Harappan and Harappan. The latter had a chronological span of [2516 (2373-2010) 1911 B.C.]. Most of the dates lie within the inner bracket (2373-2010 B.C.). The Pre-Harappan had a time spread of [3239 (2900—2300) 2021 B.C.]

[1] Sir Mortimer Wheeler, *The Indus Civilization* (3rd edition, Oxford, 1968).

[2] Sir Mortimer Wheeler, Foreword in S. R. Rao, *Lothal and the Indus Civilization* (Bombay, 1973).

[3] Michael Ralph, *MASCA Newsletter*, vol. 9, no. 1 (August, 1973).

[4] S.B. Roy, 'Astronomical Chronology of India', paper read at the Seminar of the Indian Archaeological Society, Kurukshetra, 19 November 1972. See also, Baity, 'Archaeoastronomy and ethnoastronomy today', *Current Anthropology* (October, 1973) and the author's comments thereon.

[5] S.B. Roy, 'Notes on the connection of the Vedic peoples with Ur and Larsa Kings', *Journal of the Andhra Historical Research Society* (in press).

It is perhaps not necessary to stress that while the Pre-Harappan culture evolved earlier, it continued side by side with the mature Harappan (sometimes even at the same place, e.g., Kalibangan) up to 2000 B.C.

The following tabular summary shows a sudden and discontinuous increase in the MASCA dates beyond 2230 B.C. This may be due, among others, to any one or all of the following kinds of disturbances which apparently lasted from 5500 B.C. up to 2200 B.C. : (a) in the earth's magnetism ; (b) in the earth's crust near the bristle cone forests, causing a disturbance in the constitution of the trees; (c) in the bristlecone pines themselves, affecting their power of C-14 absorption; and (d) a cosmic disturbance, affecting a change in the C-14 content of the earth's atmosphere.

TABLE 1

Corrected Radiocarbon Dates, Pre-Harappan and Harappan

Site	Laboratory No.	Uncorrected Before Present K	Corrected (S.B.R.)
1	2	3	4
	PRE-HARAPPAN		
		B.P.	*B.C.*
1. Amri	TF-864	4800	3239±223
	TF-863	4620	2993±113
2. Kot Diji	P-196	4421	2913±141
	P-179	4161	2627±151
	P-180	4083	2541±137
	P-195	3925	2367±134
3. Damb Sadaat	P-522	4387	2865±191
	UW-59	4330	2813±70
	L-180B	4348	2612±250
	UW-60	4030	2482±160
	P-523	4029	2481± 74
4. Kalibangan	TF-155	4195	2664±115
	TF-157	4120	2582±110
	TF-241	4090	2549± 90
	TF-162	3940	2394±100
	TF-161	3930	2373±100
	TF-165	3800	2230±100
	TF-156	3740	2164±105
	TF-154	3665	2081±110
	TF-240	3610	2021±110
5. Bara	TF-1205	3840	2159± 95
	TF-1204	3795	2111±155

1	2	3	4
HARAPPAN			
1. Kalibangan	TF-160	4060	2516±100
	TF-942	4055	2510±100
	TF-28	3930	2373±110
	TF-607	3930	2373±110
	TF-163	3910	2351±100
	TF-153	3910	2351±110
	TF-608	3910	2351±100
	TF-145	3895	2334±110
	TF-481	3879	2317± 72
	TF-147	3865	2301±100
	TF-948	3815	2245±100
	TF-605	3810	2241±105
	TF-151	3800	2230±100
	TF-139	3775	2202±100
	TF-947	3765	2191± 85
	TF-150	3740	2164±100
	TF-141	3705	2125±105
	TF-149	3675	2092±140
	TF-986	3675	2092± 87
	TF-142	3635	2048±100
	TF-152	3615	2026± 85
	TF-946	3605	2015±100
	TF-143	3510	1911±110
2. Mohenjo-daro	P-1179	3913	2354± 64
	P-1177	3895	2334± 64
	P-1180	3828	2260± 61
	P-1178A	3802	2232± 59
	P-1176	3801	2231± 59
	P-1182A	3702	2122± 63
	TF- 75	3600	2010±110
3. Lothal	TF-136	3915	2356±130
	TF-22	3845	2270±110
	TF-27	3840	2374±110
	TF-26	3830	2263±110
	TF-133	3740	2164±110
	TF-29	3740	2164±110
	TF-23	3705	2125±105
	TF-19	3650	2065±135
4. Surkotada	TF-1305	3890	2329± 95
	TF-1310	3810	2241± 95
	TF-1295	3780	2208± 95
	TF-1304	3645	2059± 90
(Layer of Ash)			
	TF-1297	3655	2048± 95
	TF-1294	3620	2032± 95
	TF-1311	3625	2037± 90
	TF-1307	3510	1911±105
5. Rojdi	TF-199	3590	2241±110
	TF-200	3810	1999±100

TABLE 2

Showing correction for C^{14} dates

Primary Date		MASCA Correction	Astronomical correction —x 1·1	Error in MASCA Dates
Half life 5568±30 years	Half life 5730±40 years			
1	2	3	4	5
B.C.	B.C.	B.C.	B.C.	years
550	625	765	800	+35
650	728	808	910	+102
750	831	901	1020	+119
850	934	1024	1130	+106
950	1037	(1167-1187)	1240	+63
1050	1140	1300	1350	+50
1150	1243	1463	1460	—3
1250	1346	(1526-1590)	1570	—12
1250	1449	(1659-1679)	1680	+11
1450	1552	(1722-1872)	1790	—5
1550	1655	(2000-2020)	1900	—110
1650	1758	2108	2010	—98
1750	1861	2161	2120	—41
1850	1964	(2194-2294)	2230	—14
Breakdown of the MASCA correction				
1950	2067	(2487-2537)	2340	—172
2050	2170	2610	2450	—160
2150	2237	2837	2560	—277
2250	2376	(2916-2936)	2670	—246
2350	2479	(2981-3109)	2780	—265
2450	2582	3162	2890	—272
2550	2685	(3225-3335)	3000	—282
2650	2788	3378	3110	—268
2750	2891	(3501-3541)	3220	—301±20
2850	2994	3634	3330	—304
2950	3097	3707	3440	—220
3050	3200	3770	3550	—220
3150	3303	3903	3660	—243
3250	3406	4016	3770	—246
3350	3509	4189	3880	—309
3450	3612	(4332-4352)	3990	—352
3550	3715	4415	4100	—315
3650	3818	4478	4210	—268
3750	3921	4561	4320	—241
3850	4024	(4614-4644)	4430	—199
3950	4127	(4787-4867)	4540	—237
4050	4230	(4940-4960)	4650	—300
4150	4333	5033	4760	—273
4250	4436	(5106-5166)	4870	—261
4350	4539	5259	4980	—279
4450	4642	5312	5090	—222
4550	4745	5345	5200	—145

S. B. RAY

20B, Sujan Singh Park, New Delhi.

On the Calibration of C^{14} Dates

INTRODUCTION

In recent years, very old (*c.* 5000 B.P.) trees have been dated accurately by dendrochronology. Wood material from such dated rings can also be dated by C^{14} method. Surprisingly enough, when comparisons were made between the dates obtained using these two methods, some discrepancies were observed. On the basis of this comparative study, corrections have been suggested by various workers, e.g. MASCA factor. Below, we will briefly discuss the problems, and review the present state of research.

DISCUSSION

Several calibrations have been suggested to correct the C^{14} dates. The more noteworthy among these are from Michael and Ralph,[1] Stuiver and Suess[2] and Wendland and Donley.[3] In Indian protohistory, the Harappa Culture was dated on the basis of the archaeological evidence of contact with Mesopotamia. These are definitive only during the reign of Sargon of Agade (*c.*2325 ± 20 B.C.) and the Isin-Larsa period (*c.* 2000-1900 B.C.).[4] From Mohenjo-daro, a well-known Harappan site, we now have seven C^{14} dates from the top level, giving a compounded date of *c.* 2000 B.C. The depth of the occupational deposit showing several structural phases suggests that the occupation lasted for three to five hundred years. Unfortunately, no C^{14} dates are available from the early levels of this site. If one takes a *minimum* of 300 years, the extrapolated C^{14} date for the beginning will thus be *c.* 2300 B.C. Thus, if we take the *c.* 2300-2000 B.C. time-spread, based on C^{14} dates and their extrapolation, and apply various suggested corrections we get the 'true' time-spread as given in Table 1.

It is obvious from Table 1 that all the corrections make the bracket too old to be justified on the basis of historical chronology. In fact, the corrected date for the end of Mohenjo-daro is earlier than the historically dated beginning. Only the uncorrected C^{14} dates agree with the historical bracket.

This led us to the examination of the whole evidence afresh. As Table 2 shows that the concordance of the C^{14} dates and historical dates from *c.* 1800-2000 B.C. is quite fair. The dendro-corrected C^{14} dates are too old for this period. Between *c.* 2400 and 2600 B.C., many of the C^{14} dates appear a little younger than the historical dates, whereas most of the dendro-corrected dates are 200-400 years older than the historical dates. A number of these dates, particularly those falling between *c.* 1800-2000 B.C., can be verified by astronomical dating also. Berger[5] has pointed out that 'the radiocarbon and historical chronologies go hand in hand for the entire period in which the historical time placement can be idependently verified by astronomical calculations'. He also concedes that 'the bristlecone pine calibration appears to exaggerate the magnitude of the deviations slightly'.

So far, the dendrochronological samples have been derived from only one place viz., California, from altitudes *c.* 3000 m. To check that no local/geographical factors are responsible for the indicated variations, samples of the New Zealand Kauri pine were compared with the data on Californian Bristlecone and Sequoia samples. 'The curve . . . contrasts strongly with the other two. But the New Zealand dates recalibrated against the Kauri pine curves seem to make more archaeological sense than calibration with the Bristlecone pine. Thus, a local factor seems to be at play'.[6]

The Auvernier neolithic sequences have been correlated with the Bristlecone pine by means of a 'nearest fit' comparison. 'If we assume that the same factors cause the fluctuation in both curves, and that direct correlation is valid, then we find that

[1]H. N. Michael and E. K. Ralph, 'Correction factors applied to Egyptian radiocarbon dates from era before Christ', in (ed.), I.U. Olsson, *Radiocarbon Variation and Absolute Chronology*, Proceedings of the Twelfth Nobel Symposium, Uppsala, Sweden, August 11-15, 1969 (New York, 1970), pp. 109-20.

[2]M. Stuiver and H. E. Suess, 'On the relationship between radiocarbon dates and true sample ages', *Radiocarbon*, vol. 8 (1966), pp. 534-40.

[3]W. M. Wendland and D. L. Donley, 'Radiocarbon-Calendar age relationship', *Earth and Planetary Science Letters*, vol. 11 (1971), pp. 135-39.

[4]D. P. Agrawal, *The Copper-Bronze Age in India* (New Delhi, 1971).

[5]R. Berger, 'Ancient Egyptian radiocarbon Chronology', *Philosophical Transactions of the Royal Society London*, vol. 269 (1970), pp. 23-26.

[6]J. Collis, 'Thoughts on radiocarbon dating', in Euan Mackie, John Collis, D.W. Ewer, Alan Smith, Hans Suess and Colin Renfrew, *Antiquity*, vol. XLV (1971), pp. 200-201.

TABLE 1

Suggested calibrations of Radiocarbon Dates

$C = 1{\cdot}4\,R - 1100$ (Stuiver and Suess 1966) ... (1)
$C = 1{\cdot}4\,R - 900$ (Stuiver 1967) ... (2)
$C = 1{\cdot}26\,R - 700$ (Stuiver 1970) ... (3)
$C = 112 + 0{\cdot}690 + 0{\cdot}152 \times 10^{-3}\,R^2 - 0{\cdot}138 \times 10^{-7}\,R^3$ (Wendland and Donley) ... (4)
$C = R + 350$ for the period 2099 to 1700 B.C.)
and } MASCA FACTOR
$C = R + 450$ for the period 2499 to 2100 B.C.
(Michael and Ralph 1970) ... (5)

(Where C=Corrected date, and R=Radiocarbon date)

If the above equations are applied to the Radiocarbon dates, based on half-life = 5730 yrs., for Harappan time-spread at Mohenjo-daro, we get the following results:

Calibrated time-spread using eq. (1)	2900-2480 B.C.
Calibrated time-spread using eq. (2)	3100-2680 B.C.
Calibrated time-spread using eq. (3)	2705-2327 B.C.
Calibrated time-spread using eq. (4)	2750-2350 B.C.
Calibrated time-spread using eq. (5)	2750-2350 B.C.
Uncorrected Radiocarbon time-spread	2300-2000 B.C.
Historical time-spread	2350-1900 B.C.

TABLE 2

The comparison between Radiocarbon dates and dendro-corrected dates with well-dated selected Egyptian samples

Sample No.	Radiocarbon dates, based on half-life-5730 years in years B.C.	Range of historical dates in years B.C. (Based on Helck's chronology)	Dendro-corrected[1] C^{14} dates in years B.C.
1	2	3	4
A-433,**	1892-1768	1876-1864	2242-2118
UCLA-900,**	1882-1718	,, ,,	2232-2068
BM-22,**	1840-1530	,, ,,	2190-1780
TF-564,**	1830-1620	,, ,,	2180-1870
GrN*-1178,**	1820-1716	,, ,,	2170-2066
GrN*-1157,**	1763-1649	,, ,,	2113-1899
A-220,**	2160-1850	1990-1870	2610-2200
BM-238,**	1805-1675	,, ,,	2155-1925
BM-280,**	1773-1639	,, ,,	2123-1889
UCLA-1212,**	1717-1593	,, ,,	2067-1843
BM-343,**	1965-1795	2133-1870	2315-2145
UCLA-1400,**	1920-1800	,, ,,	2270-2150
BM-342,**	1890-1750	,, ,,	2240-2100
UCLA-1399,**	1825-1715	,, ,,	2175-2065

TABLE 2 (contd.)

1	2	3	4
BM-341,**	1730-1590	,, ,,	2080-1840
UCLA-1211,	1715-1595	,, ,,	2065-1845
UCLA-1398,**	1540-1420	,, ,,	1790-1670
UCLA-1413,**	1995-1875	2133-1990	2345-2225
BM-335,	1905-1755	,, ,,	2255-2105
BM-347,**	1880-1720	,, ,,	2230-2070
BM-21,**	1880-1575	,, ,,	2230-1825
GrN*-1155,**	1875-1765	,, ,,	2225-2115
GrN*-1177,**	1875-1765	,, ,,	2225-2115
BM-317,**	1740-1560	2133-1990	2090-1810
TF-1208,	2135-1855	2100[2]	2585-2205
UCLA-928,	2375-2111	2465-2325	2825-2561
UCLA-1403,**	2165-2045	,, ,,	2615-2395
BM-401	2122-1990	,, ,,	2572-2340
BM-346,**	2110-1950	,, ,,	2560-2300
BM-139,	2737-2427	2575-2325	3287-2877
UCLA-248,	2684-2520	,, ,,	3234-3070
A-333,	2427-2303	,, ,,	2877-2753
A-521,**	2383-2178	,, ,,	2838-2628
UCLA-66,**	2345-2181	,, ,,	2795-2631
A-334,	2314-2210	,, ,,	2764-2660
A-519,**	2252-2190	,, ,,	2702-2640
UCLA-665,**	2242-2078	,, ,,	2692-2528
UCLA-667,**	2222-2058	,, ,,	2672-2408
A-330,	2190-2066	2575-2375	2640-2416
A-331,	2190-2066	,, ,,	2640-2416
A-520,**	2054-1894	,, ,,	2404-2244
A-332,	2036-1932	,, ,,	2386-2282
UCLA-1389,**	2445-2325	2575-2465	2895-2775
BM-332**	2255-2045	,, ,,	2705-2395
UCLA-1208	2240-2120	,, ,,	2690-2570
BM-324	2220-2008	,, ,,	2670-2358
BM-325	2147-1911	,, ,,	2597-2260

Key :

*Corrected sample dates

**Done by more than one laboratory

A=Arizona ; B=British Museum ; UCLA=University of California ; GrN=Groninjen

1=Correction as suggested by Michael and Ralph (1970), also called MASCA Factor

2=Historical dates as given by archaeologist concerned.

almost all the twelve readings are on the low side, six being outside 1σ range of the curve and one outside 2σ. Had these been individual dates, and not linked in a sequence, then they would have been considered several hundred years older. Thus, again there seems to be a local factor involved, either that the Bristlecone pine curve is not relevant, or that something causes unusually high reading in California and low ones in Switzerland'.[1]

Both of these examples indicate that a universal calibration of the C^{14} calendar on the basis of only Californian trees may not be valid. Besides, one does not know how reliable the tree-rings are for such calibration. Internal cell-sap, wood contamination and *in situ* production of radiocarbon in the Bristlecone pine, exposed at high altitudes, have been suggested as probable explanations for the exaggeration of discrepancies between the historical and dendro-corrected C^{14} dates.

Jansen[2] had reported on the Australian and New Zealand tree-ring results and their discrepancy with the Californian ones. During the discussion, very important facts came to light. Rafter reported the diffusion of resin in the tree-rings inwards and the variations it caused. Olsson[3] pointed out 100% atomic bomb effect in pre-bomb (1945-1950) tree-rings. These results point to the uncertainties in using tree-rings, which need to be resolved.

Walton and Baxter[4] have pointed out the discrepancies between the results of the same tree-ring samples from Arizona and La Jolla which range from 6°/oo to 70°/oo and among other laboratories between 17°/oo to 41°/oo in the reported values of δ C^{13}. Such discrepancies 'can give rise to further age corrections of 50 to 560 years over and above those already presented in the Bristlecone pine calibration of Suess . . . Results from post 3000 year B.P. samples are in substantial agreement. Until this problem is resolved, we reiterate the hazards associated with the determination of 'true ages' from radiocarbon ages'.[5]

We thus see that the tree-ring samples have not provided so far very unambiguous evidence to calibrate the C^{14} calendar.

A comparison of radiocarbon (based on 5730 half-life), historical and corrected dates shows that after *c.* 2000 B.C., the C^{14} and the historical dates are almost concordant, between *c.* 2000-2500 B.C., the C^{14} and the historical dates appear to be equidistant from the historical age, thus showing that the dendro-corrections in this range aggravate the magnitude of the C^{14}/C^{12} variations.

Other types of errors in C^{14} dating have been discussed by Sheela Kusumgar[6] elsewhere.

We are of the opinion, therefore, that till all such uncertainties are removed, the C^{14} dates should be used without any corrections. (However, the half-life used should always be indicated.) We can call it a radiocarbon calendar and its equation with the Gregorian calendar may be postponed for the time being. Any calibration at this stage therefore will create more confusion than clarity.

D.P. AGRAWAL AND
SHEELA KUSUMGAR

Physical Research Laboratory,
Navarangapura,
Ahmedabad-38009

[1]*Ibid.*

[2]H. S. Jansen, 'Secular Variation of radiocarbon in New Zealand and Australian trees', in Olsson, *op. cit.* (1970), pp. 261-74.

[3]I. U. Olsson, M. Klasson and A. Abd. Mageed, 'Uppsala Natural Radiocarbon Measurements XI', *Radiocarbon*, vol. 14 (1) (1972), pp. 247-71.

[4]A. Walton and M.S. Baxter, 'Calibration of the radiocarbon time scale', *Nature*, vol. 220 (1968), pp. 475-76.

[5]*Ibid.*

[6]Sheela Kusumgar, 'The problem of errors in radiocarbon dating', in (eds.), D. P. Agrawal and A. Ghosh, *Radiocarbon and Indian Archaeology* (Bombay, 1973).

Comments on C. C. Lamberg-Karlovsky's paper on 'Trade Mechanisms in Indus-Mesopotamian Interrelations'

Lamberg-Karlovsky's paper is one of the few thoughtful ones on the Harappan trade. It is also provocative in the sense that it tries to break away from the present hypothesis of a Direct Contact Trade between the Indus and Mesopotamia and suggests instead the dominant role of a Central Place Trade between these two regions. On a different level, not directly associated with this main problem, he also emphasizes the element of long-distance trade as a causative force of early urban growth-process.

While going through the data with Lamberg-Karlovsky one has, in fact, to wonder if the positive evidence of a Direct Contact Indus-Mesopotamian Trade is not almost non-existent. At the same time one is left with a faint suspicion that he has overstated his case. The analogy of the Assyrian merchants' establishments in Anatolia, which he cites as a model evidence of a Direct Contact Trade, may not be wholly meaningful in the Indus-Mesopotamian Context. These trading colonies were founded on a background of very old and active trade between Mesopotamia and one of her immediate neighbours, Anatolia, and reflect a situation which was seldom repeated by the Assyrians themselves anywhere else beyond their border.

The different pieces of data analyzed by Lamberg-Karlovsky and found by him to be an inadequate indication of a Direct Contact Trade may not individually connote much except an indeterminate relationship between the two regions but, taken together, they suggest to us something more than a casual indirect contact. One also notes that he has not raised in this context the issue of Mesopotamian influence on the Harappan art-form. The motifs like the hero between two tigers, the treatment of the Mohenjodaro bearded head, etc., convey a distinct Harappan awareness of Mesopotamian art-form, an awareness. which was unlikely to be the result of indirect familiarity alone. That the familiarity was not entirely indirect is perhaps indicated by such evidence as the find of a stone-head, closely comparable to the Early Dynastic Sumerian sculpture of the Diyala region, in a presumably Harappan context at Dabarkot. Lamberg-Karlovsky is also silent on the point of the depiction of an Indus humped bull before a manger on a stone vase from Tell Agrab in the Diyala region. Considerable significance was given by Childe to this item in support of the presence of the Harappan traders in the Diyala region, the terminal point of the overland trade-route from the Indus. 'In style the vase is a Sumerian work of Early Dynastic III and was presumably carved in the city by a Sumerian artist. He had therefore presumably seen the Indus cult celebrated in Mesopotamia'.[1] There should not be any theoretical objection to this. The number of unmistakably Harappan objects in Namazga Tepe, etc., may suggest to many a direct Harappan presence in the area. If the Harappans could go to South Turkemenia they could go to the Diyala region as well.

In fact, the point on which one may not agree with Lamberg-Karlovsky is that he tends to minimize completely the existence of a Direct Contact Trade between the Indus and Mesopotamia. The present data do suggest, as he has so ably shown, that the main emphasis on the Indus-Mesopotamian relationship was on trade carried through two central places, the islands in the Persian Gulf and south-eastern Iran, but surely, the emphasis need not have been exclusive.

The precise mechanism of the Indus-Mesopotamian trade is likely to be always elusive because of the poor and disjointed nature of the evidence but an interesting insight into the process may be had by studying the mechanism of trade connecting these two and their intervening areas in the nineteenth century sailing and caravan days. Some archival records should be available for that period.

In a separate context, Lamberg-Karlovsky's observation on the role of the Kulli people as middlemen in the Bronze Age east-west trade may not be acceptable to all. Both Kulli and Nal in south Baluchistan were apparently rich cultures and their wealth could come primarily through their participation in the Harappan trade with the west. About Nal's role he is positive ; about Kulli also this seems to be a reasonable theoretical premise. Incidentally, this idea was first put forward by Childe : 'plunder or trade brought the villagers a share in the surplus of the Harappan cities....', though not always has this been acknowledged to its source.

[1]V. Gordon Childe. *New Light on the Most Ancient East* (London, 1964), p. 170.

So far as the second basic premise of Lamberg-Karlovsky is concerned one wishes he could be more elaborate. According to him 'one of the important 'intensifiers' motivating the parallel but essentially distinctive rise toward urban complexes in Mesopotamia and the Iranian highlands, and the later Harappan culture was trade.' It is highly probable that long-distance trade in which sites like Tepe Yahya played an important part, brought the entire stretch from Mesopotamia to the Indus within the orbit of one broad cultural world. It is also equally probable that the 'idea' of civilization could not have moved to the Indus without this factor in the background. Only to this extent we agree that long-distance trade was a generative force of Harappan urbanism.

DILIP K. CHAKRABARTI
Department of Ancient Indian History and Archaeology, University of Calcutta, 51/2 Hazra Road, Calcutta-19.

Evidence of Horse from the Harappan settlement at Surkotada

The most controversial and sought after animal in Indian archaeology has been the horse. Some archaeologists and historians are of the view that the arrival of the horse in India is linked with the so-called 'Aryan invasion'. While a section of scholars tend to believe that the Harappans were Aryans, others would dismiss this premise on the plea that the study of animal bones from the different excavated Harappan sites had not yielded sufficient number of bones of true horse (*Equus caballus Linn.*). The latter cannot think of the Aryans without the existence of true horse.

In 1938, Mackay[1] had remarked on the discovery of a clay model of horse from Mohenjo-daro: 'I personally take it to represent horse. I do not think we need be particularly surprised if it should be proved that the horse existed thus early at Mohenjo-daro'. We repeat the remarks of Mackay for our discoveries from Surkotada as well.

Bhola Nath[2] has already reported the existence of bones of *Equus caballus Linn.* from Harappa, Ropar and Lothal, though the fragments identified are limited in number. Sewell and Guha[3] reported fragments of mandible of *Equus caballus Linn.* from Mohenjo-daro. Prasad[4] reported that bones of domestic ass had been found at Harappa and he assigned them to that of the common Indian ass (*Equus asinus Linn.*).

After the identification of Rana Ghundai fragments by E.J. Ross, to be that of the horse, Zeuner[5] in 1963 argued that this identification cannot be accepted as reliable for 'they belong to hamione, which survives in north-west India. In Rana Ghundai, only hamione existed and were hunted'. Bhola Nath[6] later on reported the remains of horse (*Equus caballus Linn*) from Harappa lying in the unworked collections of the Zoological Survey of India. He declared that that was 'the first record of true horse'. He has also reported the remains of domestic ass (*Equus asinus Linn.*) and the true horse (*Equus caballus Linn.*) from the late period of Harappa Culture at Ropar. He felt that 'the presence of true horse (*Equus caballus Linn.*) from the late period of Harappan culture at Lothal was noteworthy'.

Dr. V.V. Rao has also reported the occurrence of the true horse at Kalibangan. A detailed examination, however, is necessary before establishing the thesis.

[1]E.J.H. Mackay, *Further Excavations at Mohenjo-daro*, vol. I (New Delhi, 1938), p. 289.

[2]Bhola Nath, 'Advances in the study of Prehistoric and Ancient animals in India—A Review', *Records of Zoological Survey of India*, vol. 61 (Calcutta, 1968), pp. 3-17.

[3]R. B. Seymour Sewell and B. S. Guha, on 'Zoological Remains' in Sir John Marshall, *Mohenjo-daro and the Indus Civilization*, vol. II (Text) (London, 1931), p. 653.

[4]B. Prasad, *Animal remains from Harappa* Memoirs of the Archaeological Survey of India, no. 51, (Delhi, 1936), pp. 28-30.

[5]F.E. Zeuner, *A History of Domesticated Animals*, (London 1963), p. 299.

[6]Bhola Nath, *op. cit.* pp. 5-6.,

Recently, Alur[1] has reported the presence of horse from the neolithic chalcolithic levels at Hallur. Alur and Sharma (unpublished) could identify some *Equus caballus* bones from the Proto-Harappan site of Malvan.

Whether the Harappans were Aryans does not concern us here. Though the existence of horse bones has been reported by other workers from different Harappan sites, due to their unclear stratigraphic position, scholars have not been able to accept the evidence without reservation. In order to clear these doubts and to know the exact position of horse vis-a-vis the Harappans, concerted efforts were made at Surkotada, a Harappan settlement in the little Rann of Kutch (*circa* 2100-1700 B.C.). The excavations were carried out in 1971-72 by the Excavations Branch, Archaeological Survey of India, under the direction of Shri J.P. Joshi. Though the bulk of the material is still under investigation, sufficient number of bones of horse have been identified from the portion already studied. Apart from bones of *Equus caballus Linn.,* bones of *Equus asinus Linn.* and *Equus hamionus Khur* have also been recovered (PLS. X-XIII). Described below are the bones of *Equus caballus Linn.*

Incisors:2, One 1st and the other 3rd incisor. Both from the middle levels of Period IB (PL. XI).

Molars:4, Two from early levels of Period IC and two from early levels of Period IA (PL. XI).

Canon bones:2, One from the late levels of Period IA and the other from the middle levels of Period IC (PL. X).

First Phalanx:1, from the middle levels of Period IC (PL. X).

Second Phalanx:2, One from early levels of Period IA and the other from the early levels of Period IC (PL. X).

Third Phalanx:2, one from early leves of Period IA and the other from late levels of PeriodI C (PL. X).

From the above it could be seen that the bones of *Equus caballus Linn.* occur from Period IA to IC at Surkotada. The presence of few charred pieces is very interesting. The above evidence shows that horse was known to the Harappans at Surkotada. Associated with the horse also occured *Equus asinus* and *Equus hamionus.* Even today *Equus haminus Khur* is found in large numbers in the Little Rann of Kutch.

At times questions are asked whether our collection from Surkotada shows any evolutionary sequence. Such a question is superficial as evolution is a very slow process and 300 or 400 years of deposit cannot throw any light on this question.

A detailed study of horse-bones from Surkotada is likely to afford the desired information as to whether horse was being used by the Harappans at Surkotada only as a mode of transport or for draft purposes.

A. K. SHARMA

Archaeological Survey of India,
Nagpur

[1]K.R. Alur, 'Skeletal remains (Vertebrata)', *Proto-historic cultures of the Tungbhadra Valley* (Dharwar, 1971), pp. 107-

The Domestic Animals in the Early Cultures of India

In north-west India, domesticated animals can be traced to the early village-farming communities of the fourth millennium B.C.

Two small domesticated ruminants (sheep and goat) and cattle were already kept, but there is only a sporadic evidence of the dog. Goats were scimetar-horned ; the breed of sheep of that period is not known. Of cattle, mainly the humped species existed. Experts are very much in doubt whether these animals had been domesticated in northwest India

While sheep and goat had wild ancestors, the existence of wild cattle cannot be proved by means of archeological discoveries.

Nothing is known about the way in which cattle were kept and utilized in the early stetlements.

In the highly developed urban civilization of the Indus Valley in the third and second millenniums B.C., we have authentic proof of the following domestic animals : highly-bred cattle of different breeds ; zebus, with long and upright horns, short-horned and humpless cattle, and possibly also a long-horned "Ur"-like breed; wool-sheep, with ammon's horns and short pointed ears; goats, with long drooping ears and strong, twisted or scimetar-shaped horns; pigs, some closely connected with the wild species, but some showing already characteristics of domestication; dogs, of varying kinds, some similar to greyhounds and mastiffs ; the most common, however, were middle-sized, pariah-like types, kept like genuine domestic ated animals; and fowl, middle-sized and apparently also large and heavy.

Keeping of domesticated animals must have been of great importance in the Indus Civilization. A remarkably high standard of animal husbandry is obvious, especially in the fattening of cattle. In addition to the breeding of the most important domestic animals —cattle, sheep, goats, pigs, dogs and fowl—sometimes domestic animals were also imported, such as asses from Mesopotamia. Horses were of no importance during the time of the Indus Civilization.

As draught-animals only cattle were used. There is no evidence of domestication or taming of buffaloes, elephants, cats and peacocks. Camel were possibly also kept. Besides the economical importance of animals in old India, they were connected with cults or religion. Here, domesticated and wild animals were equally important.

Among the domesticated animals, cattle and goats were thought to have a religious meaning. Also buffaloes and elephants played a part in the old Indian cults.

Animals like tigers, rhinoceroses and garials were represented in a manner which makes it evident that they were worshipped or occasionally kept. Doves, peacocks, and other birds as well seem to have been religiously significant.*

ROSWITHA CONRAD

University of Munich,
Munich, West Germany

*This is the author's summary of the doctoral dissertation entitled *Die Haustiere in den fruhen Kulturen Indien* completed in 1968 under the guidance of Prof. Dr. J. Bressneck and submitted to the faculty of Veterinary Sciences, University of Munich.

Ancient Plant Economy at Noh, Rajasthan

INTRODUCTION

The ancient plant economy at Noh, District Bharatpur, Rajasthan, is reconstructed from the carbonized remains of food plants. The materials were kindly sent by Shri R.C. Agrawala, Director, Department of Archaeology and Museums, Government of Rajasthan, Jaipur. The material comprises four samples, the details of which are given below :

Sample 1: Carbonized plant remains, Tr.K, O'-II'; (4); Kushan levels.

Sample 2: Carbonized plant remains; Tr.K, XI', 20 x 1·80,—2·75; (7); Mauryan levels.

Samples 3 *and* 4: Two samples of burnt clay; Tr. K, XII'-XIII'. 07 x 0·72,—7.40; (5); Black-and-red Ware (pre-PGW).

No radiocarbon dates of the above layers are available but their identity with the cultural periods, as established by the excavator, is mentioned above for proper appraisal of the evidence. We are indebted to Shri R.C. Agrawala for the above materials as also for the information relating to their cultural association.

DESCRIPTION OF PLANT REMAINS

RICE

Oryza sativa. L. sub-sp. *indica L.* (PLS. XIV and XV)

The material consists of impressions of spikelets and kernels of rice in one of the burnt clay samples from the Black-and-red Ware levels and carbonized lumps of spikelets and kernels from sample 2 from the Mauryan levels. The impression of an entire spikelet is oblong, flattened and measures about 6·5 mm long and 3 mm broad (PL. XIV) and the typical chess-board pattern and the ribbed surface characteristic of rice spikelets is present. The carbonized lumps from the Mauryan levels being partially tarred, it was possible to release as many as 60 kernels of rice. The typical chess-board pattern of the rice spikelet is well preserved. The individual kernels are narrowly oblong, laterally flattened, longer than broader and strongly ribbed. The grains are variable in size ranging from 4-6 mm in length, 2-3 mm in breadth and 1-2 mm in thickenss. The long hilum is preserved in many kernels. Table 1 below, shows dimensions of small, medium and large-sized grains, and their average dimensions and L/BxT indices.

TABLE 1

Showing dimensions (in mm) of rice kernels from Mauryan levels

	Length (L)	Breadth (B)	Thick-ness (T)	L/BxT index
		Small grains		
	4·00	2·00	1·00	2·00
	4·00	2·00	1·50	1·30
	4·50	2·50	2·00	0·90
	4·80	2·50	2·00	0·90
	4.80	2·50	1·50	1·30
	4·80	2·80	1·50	1·10
Average	4·50	2·40	1·60	1·25
		Medium grains		
	5·00	2·50	1·50	1·30
	5·00	2·00	1·80	1·40
	5·00	2·00	2·00	1·20
	5·00	2·80	1·50	1·20
	5·00	2·50	2·00	1·00
	5·00	2·80	2·00	0·90
	5·00	3·00	1·50	1·10
	5·00	3·00	2·00	0·80
	5·50	2·80	2·00	1·00
	5·50	3·00	1·50	1·20
Average	5·10	2·64	1·78	1·11
		Large grains		
	6·00	2·80	2·00	1·07
	6·00	3·00	2·00	1·00
	6·00	3·00	1·50	1·40
Average	6·00	2·90	1·80	1·16

The average L/BxT index of all the 3 types of grains is 1·17. The morphological characters, viz., the shape, the size and the chess-board pattern of the carbonized grains and spikelets compare with those of rice (*Oryza* spp) and more closely with grains and spikelets of *Orzya sativa* sub-sp. *indica* L., the cultivated long grained rice. One of us[1] has recently discovered that the L/BxT index of wild and cultivated rice is of additional help in the specifie identity of spikelets and kernels of rice : the wild rices usually have a ratio higher than 2 and the cultivated ones under 2, rather much under 1·80. The L/BxT indices, as calculated for the Noh rice material, is much under 1·80, hence their reference to *Oryza sativa* based on morphological characters is amply supported by the L/BxT indices. The longer than broader grains suggest that they might have belonged to the long-grained variety of sub-sp. *indica* of *Oryza sativa.*

BARLEY

Hordeum spp. (PL. XV)

Barley is discovered only from the Kushan levels and the material consists of enormous quantity of carbonized grains. The spike remains are absent in the material. The grains are of two kinds—the hulled and naked barley.

An overwhelming majority of the grains consists of the hulled grains whereas there are a few grains which are naked. The hulled grains lack an evenly rounded outline and are angular in shape because of longitudinal ridges and grooves impressed by the palea veins. This feature is quite clearly visible along the ventral furrow. In addition to the above features, the coarse wrinkling of the paleas are found to be present in certain carbonized hulled barley. The naked barley grains are devoid of closely pressed palea and possess transverse rippling on the seed and, in addition, are evenly rounded in outline (cross-section). The dimensions of both hulled and naked barleys are shown in Tables 2 and 3 below. The hulled grains range in size from 5—8·50 mm in length, 2·25-5 mm in breadth and 1·25—4 mm in thickness. The naked grains range in size from 5—7 mm in length, 2·75-3·25 mm in breadth and 2—3 mm in thickness.

[1]Vishnu-Mittre, 'The beginnings of agriculture : the Palaeobotanical evidence from India', in (ed.) Sir Joseph Hutchinson, *Evolutionary Studies in World Crops : Diversity and Change in the Indian sub-continent* (Cambridge, 1974).

TABLE 2

Showing dimensions (in mm) of hulled barley grains from Kushan levels

	Length (L)	Breadth (B)	Thickness (T)
	5·00	2·75	1·75
	5·00	2·75	2·00
	5·00	3·00	1·75
	5·00	3·00	2·00
	5·00	3·00	3·00
	5·50	3·00	2·00
	5·50	3·00	2·50
	5·50	3·75	3·00
	5·50	4·00	2·00
	5·75	3·00	2·00
	5·75	3·50	3·00
	6·00	2·25	1·25
	6·00	3·00	2·00
	6·00	3·00	2·25
	6·00	3·25	2·50
	6·00	3·50	2·25
	6·25	3·50	3·00
	6·50	4·00	3·00
	6·75	4·00	3·00
	6·75	4·00	3·00
	7·00	3·00	2·00
	7·00	3·00	2·50
	7·00	4·00	2·50
	7·00	4·50	3·00
	7·00	4·00	3·00
	7·00	4·75	3·00
	7·00	5·00	3·00
	8·00	3·00	2·00
	8·00	3·50	2·50
	8·00	4·00	2·50
	8·00	3·50	2·00
	8·50	3·50	3·00
Average	6·48	3·58	2·00

TABLE 3

Showing dimensions (in mm) of naked barley grains from Kushan levels

	Length (L)	Breadth (B)	Thickness (T)
	5·00	2·75	2·00
	5·25	3·00	2·00
	5·00	3·00	2·00
	5·25	3·00	2·25
	5·25	3·00	2·75
	5·50	3·00	2·00
	5·50	3·00	2·50
	5·75	2·75	2·00
	6·00	3·00	2·50
	6·00	3·25	3·00
	6·75	3·00	2·00
	7·00	3·00	2·00
Average	5·99	2·99	2·18

BLACK GRAM *(Urd)*

Phaseolus mungo L. (PL. XV)

The remains of this legume have been discovered from samples 2 and 3 from the Mauryan and Black and-red Ware levels respectively: only two complete and a few fragmentary charred seeds of *Phaseolus mungo* mixed with rice grains in carbonized lumps from the former and only two cotyledons from one of the clay samples from the latter.

The carbonized seeds are subcylindric with rounded ends. The seed coat is not preserved. The tiny linear hilum scar on somewhat raised edge towards the ventral surface is seen only in some of them. The seeds discovered from the Black-and-red Ware levels are smaller in size than those from the Mauryan levels. The dimensions of seeds from the Mauryan and the Black-and-red Ware levels are shown in Table 4.

TABLE 4

Showing dimensions (in mm) of seeds of *Phaseolus mungo*

Age	Length (L)	Breadth (B)	Thickness (T)
Mauryan	4·00	3·00	2·50
	4·00	3·00	2·75
Black-and-Red Ware	3·00	2·75	2·25

HORSE GRAM

Dolichos biflorus L. (PL. XV).

Several fragmentary cotyledons of this species have been recovered only from one of the clay samples from the Black-and-red Ware levels. The seeds are kidney-shaped, compressed laterally with a small hilum scar towards the inner side. The cotyledons measure4—5mm in length, 2·50—3mm in breadth and 2 mm in thickness (*vide* Table 5 below) and compare with those of *Dolichos biflorus* both in size and shape.

TABLE 5

Showing dimensions (in mm) of seeds of *Dolichos biflorus* L.

	Length (L)	Breadth (B)	Thickness (T)
	4·00	2·50	2·00
	4·00	2·75	2·00
	4·00	3·00	2·00
	4·75	3·75	2·00
	5·00	3·00	2·00
Average	4·35	3·00	2·00

CONCLUSIONS

The plant economy of the pre-Painted Grey Ware culture at Noh, represented by Black-and-red Ware levels, approximately dated to 1100-1200 B.C., consisted of rice and the legume *Dolichos biflorus* L. We had no materials from the Painted Grey Ware levels from this site, but rice has been reported earlier from the Painted Grey Ware levels at Noh dated to 500-800 B.C. (UCLA-703A, 2554±250 ; UCLA-703B, 2771±236; TF-1144, 2440±19 and TF-993, 2675±150).[1]

The plant economy, as revealed by the overlying Mauryan levels approximately dated to about 200-300 B.C.,consisted of rice and the legume *Phaseolus mungo*.

Although the consumption of the legume *Dolichos biflorus* appears to be absent in the Mauryan times, yet rice continues to be the cereal from the Black-and-red Ware times to the Mauryan times and so does the legume *Phaseolus mungo*.

The plant economy at this site shows a remarkable change from the Kushan period, as from the Kushan levels the remains of only one and a new cereal barley would indicate. Rice or the legumes known from earlier levels are not met with here. The introduction of barley by the Kushans at Noh becomes apparent. It may be pointed out here that barley has earlier been known from Rajasthan from the Harappan site, Kalibangan (materials under investigation by us). Only rice and *Sorghum* constituted the plant economy at the Chalcolithic site Ahar in Rajasthan.[2]

The re-introduction of barley in the post-Harappan times in Rajasthan is of considerable historical interest, and there is reason to believe that it must have been introduced by the Kushans in Rajasthan.

The history of barley elsewhere in India may be of comparative interest. The Harappans in the Indus Valley, the Punjab and Rajasthan consumed barley during2300-1600 B.C. It formed a part of the diet of the neolithic peoples at Chirand, Bihar. [3] Almost continuous records of barley from the Chalcolithic, Iron Age and early historic periods are known from Atranjikhera in Uttar Pradesh, dated from 1200 to 600 B.C. [4] The early historical record of this cereal from Ter, [5] District Osmanabad, Maharashtra, is more or less of the same date as at Noh. Thus, it would appear that barley has been consumed and cultivated also more or less continuously in the north-western India from the Neolithic-Harappan times to the early historical period. [6] Its consumption and cultivation in north-western Rajasthan ceased in the post-Harappan times until its introduction at Noh in the early historical times. It is more or less around the beginning of the Christian era that this cereal was re-introduced at Noh and further down into Maharashtra. This seems to have resulted from the influx of communities from the north. Its association with the Kushans amply supports the above conclusion.

VISHNU-MITTRE AND R. SAVITHRI

Birbal Sahni Institute of Palaeobotany, Lucknow

[1]Bridget and Rymond Allchin, *The Birth of Indian Civilization* Harmondsworth, 1968).

[2]Vishnu-Mittre, on 'Remains of rice and millet' in H.D. Sankalia, S. B. Deo and Z. A. Ansari, *Excavation at Ahar (Tambavati)* (Poona, 1969), pp. 229-35.

[3]Vishnu Mittre, 'Neolithic plant economy at Chirand, Bihar', *Palaeobotanist*, 21 (1972), pp. 18-22.

[4]G. M. Butch and K. A. Chowdhury, 'Plant remains from Atranjikhera, Phase III (C. 1200-600 B.C.),' *Proceedings of Silver Jubilee Palaeobotanical Conference Lucknow*, 13 (1971); *Palaeobot.* (in press).

[5]Vishnu-Mittre, U. Prakash and N. Awasthi, 'Ancient plant economy at Ter, Maharashtra', *Geophytology*, 1 (2) (1972), pp. 170-77.

[6]F. R. Allchin, 'Early cultivated plants in India and Pakistan' in (eds.) P. G. Ucko and G. W. Dimbleby, *The Domestication and Exploitation of Plants and Animals*' (London, 1968); Vishnu-Mittre, 'Protohistoric records of agriculture in India', *Transactions of the Bose Research Institute*, 31 (3) (1968), pp. 87-106; also see, Vishnu-Mittre, 'Changing economy in ancient India', *Proceedings of the International Congress on Origins of Agriculture* Chicago, 1974 (in press); Vishnu-Mittre, 'Quaternary' Palynology and Palaeobotany in India, an appraisement' in (ed.) Vishnu-Mittre, *Late Quaternary Vegetational Developments in Extra European Areas*, Lucknow (1974). pp. 16-52.

Megaliths in Yemen Arab Republic

The megaliths in Oman in the south-eastern corner of the Arabian peninsula and the question of their possible bearing on the origin of Indian megaliths have been discussed in the pages of this Bulletin by S.P. Gupta (*4*, *1970-71*, pp. 4-16) and K.S. Ramachandran (*6*, *1972-73*, pp. 20-24). In this note I would draw attention to the megaliths that I saw in Yemen Arab Republic in the south-eastern Arabian peninsula during my three-month stay in that country in 1970. It is not my intention to suggest in any way that these megaliths had any genetic relation with the Indian ones.

2. In central Yemen, north-west of Dhamar, an important town south of Sanala, the capital of the country, on the Sana'a-Ta'izz road, is a hill called Jabal, al-Masn'a, which has extensive and typical Sabaean-Himyaritic remains of the early historical period. In addition, there is a large number of megalithic monuments, consisting of circles made of orthostats, menhirs and irregular stone slabs of enormous sizes (the largest measured by me being over 4·5 m in length, somewhat less than that in width, and 50 cm in thickness), raised to a horizontal or slanting position by props or short dry-rubble walls. The slabs were levered up from the rocks along their natural laminae, so that rocky sheltered floors were provided, perhaps for the placing of funerary deposits. As each component of these monuments is made of solid rock, there is no scope of excavating into them. Funerary deposits, if any existed, have disappeared.

3. Whether the co-occurrence of megaliths and early historical remains on the same hill indicates their contemporaneity is difficult to establish, but perhaps the indications are otherwise, as Sabaean-Himyaritic remains are not associated with megaliths anywhere else in the country, at least to my knowledge.

4. Very interesting is a group of monuments at al-Hamli, about 50 km to the north-west of Ta'izz, the largest city in the country, on the right side of the Ta'izz-Hudaida road, at the foot of the mountainous wall, in the narrow coastal strip that separates the Red Sea from High Yemen. Here are scattered stone circles of various sizes, 2 to 20 m in diameter. Sometimes, at the eastern or north-eastern point of the circles are tall boulders, perhaps marking the entrance, and often there is an upright at the centre, perhaps indicative of the spot of funerary deposits. These are reminiscent of some types of burials (not seen by me) found by different explorers in the People's Republic of Southern Yemen.[1]

5. To the east of these circles, nearer the mountains, are the ruins of a large structure of uprights, of which at least six north-to-south parallel (or a slightly radiating) alignments each some 50 m long, are identifiable. The largest of these uprights, now fallen, measures 4·35 m in height. The uprights at the northern end of the complex stand to a greater height than the rest. There is a perceptible attempt at giving the uprights a rough faceted shape of three to six sides. Immediately to the north of the rows is again a large stone circle, with an upright in the middle and two, of the same fashion as in the alignments, at the eastern end.

6. That this circle is connected with the alignments is definite. But whether it is of the same nature as those on the west (paragraph 4) is not certain. Equally uncertain is the age of the complex : while the attempt at fashioning the uprights into a shape does indicate the use of metallic tools (whether they were of copper-bronze or iron cannot be decided), the absence of inscriptions so prolific at all Sabaean-Himyaritic sites is significant and does in all probability indicate a prehistoric origin. The same remark would apply to the western group of stone circles (paragraph 4).

7. About 25 km. to the east of Sana'a, in the north-eastern part of the country, on a plateau between the villages Maroba and Salahi, is a cluster of stone enclosures, seemingly burials. They are sometimes circular, about 4 m in diameter and often rectangular, about 20 m in length, all surrounding cairns and marked off by unfashioned vertically-placed stone blocks, rarely more than 75 cm in height.

8. Stone enclosures, such as those mentioned in paragraphs 4 and 7 are usually classed in India under megaliths; that is my justification of including them in this note. No excavation has taken place at any of these sites. Photographs and drawing should have accompanied this note, but I have neither. The remains of Jabal al-Masn'a and al-Hamli are recorded with good illustrations by Gualtiero Benardelli and Antonino E. Parrinello;[2] they had visited the two sites earlier than myself. I am thankful to Mr Isma'il

[1]Richard LeBaron Bowen Jr. and Frank P. Albright, *Archaeological Discoveries in South Arabia* (Baltimore, 1958), pp. 133-36.

[2]Gualtiero Benardelli and Antonino E. Parrinello, *Annali dell' Istituto Orientale di Napoli*, Naples, 30 (1970), pp. 117-20.

al-Akwa'a, Director of Antiquities in Yemen Arab Republic, for having me to see them. The third site, that between Maraba and Salahi, was accidentally seen by me when I was travelling in that region with Professor Pietrov Gryaznevich of the Institute of Oriental Studies, Academy of Sciences in USSR, Leningrad.

9. The only intention of this note is to draw the attention of Indian archaeologists to the existence of different types of megaliths in a corner of the Arabian peninsula opposite the one which has been discussed in the pages of this Bulletin. I repeat, I have no intention of drawing any conclusions on the genesis of Indian megaliths.

A. GHOSH

"Bankuli",
Gurgaon Road, New Delhi-110037

Cairn Burials of Baluchistan Makran and South-east Iran : their Character and Chronology

Burial cairns are spread over a vast area in Pakistan, Baluch and Persian Makran and South-east Iran, extending along the Makran coast in the south and from Bushire in Iran to Fort Sandeman in the north; these occur also in the valleys of Mashkai, central Jhalawan and Dashtiari as far as Turbat and Fars. The northernmost site happens to be Chah Darat in south-east Iran on the west and Moghul Ghundai and Periano Ghundai (in Pakistan) in the east. The area covered forms a rough parallelogram connecting Zarand, Bushire, Kulli and Periano Ghundai. Heaviest concentration of these cairns is seen in the Dashtiari valley along the Makran coast. Normally, these are located on a hill slope or ridge and more often than not near a potential source of water.

Stein excavated many cairns in this area. At Gatti[1] the cairns ranged between 1·52 to 2·13 m in diameter and rose to a height of about 0·6 m. Of the half-a dozen cairns examined here they were found to contain fragments of copper/bronze vessels and pieces of pottery. One contained a piece of bluish green glass and a fragment of ribbed potsherd. Besides, the cairns also entombed iron vessels, horns and green glazed bottle of elegant shape. At Take Dap[2] the cairns contained loose earth in the centre with broken shells of crustacea, under which were noticed human bones, coarse plain pottery and copper pin, all in fragments.

Jiwanri[3] was the major site excavated. Here one hundred and seventy-eight burials were dug. Two types of monuments were observed—one circular and the other roughly quadrangular/rectangular. All the cairns had walls of rough calcareous sandstone and were filled up with earth. Diameters of the circular cairns ranged from 24 to 3·65 m (outer) to 0·9 to 1·5 m (inner). The rectangular structures also, of coursed stones, rose to a height of about 90 cm from the surrounding ground-level and were similar to those at Dambah Koh. The grave goods consisted of bones (femurs, humeri, patella, etc.), broken potsherds and full pots of coarse red fabric. Shapes included : large flat-bottomed pots, some of them spouted, narrow-mouthed flasks ; flat water bottles with three ears along the periphery with a groove running through them to facilitate running of a cord for hanging purposes ; *lota*-shaped vessels ; flat dishes of dark grey ; small jars of grey ware ; stands, etc. Painted designs in black pigment or sometimes in dark buff consisted of volutes, parallel bands bordering the volutes, vandykes, simple wavy lines within parallel bands, parallel lines and hachured triglyphs, vertical hachures, stylized birds. Other finds included: iron hooks ; fragments of two copper bracelets; several thin rings joined together; copper ring; carnelian beads, etc.

Skeletal remains were of the post-excarnated variety. Of the four hundred and ninety cairns at Zangian[4] in Kej valley, sixty-nine were opened. The walls of these cairns were of heaped up stones, and the cairns were roughly oblong in shape. Skeletal remains inside consisted of fragmentary calcined bones. Ceramic

[1]Sir Aurel Stein, *An Archaeological Tour in Gedrosia,* Memoirs of the Archaeological Survey of India, no. 43 (Calcutta, 1931), pp. 74-75.

[2]*Ibid.,* p. 76 ff.
[3]*Ibid.,* pp. 77-86.
[4]*Ibid.,* pp. 86.

contents were similar to those found at Jiwanri. But the pigment of the painted designs varied from buffred to black. The design repertoire consisted of hanging triangles. Incised decoration was represented by zigzag lines. Shapes of the pots were also similar to those at Jiwanri. Particular mention may, however, be made of a tea-pot and a jug. Other finds included : fragments of copper and iron (a badly rusted. large, broken sword-blade, another with bronze hilt) ; beads ; and terracotta animal figurines and heads of horses (in two cairns).

The cairns at Kulli[1] contained bone fragments,

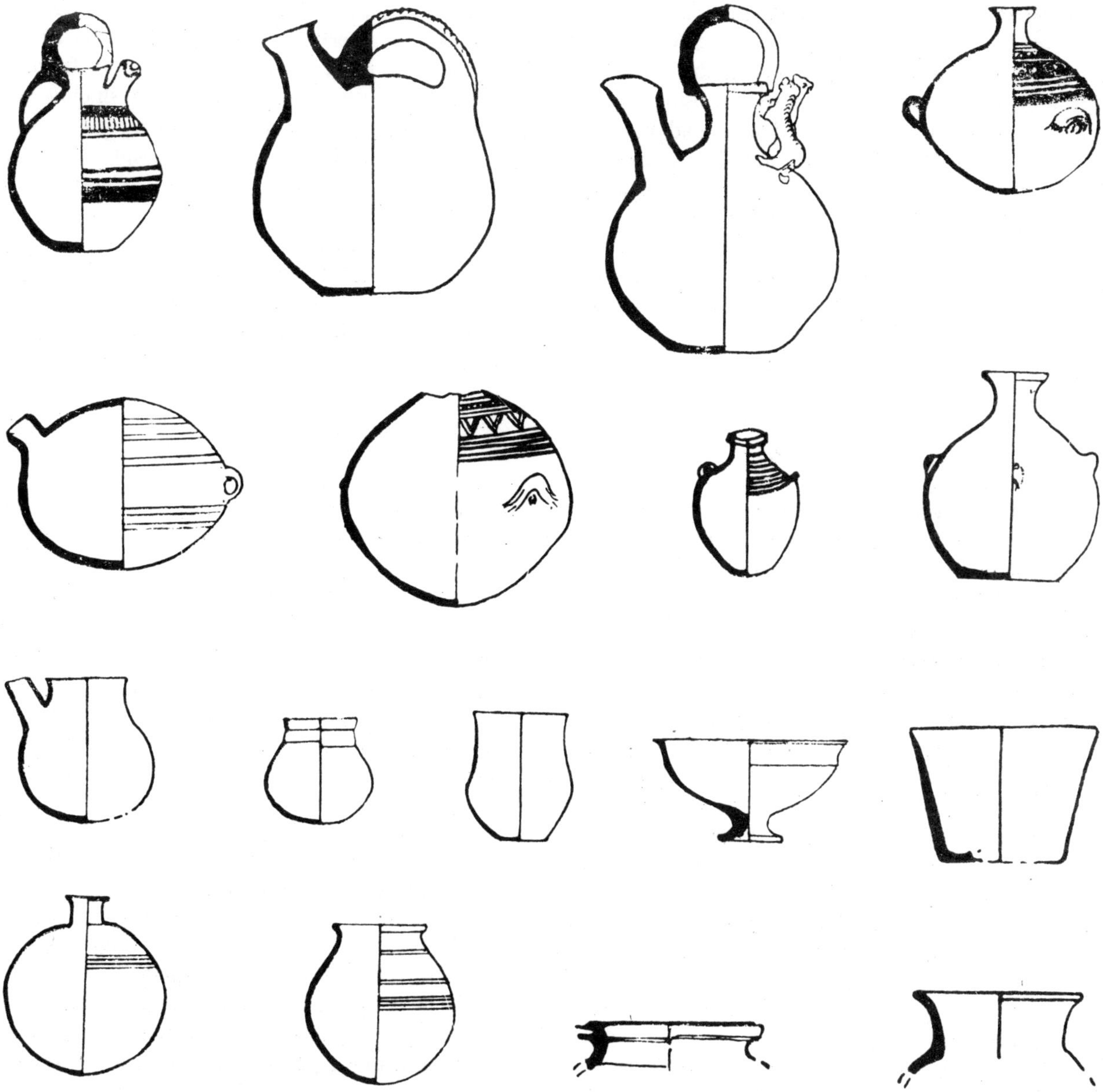

FIG. 1

[1]*Ibid.*, pp. 119 ff.

ash and plain pottery. Those near Gwarjak[1] also contained calcined bones, ashes and charred dates.

The cairns at Sunstar[2] are of the simple type, constructed of rough circle-stones enclosing a low heap of earth. Contents were small pieces, of human bones and potsherds. Part of a wooden comb and a pedestalled bowl are noteworthy finds.

Dambah Koh[3] is a major site containing more than thousand burial cairns. These are all constructed of undressed stones and vary in constructional details. They are of two types : (i) the circular/oval ; and (ii) rectangular. The first type was in the shape of small mounds of undressed stones enclosing loose earth concealing burial deposits. The second was of dry masonry constructed of irregular slabs enclosing roughly an area of 0·46 to 0·55 sq. m ; height of these varied from 1·2 to 1·52 m. The cairns were covered with slabs on top. Often one of the side-walls had a small opening which was closed by stones. Inner filling was of loose earth. Grave goods consisted of fragmentary human bones, pots and potsherds, green glazed, ribbed and grey and red wares ; and iron objects. Shapes in pottery comprised lugged pots with handles of animal motif. Several of the potsherds bear paintings showing annular wavy lines with hatching, etc. Other objects consisted of vessels and javelin-heads of iron, stone vases, beads, shell rings, steatite and terracotta beads, etc. Important among the finds from these cairns is a Parthian copper coin found by Mockler and another much corroded copper coin identified by Allan as belonging to Sinatruces (77-70 B.C.).[4]

Similar tombs were also noticed at Darmani Ban and Jooni.[5] Those at the latter site are built up ones. The grave goods consisted of pots and potsherds, iron objects, copper bracelets, shell ornaments, copper lamp, carnelian beads, etc. Two of the copper bracelets showed snake head patterns.[6]

At Damban, the contents of the cairns were similar to those in the cairns at Dambah Koh. Among other things, silver ornaments of twisted wire and folded silver plaque/buckle were found.

[1]*Ibid.*, pp. 149 ff.

[2]Sir Aurel Stein, *Archaeological Reconnaissances in the North-western India and South-eastern Iran* (London, 1937), pp. 71-72.

[3]*Ibid.*, pp. 37 ff; see also, Mockler, 'On Ruins in Makran', *Journal of the Royal Asiatic Society*, 1877, pp. 121-34.

[4]Stein, *op. cit.* (1937), p. 37.

[5]Mockler, *op. cit.*, p. 132.

[6]Stein, *op. cit.*, (1937), pp. 61-62.

Cairns at Sar-i-Asiab[7] were excavated by Stein and recently by Lamberg-Karlovsky. The cairns were circular/roughly rectangular. In height, these were about 1 m and in diameter, 5 m. The cairns excavated revealed some constructional peculiarities. The inner area of the retaining circle of stones of one cairn was divided into two by a line of stones along east-west. Again, the southern half was similarly divided into two. The northern half contained haphazardly piled up stones. The grave goods consisted of : on the floor, in the south-east corner, two pieces of copper/bronze wire and in the south-west corner, a bone bead, two incisors and fragmentary bones. The other cairn contained a shallow pit and entombed copper/bronze ring, much rusted iron piece, terracotta beads, blue glass bead and some animal bones but no human remains. Ceramic contents were wheel-made, whitish ware with incised decorations. The third cairn, similar in construction as the above, did not contain anything.

To sum up, cairns fall into three main types. The first type resembled a simple pile of stones,varying from circular to oval on plan. Here, within a circle of retaining stone over the burial furnishings and human remains were dumped loose earth capped by stone rubble. A variation of this type is the bifurcation of cairns in one axis and again division of one of the halves into two by a series of stones in alignment. The latter was noticed at Sar-i-Asiab. In some sites the circle of retaining stones, instead of being single boulders were of coursed dry masonry of uncut slabs of stones. The cairns normally varied in diameter from 1·2 to 4·57 m, and the height of the cairn ranged from 0·6 to 0·9 m above the surrounding ground level.

The second type was a rectangular structure of coursed dry masonry enclosing a hollow space and covered by capstones of slabs. The dimension of these ranged from 1·2 to 4·2 m square with a height varying between 1·2 to 1·5 m. Major Mockler reports a low doorway on one side with long slabs for a lintel hoisted on jambs of carefully laid stones. This fact, however, is disputed by Stein. A variation of this type was noticed at Hajjiabad where the inner sides were stepped in crude imitation of a corbelled vault. The chamber entombed skeletal remains and other burial furnishings. Filling inside was of loose earth.

A third type, confined to Fars valley, but found

[7]C. C. Lamberg-Karlovsky and James Humphries, 'The cairn burials of South-eastern Iran', *East and West*, 18, nos 3-4 (1968), pp. 269-76 and also Stein, *op. cit.* (1937), pp. 61-62.

together with the first, comprises neatly piled circular platforms of about 1·5 m in height over which was a similar but smaller platform. Occasionally, a similar third tier was also noticed. Inside, a series of tunnel-like chambers were found which contained the mortal remains and other furnishings.

Ceramic contents of these cairns consisted mainly of thick coarse red, dark grey and grey wares. Some of the red wares had whitish slip. Occasionally, bluish green glazed sherds were also found besides some sherds of ribbed pots. Pots were both plain and decorated ; the latter comprising painted and incised designs. The shapes and the decoration of the pottery has already been explained above (p. 82).

Other grave furnishings comprised : copper objects, viz., pins, bracelets or anklets, basal ring, lamp ; decorated disc of bone or shell ; beads of terracotta, steatite, glass, carnelian, etc. ; terracotta animal figurines ; shell rings, stone vases ; ornaments of small thin silver, rings stuck together; silver ornaments of twisted wire; folded silver, plaque resembling a buckle ; and fragment of a wooden comb. Iron objects consisted of vessels, weapons, etc. Most of the metal objects were fragmentary.

CHRONOLOGY OF THE CAIRN BURIALS

Paucity of datable evidence is a deterrant factor in dating these cairns with any certainty. However, from a study of comparable ceramic-types and other associated objects a broad chronological horizon can be postulated. The cairn-burial people have been equated with the Londo-Ware using folk.[1] The Londo Ware, deriving its name from the type site, is red in surface colour. This handmade ware, fashioned out of pinkish red paste, containing some gritty substance, has an uneven surface. The ware is well-fired, slipped wholly or partially and bears paintings in black or polychrome. Popular shapes in this ware are copies of metal prototypes. Representative forms are : carinated bowls ; beakers ; and pedestal-footed goblets. Design repertoire comprised parallel bands, hachured triangles, pot-hook spirals or voluted scrolls and discs with rays. Below this occur a variety of designs which appear to be a hybrid version of the distinctive Sialk B pottery. In the context of its late date the technique of manufacture and finish is perhaps indicative of a general backwardness of the region.

The Londo Ware sites are distributed along the Kej valley to the Jhalawan and Sarawan and the western districts of Kharen.[2] Such sites are not found either in Sind or in Persian Makran. Further, the Ware seems to be wholly different from other prehistoric wares of Baluchistan. Therefore, one is led to the conclusion that it is entirely regional.

From none of the numerous excavated cairns, Londo Ware was recovered. The sherds found at Dambah Koh are surface finds. However, certain painted designs, viz., curvilinear patterns from Basot and Dambah Koh, Harmardi, Rudbar, Jiwanri, etc., might have been inspired by the Londo Ware. According to Gordon, volutes are late and uncommon in cairns and spiral decorations are not noticed beyond the Nihang valley. Even at Zayak, spiral decorations are absent. The animal motifs seemingly recalling similarities with Sialk VI B, differ in detail. According to de Cardi, the Londo Ware people came into contact with Sialk B people and 'being displaced by them migrated to Baluchistan.'[3] Further she denies emphatically any resemblance between Londo Ware and the cairn-burial pottery.[4]

SIALK

Sialk influence on pottery and grave goods from the cairn burials can be recognized. For example, jugs with flattened spouts from Zangian and Jiwanri are found in Sialk B. Here it is worthwhile to consider the date of Sialk B. Ghirshman has dated this to *c.* tenth-ninth century B.C. on the grounds that (i) Sialk B succeeds Sialk A and hence later than 1000 B.C.; (ii) Sialk B people were Medes, an undisputed fact; and Medes are mentioned for the first time in 834 B.C.; and (iii) the presence of an Assyrian cylinder seal of the ninth century. Dyson,[5] however, objects to the postulates (i) and (iii) and argues that the Medes of 834 B.C. need not necessarily be the same Medes of Sialk B, and the cylinder seal is one typical object and therefore does not warrant an acceptable dating object for the whole assemblage. On the basis of ceramic similarities at Ziwayeh and Persian Village I (*c.* seventh century B.C.),Sialk B is dated by him to

[1]N. R. Banerjee, *Iron Age in India*, (Delhi, 1965), pp. 44 ff.

[2]Beatrice de Cardi, 'A new prehistoric Ware from Baluchistan, *Iraq*, XIII (1951), pp. 63-75.

[3]*Ibid.*

[4]*Ibid.*

[5]Robert H. Dyson, 'Problem of protohistoric Iran as seen from Hasanlu', *Journal of Near Eastern Studies*, XXIV, 3 (1965), pp. 193-217.

the eighth century B.C. However, there are dissimilarities in weaponry and population. Yet, a few metal arrow-heads, spear-heads, a bit type and harness button do show affinities. At Baba Jan[1] in Central Luristan, Iron Age II is represented by Baba Jan B culture. Here, the ceramics comprise pottery of *genere* Luristan, and medium and coarse wares. Common ones are of medium thickness, and are fashioned out of well-levigated clay. The pottery is either handmade or turned on slow wheel. Colour of the wares ranges from off-white through cream to peach, orange, light reddish brown and buff. Surface is smooth and rarely slipped. Some of the finer specimens are burnished. Pigment of painting is of reddish brown ; rather greenish, over vitrified specimens. Painted designs are crude, showing lack of dexterity and imagination.

The medium wares are dirty buff or reddish brown in colour. Mainly storage jars belong to this variety. Decorations comprised applied cordon and impressed designs. Colour of the coarse wares ranged from reddish brown to black.

Design repertoire is limited. Kites,often combined with Kassite cross, hanging triangles, dotted band are the normal patterns. Less frequent are zig zags, cross hatchings, net, checker, double arc or butterfly arrangement and large blobs in lines or on apexes of triangles.

Baba Jan A pertains to Iron Age III (*c*. 700-400 B.C.). Bulk of the pottery is wheel-made and consists of medium and coarse wares. Medium wares are medium textured,surface being smoothed or burnished. These are thick walled and are heavy. Pots in common use are fine, hard and are fashioned out of well-levigated clay. Colour ranges from buff through deep peach pink or pale or dark orange. Fine specimens are burnished. Coarse ware is rare. Storage jar is the common shape. Ribbing, and cable decora-

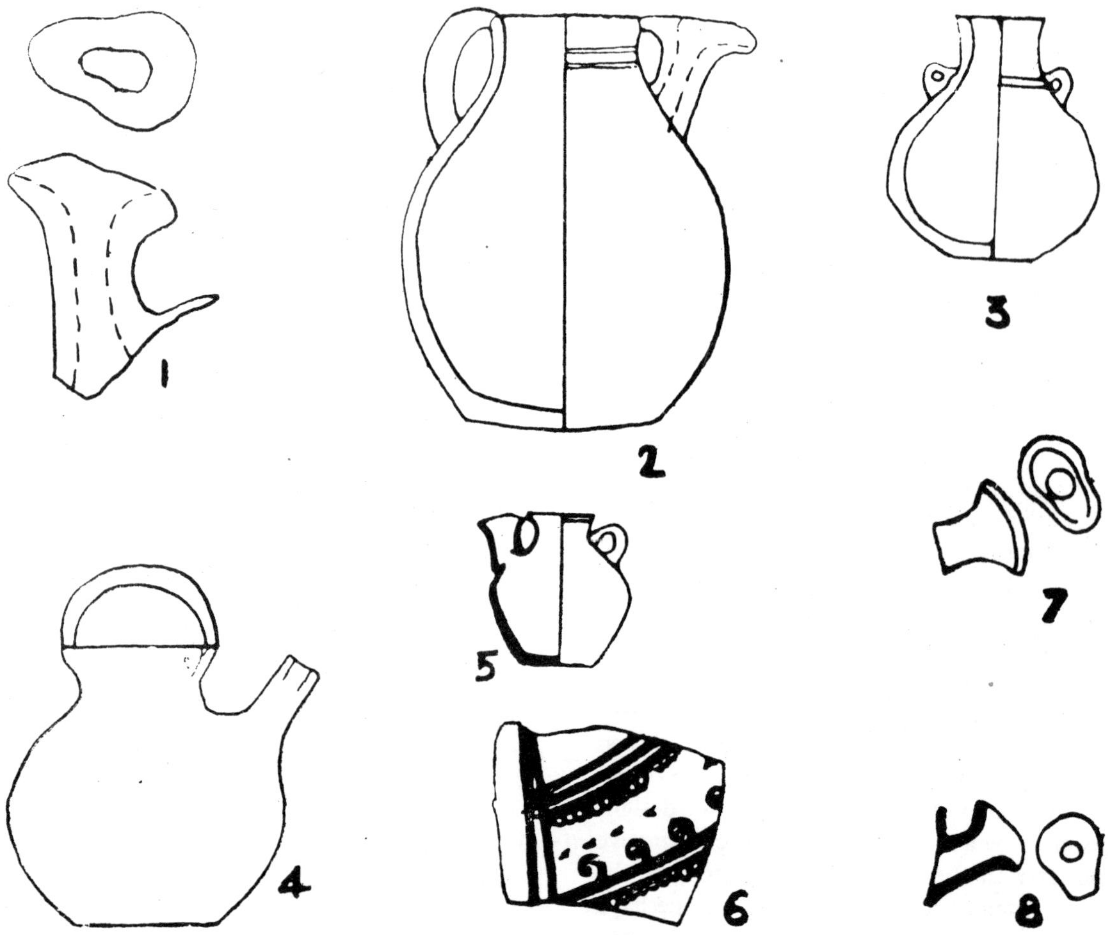

FIG. 2

[1]Clare Goeff Meade, 'Luristan in the first half of the first millennium B. C., *Iran*, VI (1968), pp. 105-34.

tions are found at all levels. Red Ware is also rare. Shapes included open bowl, sometimes carinated, ledge/nail-headed rim bowls with inturned rims, hemispherical rims with horizontal loop handles. Less frequent shapes are jars with trefoil spout and jars with upright spouts.

In ceramics, there is a definite development from Baba Jan B to Baba Jan A.

Baba Jan A is comparable to Hasanlu IIIB and Ziwayeh where ledged rim, trefoil spout and strait spout are common. Spouts are also available at Achaeminid village II-III (fourth century B.C.) at Susa. Trefoil spout has parallels at Pasargade in the upper levels (sixth century B.C.).

Painted designs distinctive of Iron Age III sites in Pish-i-kui include dashes and solid triangles on the rims of bowls, pot hooks, and hanging loops. These are again comparable to Hasanlu IIIB and Ziwayeh and the Achaeminid Village I, datable to seventh century B.C. This culture has spread throughout the eastern Pish-i-kui and the plains of Mahi Dasht.

Baba Jan B has been dated to the eighth century B.C. perhaps with an early beginning in the ninth century B.C. This culture had died out by 650 B.C. Baba Jan A has been assigned to the sixth century B.C. Pottery from the cairn-burials exhibit some affinities in form and painted motifs with Baba Jan A. Pots with upright spouts from Zangian, horizontal loop handles/lugs from Jiwanri, rope (basket) and strap handles from Zangian, handles with animal motifs from Dambah Koh, trefoil spouted jar with handle from Jiwanri are noteworthy. Pot hooks and hanging triangles from Jiwanri, dashes within bands at Zangian and Jiwanri and zig zags from the latter site are some of the design patterns showing similarities.

Now, considering the difficult topographical terrain of the Zagros, a minimum of at least a century should be allowed for these traits to travel to Baluchistan. Therefore, the cairns can be dated to the latter half of of the sixth or early fifth century B.C.

The bronze basal ring with engraving of a man with headdress and carrying a bow and a spear and facing a woman could be put in a time bracket of fifth century to the middle of the second century B.C.[1] Whereas the adjustable bracelet is known to date in West Asia and Caucasus from the middle of the second millennium B.C.[2]

The bronze tripod vessel from Moghul Ghundai has been compared to similar bronze and clay vessels from Sialk B.[3] But a more convincing stylistic-affinity of the Moghul Ghundai vessel has been establ lished with Sirkap (Taxila) by Alcock.[4] As a supporting evidence similarities of the pedestalled bowls from Fanuch and Sunstar with those from Taxila have been cited.[5]

The bowl decorated with Hellenistic motifs from Moghul Ghundai[6] could be dated to the last centuries B.C. The presence of green glazed ware in some cairns would definitely warrant a late date. Similarly the coin of Sinatruces (77-70 B.C.). from a cairn in Dambah Koh would bring down the date to the first century B.C. Again, another coin of Yazdagird III, from a cairn at Bishezard, would further lower the date, bringing it to the seventh century A.D.

On the above considerations the cairn-burials of Baluchistan may be assigned to sixth-fifth century B.C. to seventh century A.D.

K. S. RAMACHANDRAN
Archaeological Survey of India,
Janpath, New Delhi--110011

[1]D. H. Gordon, *The Prehistoric Background of Indian Culture* (Bombay, 1958), p. 160.
[2]*Ibid.*
[3]Stuart Piggott, *Prehistoric India* (Harmondsworth, 1952), p. 240.
[4]A. Alcock, 'The 'Dark Age' in North West India', *Antiquity*, 26 (1952), pp. 93-95.
[5]Lamberg-Karlovsky, *op. cit.*, p. 274.
[6]Sir Aurel, Stein, *An Archaeological Tour in Waziristan and Northern Baluchistan*, Memoirs of the Archaeological Survey of India, no. 37, pp. 47-58 and Lamberg-Karlovsky, *op. cit.*

Some Theoretical Aspects of Early Indian Urban Growth

The present brief paper proposes to deal with the comments made by Banerjee, Krishna Deva, Ghosh, Thapar and Joshi on the early Indian urban growth in the *Puratattva*, no. 6 (1972-73), pp. 32-36. This also takes into consideration the hypotheses formulated by Gupta and Agrawal in the same number of the Bulletin. The discussion will be basically on three separate issues : the Harappan genesis and its relationship with the pre-Harappan village-settlers (Agrawal, Gupta, Thapar); the role of the political power in the growth and consolidation of the earliest historical cities (Banerjee, Krishna Deva, Ghosh, Joshi); and finally, the problem of the applicability of the term 'urbanization' in the Indian context (Ghosh).

One entirely agrees with Agrawal that the pre-Harappan villagers did not go out of the scene with the advent of the Harappans but co-existed with them, at least for some time. But one may not agree with his broad cultural statement that the Harappans and the pre-Harappans were 'urban and folk (rural) facies respectively of the same cultural phenomenon'.[1] Of 250 odd Harappan sites[2] only very few may be considered urban. The point is that the Harappans themselves, as we know them, had a demonstrable rural facies and in the present state of knowledge one cannot simply say that this rural facies was composed only by the pre-Harappan village-settlers. In this context Gupta's idea is apparently more justifiable ; only to '*somе* of the so-called pre-Harappan settlements in the same vicinity' [3] he is willing to assign a peasant status in the Harappan framework. Incidentally, both Agrawal and Gupta seem to be unhappy with the term 'pre-Harappan'. Technically there is nothing wrong with this term. At all the relevant excavated sites, this level is demonstrably earlier than the Harappan level. In absolute chronological terms also this goes back to the beginning of the third millennium B.C., a point in time which cannot be attributed to any of the Harappan levels. Their obvious existence even after the Harappan growth, as pointed out by Agrawal and Gupta, does not alter their pre-Harappan status.

An important aspect of Gupta's six 'stages' within his evolutionary model of the first or Harappan phase of Indian urban growth is that these 'stages' are not bound by any directly causal relationship, not at least up to the formation of the Harappan civilization. One is, however, wary in accepting the validity of his last 'stage', 'Dispersal'. Within this stage he puts the Ochre Colour Pottery complex, the Siswal-Mitathal level and the lesser Harappan sites, apparently marking the end of the Harappan civilization. The problem is : does one know enough of these horizons to put them within one broad cultural stage ?

In his discussion, Thapar rightly emphasizes the need 'to study the traits of the loosely-termed pre-Harappan communities in the various regions, and to establish points of interrelationship and lines of communication between each.[4] Till such a study is made it is not possible to assess with any degree of accuracy the role of the pre-Harappans in the Harappan make-up. And, without such an assessment the Harappan urbanism has got to be accepted as an illustration of Barraclough's contention that 'continuity is by no means the most conspicuous feature of history.[5]

Banerjee, Krishna Deva, Ghosh and Joshi have criticized the present author's hypothesis that of all the factors leading to the growth of the earliest historical cities like those of Rajagriha, Varanasi, Kausambi and Ujjayini, the primary emphasis should perhaps be given on the factor of political power. According to them the basic causative force behind these cities was the socio-economic factors. Joshi, in fact, goes to the length of saying that 'the deciding factor in calling a particular culture as urbanized should be the existence of a monetary exchange rather than any other feature, may that be script or monumental architecture'. [6] The importance of the socio-economic factors like those of an effective rural-agricultural base, the increasing importance of trade and trade-routes, an elaborate growth of merchants and artisans, etc. is, of course, obvious behind any urban scene. But as one notes, all these earliest fortified urban settlements were also the centres of some centralized power-structure. The spark which set off the process of early historic urban growth was this element of political consolidation. After all, the socio-economic factors could be effectively integrated within one social complex and given a centralized direction only under the aegis of a consolidated power-structure. In any case, the element of monetary exchange cannot be taken as the most crucial urban index. A standardized monetary medium cannot function without an organized control within the framework of a political structure.

One of the issues raised by Ghosh is rather a crucial one. 'In the first place, I would hesitate to use the word 'urbanization' in the Indian context. In both the periods, the Indus and the early historical,

[1]D. P. Agrawal, 'Genesis of Harappa Culture', *Puratattva* no. 6 (1972-73), p. 41

[2]B.M. Pande and K. S. Ramachandran, *Bibliography of the Harappan Culture* (Florida, 1972), pp. 37-43.

[3]S. P. Gupta, 'A model for Understanding the First Urbanisation in India, *Puratattva*. no. 6 (1972-73), p. 45

[4]B. K. Thapar, Comments, *Puratattva*, no. 6 (1972-73), p. 36A.

[5]G. Barraclough, *An Introduction to Contemporary History* (Harmondsworth, 1267), p. 11.

[6]M.C. Joshi, Comments, *Puratattva*, no. 6 (1972-73) p. 36B.

there was no large-scale drift to the city, as the word would lead us to expect. The vast population continued to be rural and nothing altered the predominantly rural character of the land'.[1] The significant word here is 'large-scale'. Is the term 'urbanization' to be used only in a context where one can postulate a 'large-scale' rural-urban migration? Ghosh is obviously imposing the notion of modern urbanization on the ancient context because before the modern industrial period there was no 'large-scale drift to the city' anywhere. In any ancient context the landscape was predominantly rural, and the rural element was quite strong even within the cities. Mumford[2] has analyzed how even the Greek cities of the fifth-fourth centuries B.C. were close to rural ways, and according to Max Weber 'the full urbanite of antiquity was a semi-peasant'.[3]

Ghosh also apparently ignores the fact that in every period of early Indian history, when the situation was favourable, there was a growth of cities. One can understand this feature rather clearly in the context of early historic cities. On the basis of the available archaeological data, the present author has distinguished three distinct phases of early historic urban growth.[4] The first phase corresponds to the sixth-fifth centuries B.C. Beginning primarily along a belt stretching from Champa and Rajagriha to Ujjayini through Kausambi, this soon included the upper Gangetic valley and the Indo-Gangetic divide. This was also the period when the Achaemenid annexation of the north-west might have given rise to an urban nucleus there. The third-second centuries B.C. seem to mark the next phase of growth. This period witnessed the further growth of settlements in the areas which already came within the urban fold in the preceding phase. The basic importance of this phase, however, seems to be the fact that during this period many new regions,where the precise beginning of early historic period is still uncertain, came to develop or was about to develop a clear and unmistakable urban base. The regions which should fall in this category are the Punjab plains, Sind, lower Gangetic valley, Rajasthan, Gujarat, Maharashtra and Orissa. That was also the twilight period of early history in Mysore, Kerala, Madras and Andhra. The third and final phase of urban growth in our chosen period seems to have developed in the early centuries A.D., characterized by a general urban prosperity throughout the subcontinent. One also detects now the indisputable evidence of urban settlements in the areas like Mysore, Kerala, Madras and Andhra where the earlier evidence seems to lie vague and doubtful. There is also some possibility of the growth of an urban core in the Brahmaputra valley in about this period.

So far as the general historical process is concerned it should be obvious that these three phases belonging to the sixth-fifth centuries B.C., third-second centuries B.C. and early centuries A.D., correspond to three significant politico-economic and cultural phases in early Indian history—the periods of the first emergence of historical light, the consolidation and spread of the Mauryan hegemony and the Indo-Roman trade, supplemented by close trade-contacts with Central Asia, China and South-east Asia.

The archaeological pattern of early historic urban growth is, in fact, in no stage divorced from the corresponding historical realities of the country. Up to the Guptas, the historic urban growth in India was a continuous process in which may be discerned three peaks. There was a drift from the village to the city over all these centuries of early Indian history. The drift might not have been 'large-scale' but in no ancient society was this drift so. We, on our part, find no hesitation to use the term 'urbanization' in the early Indian context.

DILIP K. CHAKRABARTI

Department of Ancient Indian History and Archaeology
University of Calcutta,
51/2 Hazra Road, Calcutta-19

[1]A. Ghosh, Comments, *Puratattva*, no. 6 (1972-73), p. 34.
[2]L.Mumford, *The City in History* (London, 1961),pp. 126-33.
[3]Max Weber, *The City* (New York, 1961), p. 78

[4]Dilip K. Chakrabarti, *Early Urban Centres in India, an Archaeological Perspective, c. 2500 B.C. — c. 300 A.D.*, Ph.D. Thesis, University of Calcutta (unpublished).

Early Historical Urban Growth in India : Some Observations

In his rejoinder, Chakrabarti has discussed the problems relating to early Indian urban growth and has advanced further arguments in support of his hypothesis emphasizing the factor of political power for urban growth. He raises two important issues : (i) the earliest fortified urban settlements were also the centres of some centralized power-structure ; and (ii) it was the element of political consolidation which served as the principal governing factor for early historical urban growth.

Thus, in his opinion, a fortification was an essential feature of an urban settlement ; but, as a result of archaeological excavations, we now know definitely that many early Indian cities of political significance e.g., Taxila, Sravasti, Vaisali or Ahichchhatra were without fortifications in the sixth-fifth century B.C. Besides, there was a non-urban fortified settlement at Eran in the chalcolithic age, much before the early historical period. Around the sixth-fifth century B.C., most of the early cities of north India did function as centres of political power, yet this feature does not necessarily imply that every fortified habitation[1] was an urban settlement and every urban settlement was the hub of a centralized power-structure. The basic reason for the birth of a city/township was economic necessity whereas in case of a fortification it was the political/defensive factor. The following reference (preserved in early Pali literature) to townships and cities located on a trade-route connecting Assaka and Magadha *Mahajanapadas* deserves special mention in the present context :

Allakassa Patitthanam purim Mahissatim tada
Ujjenim chapi Gonadhdam Vedisam
Vanasahvayam ॥
Kosambim chapi Saketam Savatthim
chapurottamam ॥
Setavyam cha Kapilavatthum Kusinaram
cha mandiram ॥
Pavam cha Bhoganagaram Vesalim
Magadham-puram ॥
Suttanipata, Vatthugatha, 36-38

These verses clearly show that some time during the period of the Buddha many places like Allaka (also read as Mulaka sometimes), Gonadhda, Vidisa, Vanasa, Saketa, Setavya and Bhoganagara were only market-towns and not the headquarters of any centralized power. Similarly, Veranja, Sankasya, Soreyya and Prayaga-Pratishthana (Jhusi near Allahabad) situated on another trade-route were also only commercial towns or townships.

The genesis of the urban growth therefore does not seem to lie in the political consolidation, as suggested by Chakrabarti. The rise of four important monarchical powers was primarily a result of the urban transformation. The merger of Kasi into Kosala and conquest of Vajji by Ajatasatru were mainly conditioned by economic reasons. An interesting reference to this effect is preserved in the *Piyajatika Sutta* : Queen Mallika once asked her husband king Prasenajit the reason for his love for Kasi and Kosala. The latter replied that it was so because he could get luxury items like *mala* (garlands), *gandha* (scent), *vilepana* (lotion) including *Kasika-chandana* only on account of the prosperity of the two peoples.

The consolidated power-structure, for the emergence of which Chakrabarti does not assign any reason, was thus itself an outcome of the urban growth which could be marked in increased trade activity based on monetary exchange. The field of trading activity around *circa* sixth-fifth century B.C. covered a much larger area than the political limits of one or two kingdoms and it was, therefore, beyond the control of a king or a ruling chief to determine the value of money. The trader or the trading group and international trade situation served as principal factor in this regard. The system of issue and circulation of the earliest currency of India, viz., the punch-marked coinage was in conformity only with this kind of economic structure under well-organized guilds.

The urban growth in India duriug the early historical period is not to be merely interpreted in the emergence of township in *doab* or elsewhere; it is to be understood as an economic phenomenon which transformed the barter-based rural economy of a vast area and interlinked it with the international trade exchange structure of those days.

[1]The early Pali literature preserves two terms for fortification, viz., *pakara* (Skt. *prakara*) and *nagarupakarika*. In the context of urbanism the latter is particularly significant as it appears to have originally stood for a fortification which was raised around an already established urban settlment for its betterment.

In this respect the existence of a city or a township with a specific personality was only a secondary element. In the initial stage, when there was no well marked city, probably the villages located on trade-route functioned as trading centres. The fundamental factor which ultimately led to the birth of urbanism in north India was nothing but the use of iron technology resulting in surplus production as suggested by R.S. Sharma.[1] For the proper utilization of this surplus-yield[2] monetary exchange was adapted so that the new trader, who was an agriculturist[3] (*vaisya*), could procure the items of his comfort and luxury. With the adoption of monetary exchange,[4] urban transformation commenced and with the establishment of Nigamas, Nagarakas and Nagaras, etc., the agricultural trader emerged as a *sresthin* or *sarthavaha* with an organized guild. Hence to us the existence of monetary exchange remains to be the determinant trait of urbanism.

M. C. JOSHI

Archaeological Survey of India,
Purana Qila, New Delhi, 110011

[1]Ram Saran Sharma, 'Material background of the origin of Buddhism', in (eds.) Mohit Sen and M. B. Rao, *Das Kapital Centenary Volume - a Symposium* (Delhi-Ahmedabad-Bombay, 1965), p. 61.

[2]According to A Ghosh, *The City in Early Historical India* (Simla, 1973), p. 20, the surplus could not have been produced unless there was need for it. We, however, do not agree with him, for, the idea of surplus-yield is itself present in the very concept of agricultural production. This is also attested by a number of Vedic hymns wherein a sacrificer always desires to possess as much cattle and agricultural wealth as possible.

[3]The origin of the term *karshapana* or *kahapana*, the early currency of India from the verbal roots *krish* (to cultivate) and *pan* (to exchange or barter and to bargain), also suggests that it was the early Iron Age cultivator who became a trader and introduced this word for the coin with the adpotion of the monetary exchange.

[4]The later date for the beginning of urban transformation in south India than that of the north in spite of contemporaneity of the knowledge of iron technology in two parts may be due to non-replacement of barter system by money and proper utilization of trade routes till the second-first century. B.C.

Stratigraphical Position of the N.B.P. Ware in the Upper Ganga Basin and its Date

This paper attempts to study the N.B.P. Ware and a few associated types in their stratigraphical context and to correlate the available literary evidence for determining the date of the Ware.

In the upper Ganga basin, the important excavated sites yielding the N.B.P. Ware are Hastinapura, Alamgirpur, Purana Qila, Mathura, Khalaua, Atranjikhera, Ahichchhatra, Kanuaj, Kausambi, Sravasti, Ayodhya, Sohagaura, Rajghat, Sarai Mohana, Prahladpur and others. The stratigraphical position of the N.B.P. Ware and its associated shapes and types of different wares along with their complex of cultural traits vary a great deal from region to region and site to site. Of these sites, Hastinapura, Atranjikhera, Sravasti and Prahladpur are considered here as type sites.

The appearance of the N.B.P. Ware takes place in four different contexts as given below :

1. On some western sites, the N.B.P. Ware phase comes stratigraphically after the P.G. Ware phase with a break in between the two, with the result that both represent two different cultural horizons. The type site is Hastinapura.

2. On certain sites, it overlaps with the P.G. Ware assemblage, but an earlier independent P.G. Ware horizon is absent. The type site is Sravasti.

3. On a few sites, it appears in both the contexts referred to in 1 and 2 with a little difference. Here N.B.P. Ware is preceded by the P.G. Ware phase in an indepdendent cultural horizon and thereafter overlaps with the P.G. Ware assemblage and finally continues as an independent phase, the difference being that there is no perceptible gap between the two as is found in 1. The type site is Atranjikhera.

4. Lastly, on a few other sites of the eastern region, of which Prahladpur is considered as the type site, N.B.P. Ware phase is preceded by black and red ware phase (layers 5 and 6) without any perceptible gap. On such sites, P.G. Ware is conspicuous by its absence, but in this phase, most of the cultural traits are found in common with those of the independent P.G. Ware of the western region as found in Prahlad-

pur Sub-period IA. In the later deposit (layers 4 and 3) which yields N.B.P. Ware, some of the earlier traits also continue in a diminishing order and lastly in Sub-period IC, N.B.P. Ware continues in a new cultural horizon.

Thus, the combined stratigraphical testimony indicates the existence of the N.B.P. Ware in two cultural horizons. Of these, the earlier is accompanied by the traits of the preceding period, while the latter shows new traits to the exclusion of the earlier ones.

These two sub-phases become clearly perceptible on a closer examination of the stratigraphical position of certain characteristic shapes, usually associated with the N.B.P. Ware. In the present study, only three such shapes or types have been considered : (i) flat-based bowls (or lids) with thread marks at the base, with or without incurved rims; (ii) pear-shaped vase generally called Ahichchhatra 10 A, in red ware ; and (iii) carinated *handi* with featureless rim in grey, red and N.B.P. Ware fabrics. The exact stratigraphical position of these individual shapes are not clearly reported at most of the sites. At Hastinapura, all these shapes are reported from the early levels of Period III. However, our study of pottery at Atranjikhera reveals that all these shapes do not occur in the early levels of the N.B.P. Ware deposit. The characteristic type, associated with the earliest N.B.P. Ware at the site, is the miniature bowl with incurved rim and flat base, bearing thread marks, and this feature is more significant. It is found in both red and grey ware fabrics.

The significance of this flat base bowl lies in the fact that this shape does not require additional labour in finishing it, whereas almost all the pottery shapes of the preceding cultural periods, to our knowledge, are hand finished at the base. In other words, with the introduction of the N.B.P. Ware, a new potting technique was introduced, resulting in the production, on a mass scale, of utilitarian pots. However, the remaining pottery complex of this level remains the same as is found in the preceding P.G.W. period, though in a diminishing order. Although such kind of miniature bowl is reported earliest in Pd. II of Sravasti, but a shape called lid-*cum*-bowl of grey ware, with tapering sides and flat base has been reported from Period I.[1] At Prahladpur also the flat-based type with little modification is reported from the early level of Sub-period IB.[2] At Sarai Mohana, the shape is reported from the Sub-period IB.[3] Thus, the stratigraphic position of this associated type at Atranjikhera stands corroborated from these sites as well. It may also be mentioned here that Ahichchhatra 10A and the carinated *handi* are conspicuous by their absence in the early deposits yielding the N.B.P. Ware.

These two latter shapes, Ahichchhatra 10A and carinated *handi,* seem to have been introduced in the comparatively later deposits at Atranjikhera. These shapes are reported from the early levels of Hastinapura III, Atranjikhera IVB, Sravasti II, and Prahladpur IC.[4] Regarding Sravasti II, it may be observed that K.K. Sinha put this period as 'post-N.B.P. Ware phase'[5] but type 8 and 8A of figure 5 which are of N.B.P. Ware, belong to Period II as given in the report. Thus, according to our estimate, Period II at Sravasti would represent the late phase of the N.B.P. Ware. Thus, these characteristic shapes generally associated with the N.B.P. Ware, are in fact associated with the Ware only in the later phases. Accordingly, any deposit of N.B.P. Ware which also contains these two shapes should be considered as the later N.B.P. Ware deposit.

Phase A or the earlier phase is characterized by the continuation of the P.G. Ware, in diminishing proportions, along with its shapes and pottery complex in the western region, and by the continuation of the black-and-red ware traditions and shapes in the eastern region. In this phase the N.B.P. Ware is found in richer variety. Certain new shapes like flat-based bowls, etc., and others were introduced. It is marked also by the absence of punch-marked coins and structures of either mud brick or baked brick. This phase is represented by Atranjikhera IVA, Sravasti I, and Prahladpur IB, and is absent at Hastinapura, probably covered by the gap between Periods II and III.

Phase B or the later phase, is characterized by the absence of P.G. Ware and the black-and-red ware, greater use of coarse grey ware and emergence of some new shapes like Ahichchhatra 10A and carinated *handi* etc. In this phase, the N.B.P. Ware occurs in lesser frequency and is generally thicker in fabric. It is in this phase that punch-marked coins and mud brick structures are found. This phase is represented by Hastinapura III, Atranjikhera IVB, Sravasti II and Prahladpur IC.

Having established the stratigraphical context in which the N.B.P. Ware is found, let us make an attempt

[1] K. K. Sinha, *Excavations at Sravasti 1959* (Varanasi, 1967), fig. 11, type XLVIII, p. 39.

[2] A. K. Narain and T.N. Roy, *The Excavations at Prahladpur* (Varanasi, 1968), fig. 12, T.6A, and T. 6B, p. 34.

[3] *Indian Archaeology 1967-68—A Review*, pp. 48-49.

[4] Narain and Roy, *op. cit.*, p.23.

[5] *Ibid.*, p. 15.

to find out if there is any reference to N.B.P. Ware or any of its associated shapes in our literary evidences.

There are certain literary evidences which indicate that N.B.P. Ware and the carinated *handi* was already in use during the life-time of Gautama Buddha. Fa-hien's and Yuang Chwang's accounts, though comparatively late, preserve certain traditions which can be traced up to Buddha's time.

Yuang Chwang[1] makes a statement in connection with his description of Bodh Gaya that when Buddha declined these bowls (golden and other costlier bowls offered to him to hold his food) as unsuitable for religious mendicants, the Devaraja's brought from their palaces a stone bowl of dark violet colour, bright and lustrous, which he accepted. This tradition can be traced back to a similar tradition contained in the *Chullavagga* (1.4.4.)

Fa-hien gives the following description when he was at Peshawar. Buddha's alms-bowl was an object of worship, it holds two pecks and is of several colours, chiefly black. It is almost 1/5th of an inch thick, of transparent brilliance and of glossy lustre. These descriptions indicate that probably Buddha's alms-bowl was of N.B.P. Ware, since it is the only Ware which satisfies most of these descriptions.

Now let us consider the shape and the general features of the alms-bowls used by Gautama Buddha or the Buddhist monks in general. The following are the characteristics of the alms-bowls used by the monks in general, as revealed by *Chullavagga* in its Fifth *Khandhaka*.[2]

1. It could either be of iron or clay.

2. Its shape was of such a type that an additional support was required to keep it in position.[3]

3. When the *bhikshus* put away these bowls without water in them the bowls were spoilt, and when they were dried in the sunshine with water, it used to become evil smelling, and when placed in the warm place the colour of the bowl was spoilt.[4]

4. When bowls were left in the open air without any support, the bowls were turned over by whirlwind and broke, when placed on the edge of the steeping benches, the bowls fell down and were broken, when turned upside down on the ground, the lips were out, and these bowls were often carried by the monks in bags.[5]

It implies, therefore, that these alms-bowls were of fragile nature, probably an earthen ware pot with a round or convex base.

There is also a reference that when the monks went on their round for alms they carried with them *ghati kapalam*.[6] There is another reference in the same text that during this period certain monks who had taken upon themselves a vow to wear or use nothing except that they could procure from dust heaps or cemeteries, when on their round for alms, carried a bowl made of human skull, and were advised not to do so by the Blessed One because such was the practice adopted by the devil worshippers.[7] Now this would mean that even when the human skull was discarded as a begging-equipment, the term *kapalam* continued to be used for the begging pot. It was done more so because the alms bowl which replaced the skull might have resembled it in shape. And as pointed out earlier, it was an earthern ware pot having round or convex base. Hence it was technically called *ghati kapalam*. An earlier reference to *kapala* is to be found in the *Ashtadhyayi* of Panini.[8] Kautilya[9] also refers to *kapala* in the workshop of goldsmith. According to him it was a pot used for begging alms also.

Now, in the light of these literary evidences, the author is inclined to identify this alms bowl with the carinated *handi* of N.B.P. Ware since it satisfies most of the features described above.

Thus, if the above conclusions are accepted, it would naturally imply that N.B.P. Ware and carinated *handi* was already in use during the life-time of Gautama, Buddha. But the archaeological data, as indicated earlier, suggests that this shape was introduced at a later phase of the N.B.P. Ware deposits. Consequently, the early N.B.P. Ware phase would have to be pushed back in point of time to the pre-Buddha's period by a century or so at least if not earlier. This conclusion is in complete accord with the data proposed by B.B. Lal[10] for Hastinapura III, and, in fact, provides an additional corroborative evidence for the same, because according to reasons ascribed above, Hatinapura Period III represents the comparatively later phase of the N.B.P. Ware period. The date proposed here is also in conformity with the date

[1]Thomas Watters, *On Yuang Chwang's Travels in India*, (*A.D. 629-645*) (reprinted, Delhi 1961), pp. 130-31.

[2]T.W. Rhys Davids and Hermann Oldenberg (trans.), *Vinaya Texts*. Sacred Books of the East (Oxford, 1885), vol., XX, pp. 66-90.

[3]*Ibid*., pp. 82-83.

[4]*Ibid*., p. 84.

[5]*Ibid*., p. 85.

[6]*Ibid*. p., 88.

[7]*Ibid*., p. 89.

[8]*Ibid*., 6.2.29.

[9]*Arth*. 2.13.

[10]B.B. Lal, 'Excavation at Hastinapura and other Explorations in the Upper Ganga and Sutlaj Basins 1950-52', *Ancient India*, nos. 10 and 11 (1954-55), pp. 22-23,

proposed for this Ware in Bihar.[1]

But the C^{14} dates do not fully support this hypothesis, since concentration of the majority of dates lies between 500-50 B.C. But since certain samples from certain sites have been dated to the sixth century B.C. also, and considering the margin of error of these dates, and the human error of the archaeologist, if there be, there appears to be no contradiction on this account. It may further be pointed out that any conclusion based simply on the concentration of majority of the C^{14} dates within a limited time-bracket, without taking into consideration the relative stratigraphical position of the deposits from which each of the samples were derived, may be erroneous.

M. D. N. SAHI

Aligarh Muslim University,
Aligarh

[1]Sachchidanand Sahay, 'Origin and spread of the Northern Black Polished Wares', in (ed.), B. P. Sinha, *Potteries in Ancient India* (Patna, 1969), p. 148.

A Note on Some Ancient Indian Mirrors

Mirror is an important object of toilet equipment. The note intends to discuss the evidence of mirrors obtained from the early historical period (*c.* 200 B.C.-A.D. 200).

These mirrors are made up of a circular disc, with a tang at the base which is fitted into a handle made of bone, ivory or wood. The mirror or the disc part is a little convex at the back, often with a broad wavy rim and raised boss (or miniature knob). The rim is intended perhaps to preserve the polish on the mirror.

The metal used for the manufacture of the mirror is bronze or copper and it is very likely that the portion is coated with some preparations viz., mercury which gave it a silvery lustre. But, so far, none of the mirrors has been found with any shining effect left on them.

Mirrors have been reported from Taxila, Adichanallur, Basarh, Brahmapuri, Rairh, Taxila, etc. Of these, the Taxila[1] specimen had an intact ivory handle, while the other examples are without handle.

At Rairh[2], two bronze mirrors have been found fitted with a tang. They have a flat circular rim all around. They came from Sunga-Kushana levels. All the mirrors at Taxila[3] come from Saka-Parthian levels at Sirkap, datable to *c.* 100 B.C.-A.D. 100. Marshall[4] suggests that they were copies of western prototypes. They have round rims with *omphalos* at the centre. One of them[5] with ivory handle is of importance. Another has a wavy rim[6] around. Similar one, said to be belonging to Sunga date, comes from Bulandibagh,[7] Patna. All the mirrors at Taxila are made of copper.

A number of handles, perhaps used for mirror, have been reported from Taxila.[8] They are prepared from ivory, bone or wood. Handles of bone and ivory have been decorated with incised bands, hatchings, mouldings or with figure carvings in relief. Mirrors have not been found at Taxila after the first century A.D.

Three specimens come from a hoard at Brahmapuri[9] from late Satavahana levels, datable to *circa* first-second century A.D. All of them are of bronze and have excellent finish. It appears that the surface was polished after fashioning them on lathe. One of the mirrors[10] with *omphalos* has a lovely finish. It has a wavy rim with *omphalos* in the centre.

[1]Sir John Marshall, *Taxila* (Cambridge, 1951), vol. III, pl. 182b.

[2]K. N. Puri, *Excavations at Rairh* (Jaipur, 1940), p. 43, pls. XX,15 and XXI, 14.

[3]Marshall, *op. cit.*, vol. II, pp. 584-85.

[4]*Ibid.*, p. 584

[5]*Ibid.*, vol. III, pl. 182 b.

[6]*Ibid.*, pl. 181f.

[7]*Ibid.*, vol, II, pp. 484-85.

[8]*Ibid.*, vol. II, pp. 508, 658-59, vol. III, pls. 142 hh, 203 k-n, 199, 49-52 and 54-56; also see, A. Ghosh; 'Taxila (Sirkap) 1944-45', *Ancient India*, no. 4 (1947-1948), p. 81 and pl. XXI, *13*.

[9]Karl Khandalawala, 'Brahmapuri', *Lalit Kala*, no. 7(1960), pp. 62-63 and pl. XVI *14,15* and *17*.

[10]*Ibid.*, pl. XVI, *14*.

Omphalos is commonly found in Roman metalwork and was perhaps derived from earlier articles of Graeco-Roman workmanship. It has been suggested to be made at Alexandria and was brought by way of trade. An identical one at Sirkap[1] has been considered to be of Graeco-Roman origin. Another is a small one,[2] as compared to the above and is suggested to be a local product on the basis of its make and finish. The third one,[3] in addition to the *omphalos,* is decorated with a design of concentric rings on its surface. It is a common decorative feature found in Roman metalware. It is not clear whether it is an imported or a locally made specimen, but the design suggests extraneous workmanship.

At Adichanallur,[4] urn-burials have yielded a few similar mirrors. They consist of five circular bronze specimens with projecting tangs and central bosses (*omphalos*). These have been incorrectly recorded as frying pans and bronze plaques by the excavator. All of them have circular beaded rims. Two of them are exactly similar to those from Brahmapuri and Rairh. One with *omphalos*[5] and circular ring at centre can be compared with the example from Rairh.

A copper mirror has also been reported at Basarh[6] from Mauryan levels. It has been described as 'a circular disc with a handle attached to it and a knob in the centre'. It is evidently a mirror with *omphalos* at centre. It is similar to the specimens from Adichanallur and Brahmapuri.

The foregoing account clearly suggests the use of mirrors of copper and bronze during the period ranging between *c.* 200 B.C. and A.D. 200. They indicate that mirrors were made locally for household use. Marshall[7] suggests that mirrors with *omphalos* at Taxila represent copies of Graeco-Roman prototypes. At the same time, similar Taxilan mirrors have been reported in earlier levels at Adichanallur, Basarh, etc. where they were recorded in levels of the third-second century B.C., thereby suggesting their local manufacture.

In addition, supporting evidence comes from sculptures also. Scenes of toilet depicting ladies holding mirrors and adjusting ornaments and arranging coiffure are a familiar theme in the early schools of Indian art, particularly at Amaravati,[8] Bharhut,[9] Mathura,[10] and Nagarjunakonda.[11] The motif is also seen in Begram[12] ivories. All these are datble to *c.* third-second century B.C. and the second century A.D. This archaeological and sculptural coincidence of the mirrors and their shape is quite striking and in a way reveals the indigenous origin of some of them, though the elaborate ones seem to be imported from the Graeco-Roman world.

C. MARGABANDHU
Archaeological Survey of India,
Nagpur

[1]Marshall, *op. cit.*, pl. 181f.

[2]Khandalawala, *op. cit.*, pl. XVI 17.

[3]*Ibid.*, pl. XVI 15.

[4]*Archaeological Survey of India, Annual Report* (hereafter *ASIAR*), 1902-03, pp. 128-29 and figs. 12 and 13.

[5]*Ibid.*, fig. 13.

[6]*ASIAR*, 1903-04, p. 99, fig. 15; K. de B. Codrington, 'Ancient Indian hand mirrors', *Man*, vol. XXIX (1923), pp. 170-71.

[7]Marshall, *op. cit.*, II, p. 584.

[8]C. Sivaramamurti, *Amaravati Sculptures in the Madras, Government Museum*, General Section, vol. IV (Madras, 1956), pl. IX 17.

[9]B. M. Barua, *Barhut* (Calcutta, 1937), pt. III, pl. LIX 68; A. Cunningham, *Stupa of Bharhut* (reprinted, Varanasi, 1962), pl. XXIV 4; *ASIAR* 1925-26, pl, LVIII.

[10]J.Ph. Vogel, 'The Mathura school of sculpture', *ASIAR*, 1906-07, pl. LI a.

[11]A.H. Longhurst, *The Buddhist Antiquities of Nagarjunakonda*, Memoirs of the Archaeological Survey of India, no. 54, Delhi, 1938, pls. XXVIII b and XXXII a.

[12]Moti Chandra, 'Ancient Indian ivories', *Bulletin of the Prince of Wales Museum*, vol. VI (1957-59), pp. 31-36; also see, Jeanine Auboyer, 'Ancient Indian Ivories from Begram, Afghanistan', *Journal of the Indian Society of Oriental Art*, vol. XVI (1948), pp. 34-46 and figs. 73-75.

The Domestic Art* Delineated in the Gandhara Reliefs

INTRODUCTION

The term Gandhara appears for the first time in the *Rigveda*[1] wherein it has been defined as a region on the north-western frontier of India. However, a more specific definition of the term is available from the accounts of the Chinese pilgrim Hiuen-tsang who visited India in the early seventh century A.D. According to him, the kingdom of Gandhara constituted the tract of country lying on the west bank of the Indus which includes the Peshawar valley and the modern Swat Buner, and Bajaur.[2] Thus, situated on the borderland between India and Western Asia, Gandhara belonged as much and as little to the one as to the other. However, the art that thrived at Gandhara was not the first to arise on Indian soil. Even earlier, the ancient schools of Indian Art are represented by the sculptures of Barhut,[3] Bodhgaya,[4] Sanchi,[5] the facade of the rock temples of Orissa[6] and the Konkan[7] and the pre-Kushana sculptures of Mathura.[8] The school of Gandhara on the other hand, though later in date, does not appear to be the natural continuity of these early art schools. It reveals the clear impact of the Hellenistic influence, displays comparatively evolved technical skill, and introduces new foreign motifs. Nevertheless, it is primarily religious in character, serving the Buddhist faith.[9] Thus, the form is strongly Hellenistic, while the matter is yet Indian. Consequently, this intimate fusion of the widely divergent elements, unmistakably dominates the material culture depicted in the Gandhara reliefs. Obviously, therefore, religion, some foreign elements and indigenous traits have caused indelible impressions on the society and civilization of the Gandharans as visualized in the sculptures.

An attempt has been made in this paper to study the extent of the impact of these factors in respect of the domestic art delineated in the Gandhara reliefs. An endeavour has also been made to locate the contemporary plastic parallels and finally to confirm the archaeological data with the literary one.

*The domestic art here is understood to have included domestic vessels and the other household objects.

[1]A.A. Macdonell and A.B. Keith, *Vedic Index of Names and Subjects*, 1958, vol. I, p. 219. In the *Rigveda* the good wool of the sheep of the Gandharians is referred to (1.126.7). The *Atharvaveda* mentions the Gandharians with the Mujavants, Angas and Magadas (v, 22,14). They also occur in *Srauta Sutras, Hiranyakesi Srauta Sutra*, XVII, 6 : *Apastamba Srauta Sutra*, XII, 18 and *Baudhayana Srauta Sutra*, XXI-13. Zimmer considers that they were settled in Vedic times on the southern bank of the *Kupha* upto its mouth in the Indus and for some distance down the east-side of the Indus itself. They later formed part of the Persian Empire (Altindish *Leben*, pp. 30-31).

[2]Harold Ingholt, *Gandharan Art in Pakistan*, (New York, 1957), p. 13. To the north, the east and the west Gandhara is hemmed in by tall mountains, but to the south the flat Indus valley spreads out for some seven hundred miles until it reaches the Indian Ocean. See also John Marshall ; *The Buddhist Art of Gandhara* (Cambridge, 1960), p.1.

[3]*C.* middle of second century B.C.

[4]Early first century B.C.

[5]Later half of the first century B.C.

[6]*C.* first century B.C.

[7]Later half of the first century B.C.

[8]Middle of second centuly, B.C. onwards.

[9]Marshall, *op. cit.*, p. 42.

DOMESTIC VESSELS

The vessels depicted in the reliefs are varied, and typologically include: (i) bowls and saucers; (ii) wine-cups; (iii) goblets; (iv) drinking horns; (v) mugs; (vi) amphorae; (vii) *kujas*; (viii) spouted vessels; (ix) vases; (x) pots; (xi) incense burner; (xii) troughs; (xiii) krater, (xiv) wine-vats; (xv) wine-skins or wine-bags.

(i) *Bowls and Saucers* : In the reliefs, the bowls appear frequently. In the panels[10] representing 'offering of the four bowls to the Buddha' and 'conversion of Nanda', the bowls, probably containing rice soup or similar other edibles, are illustrated as being offered to the Buddha by the princes and Nanda. The bowls have incurved featureless rim and round base (FIG. 1, *1*). These bowls can be identified as *thalika*[11] of the Buddhist literature.[12] Similar bowls are represented in the sculptures of Barhut,[13] Amaravati,[14] Nagarjunakonda,[15] etc.

[10]Ingholt, *op. cit.*, 69, 123, xx.1 and Marshall, *op. cit.*, Pl. 86 fig. 121; pl. 53 fig. 77.

[11]S.B. Deo, 'Pots and utensils from Jaina literature', *Bulletin of the Deccan College Research Institute*, vol. XIV (June 1952), no. 1, p. 41. In Jain literature, bowls *Padiggha* are mentioned in different context.

[12]*Vinaya* Texts, 11, p. 51, IV. 12.1.

[13]Benimadhab Barua, *Barhut, Aspects of Life and Art* (Calcutta, 1934-37), pl. XCI-138-140.

[14]C. Sivaramamurti, *Amaravati Sculptures in the Madras Government Museum* (Madras, 1956), pl. V, fig. 26 : Jasmes Burgess, *The Buddhist Stupas of Amravati and Jaggayyapeta* (London, 1887), pl. XV, 2, XVI, 2.

[15]K.Krishna Murthy, *Life under the Ikshvakus as depicted in the Nagarjunakonda sculptures*, Ph.D. Thesis, Nagpur University, 1969 (unpublished) pp. 421-22.

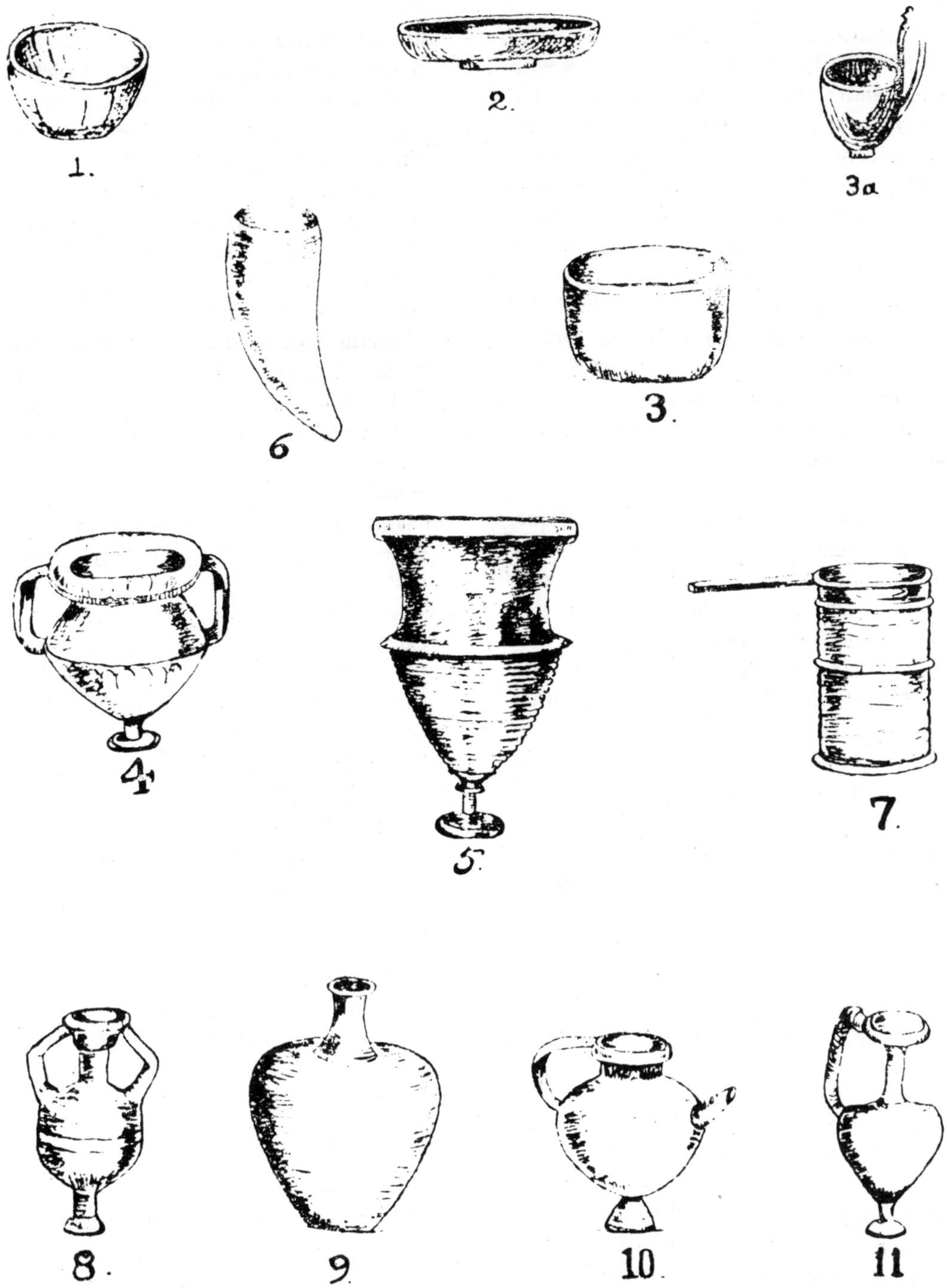

FIG. 1

Again, the toilet tray,[1] illustrating the crowded drinking-scene, offers a saucer evidently of Greek origin. A man is shown drinking wine from the saucer. This saucer with incurved sides and sharpened rim with flat base (FIG. 1, *2*) may represent Greek '*phiale*'.[2] Such drinking vessels, made in the form of saucers or bowls, are very common in Greek vessels. The present example of *phiale* has also close resemblance to Roman *patera*.[3]

The *phiale* appears in Chiot and Corinthian pottery at the beginning of the sixth century B.C. and later occasionally in Attic pottery.[4]

[1] Marshall, *op. cit.*, pl. 14, fig. 16.

[2] Oskar Seyffert, *A Dictionary of Classical Antiquities* (London, 1957), p. 685, figs. 1-2.

[3] *Ibid.*, p. 685

[4] R.M. Cook, *Greek Painted Pottery* (London, 1960), p. 239. The name *Phiale* seem appropriate since it was applied by the Greeks to pots for pouring libations, and vase paintings show this shape. Interestingly, Romans also used *patera* for similar purposes.

In another instance, a *nagini* appears with a different variety of bowl.[1] The bowl is bigger in size with a luted, slender handle reaching from the rim to the foot on either side. It again appears to be a Greek vessel. It can be identified as *'carchesion',*[2] a vessel which is generally used for drinking wine. A kneeling woman from Taxila[3] offers a hemispherical bowl. It has featureless and externally grooved rim and round base. The woman appears to be a foreigner wearing a foreign dress. The bowl which she holds again could have been of Hellenistic origin. Similar bowls devoid of handles and with or without a ring-foot are common in Hellenistic black-painted ware. The so called Megarian bowl has comparable parallel to the present example (FIG. 1 *3*.).[4]

(ii) *Wine-cups*: The wine-cups depicted in the reliefs are of Greek or Graeco-Parthian origin. Thus, in two panels, representing drinking scence on toilet trays, can be seen a cup with a single handle presumably raising high above the rim (FIG. 1, *3a*). This may be *'cyathus'*, the Greek cup.[5]

The panels[6] illustrating 'Head of Dionysus and 'Dowager and man with bowl' represent another variety of wine-cup. They have two handles with or without carinated profile and pedestal or ring-base (FIG. 1, *4*). These cups are evidently the *'kantharos'*[7] of Graeco-Parthian period.

The *kantharos* becomes common only in the fourth century. In the Hellenisitic period, it looses its importance to the *Megarian* bowl.[8] However the specimen represented in the reliefs can be dated to 300 B.C. It appears, the Greeks knew four kinds of wine-cups, namely, *skyphos, kotyle, cylix* and *kantharos*.[9] In Buddhist literature, words *chashaka* or *panapatra* stand to mean wine cups.

However, in early Indian art wine-cups are depicted in profusion. They appear in Sunga,[10] Satavahana[11] and Kushana art as also in the ivories from Begram.[12]

(iii) *Goblets*: Goblets found in the Gandhara reliefs are typical of the Parthian perriods. They have carinated bodies, deeply flared mouths, horizontal flutings or bands and pedestal bases (FIG. 1, *5*). Thus, a few panels[13] representing these Parthian goblets were evidently used as wine cups. These goblets have close resemblance to the Greek goblet *holmose*.[14]

(iv) *Drinking horn* : A solitary example of a *nagini* holding a drinking horn in her right hand occurs in the reliefs.[15] The drinking horn has a wide mouth with the sides tapering towards the bottom. (FIG. 1, *6*). It represents the Greek rhyton. The Romans borrowed most of their drinking vessels from the Greeks. The drinking horns were generally fitted with silver, and during the imperial times they were often embellished with finely cut gems.[16]

In art, we find a similar specimen in the Nagarjunakonda sculptures.[17]

(v) *Mugs* : Mug is depicted in the reliefs only once. The panel[18] illustrating 'drinking-party of nine figures' represents a foreigner holding a mug. The mug is cylindrical in shape with multi-ribbed exterior, It has a big handle luted to the brim of the rim and profile (FIG. 1, *7*). The base is flat and the very appearance suggests that the mug was probably made of some metal. It has unmistakable Hellenistic origin. It is noteworthy that the metal tankards of similar type still survive in Kashmir and North-west Frontier.

(vi) *Amphorae* : In one instance,[19] a lady is shown holding an amphora vessel in her left hand. It has a vertical neck, globular body and pedestal base. It is also provided with two handles. They are luted to the rim and the body (FIG. 1, *8*). The specimen represented in the relief appears to be a Greek amphora. It is generally either buried up to the middle in the ground or set up slanting against the wall. It served to keep oil, honey and more especially the wine drawn off from the big fermenting vats.[20] Generally, the amphora is of two main classes, namely, the neck-amphora and one-piece amphora. Besides nikosthenic, villanvan, amphoriskoi, amphorae were also known.[21] The Romans used *cadi* for storing Greek wines.

[1]Marshall, *op. cit.*, pl. 56. fig. 83.
[2]Seyffert, *op .cit.*, p. 685, fig. 1,11.
[3]Ingholt, *op. cit.*, 402.
[4]Cook, *op. cit.*, p. 239.
[5]Seyffert, *op. cit.*, fig. 1, 10, 13-15.
[6]Marshall, *op. cit.*, pl. 24, fig. 29; Ingholt, *op. cit.*, 422.
[7]For comparison, see Seyffert, *op. cit.*, fig. 1, 12.
[8]Cook, *op. cit.* p. 238.
[9]*Ibid.*, p. 235.
[10]Barua, *op. cit.*, pl. XXXVI-30.
[11]Sivaramamurti, *op. cit.*, pl. V, 20, Burgess, *cit.*,XVI.2, for Amaravati; Krishnamurthy, *op. cit.*, pp. 435-37.
[12]J. Auboyer, 'Ancient Indian Ivories from Begram, Afghanistan', *Journal of Indian Society of Oriental Art*, vol. XIV (1948), pl. IX, nos. 65-69.
[13]Marshall, *op. cit.*, pl. 27, fig. 40, pl. 28, fig. 42 and pl. 56, fig. 83; Ingholt, *op. cit.*, IV.I.
[14]Compare, Seyffert, *op. cit.*, fig. 9.
[15]Marshall, *op. cit.*, pl. 56, fig. 83.
[16]Seyffert, *op. cit.*, p. 686a.
[17]Krishnamurthy, *op. cit.*, pl. XII, 17.
[18]Marshall, *op. cit.*, pl. 27, fig. 40.
[19]*Ibid.*, pl. 31, fig. 49.
[20]Seyffert, *op. cit.*, p. 30; fig. 2, a, b,
[21]Cook, *op. cit.*, p. 220; cf. pls. 3a, b, 21, a, b, 22, a, 34, a : 54.

(vii) *Kujas*: *Kujas* are represented in the reliefs profusely. Generally they are seen with sages or ascetics, monks, Brahma and Maitreya.[1] For Brahma and particularly to Maitreya *kuja* appear to be an inevitable appendage. The *kuja* illustrated in the relief has a long neck, globular body and flat base (FIG. 1, *9*). The *kujas* could have been used either for carrying drinking water or wine. These may be identified as *Sarka*[2] and probably the Persian word '*Surahi*' is related to this.

The *kujas* with their polished surface, thin section and fine fabric may represent Samian wares.[3] Many *kujas* or sprinklers of 'Red Polished Ware,' which is said to be the Indian imitation of Roman Samian ware, are reported to have been recovered from the excavation in western India and the Deccan in *c.* first-second century A. D. At Amaravati, Samian ware is available.

In early Indian art, however, the depiction of *kujas* are in plenty. The specimen found in the reliefs of Gandhara are to be seen in the sculptures of Sanchi,[4] Amaravati,[5] Nagarjunakonda,[6] etc.

(viii) *Spouted Vessels*: Spouted vessels occur in the reliefs more than once.[7] They have vertical necks, globular bodies and pedestal or ring bases. A spout is luted to the body. A handle is also provided in order to provide a grip. It is luted to the rim and the body (FIG. 1, *10*). These spouted vessels with the handles on the side may represent *Bhinkara* of the Buddhist texts.[8]

In art, the depiction of the spouted vessels are in plenty. The sculptures of Sanchi, [9], Barhut,[10] Amaravati,[11] Nagarjunakonda,[12] Mathura, depict *kujas* similar to those found in the Gandhara reliefs.

Apart from this, the panel[13] representing drinking scene on a toilet tray illustrates a *flagon* evidently of Greek or Roman origin. It is having high vertical neck, globular body, and prominent pedestal base. It has a handle provided at the side and luted to the rim and profile (FIG. 1, *11*).

This may represent *oinochoe* of the Greek.[14] The name *oinochoe* in Greek means 'wine-pourer' and similar utility is seen in the case of the present example also. It is noteworthy that the Roman *flagons*[15] of the early centuries of the Christian era also betray resemblance to the present example.

Sometimes, the spouted vessels have handles on the top[16] (FIG. 2, *12*) instead of at the sides as seen above. This type of spouted vessel with the handle on the top may be identified as '*kamandalu*', the survival of which can be seen in the *kamandalus* used by the Indian ascetics and *fakirs*. In Buddhist literature its is represented as *Dhammakaraka*.[17] In art, the depiction of the spouted vessels with handles either on the side or in the top are profuse and appears in the sculptures of Sanchi,[18] Barhut,[19] Amaravati,[20] Nagarjunakonda,[21] Mathura,[22] etc.

(ix) *Vases*: Vases that occur in some reliefs[23] have close resemblance to the proto-Corinthian[24] and Sassanian[25] silver vases.

[1]Marshall, *op. cit.*, p.. 34, fig. 54, pl. 22, fig. 25, pl. 71 fig. 101, pl. 81, fig. III, pl. 89, fig. 124, pl. 103, fig. 142, Ingholt, *op. cit.*, 289, 290 etc.

[2]R. L. Mitra, *Indo Aryans*, vol. I (Calcutta, 1881), pp. 272-73.

[3]In A. D. 77 Pliny writes ; 'The greater part of mankind uses earthern ware. The Samian is to this day appreciated as a table-ware, (Pliny, *Natural History*, Book XXXV, 12(46), 160). The word *Samian* is used in association with the names of other places such as Arretium, a known pottery centre. The geographical context makes it certain that here the word can only mean of *Samos*. As early as in second century B.C. (in the plays of Plautus) *Samian* is clearly used in the generic sense of '*made of clay*. The statement of Pliny and other older references suggest that even as early as the 2nd centuty B.C. the wares of *Samos* were so familiar initially that the word *Samian* became synonyms with '*clay*'. The pottery excavated in the town site of Priene in the Asia Minor has been equated with that of *Samos*. (R.J. Charleston, *Roman Pottery* (London), p. 18). Therefore, the presence of such Samian ware *Kujas* in the Gandhara reliefs cannot be out of archaeological context.

[4]Sir John Marshall and Alfred Foucher, *The Monuments of Sanchi* (Calcutta, 1940), pl. XL, XXIX.

[5]Burgess, *op. cit.*, pl. XXIII-2.

[6]Krishna Murthy, *op. cit.*, pl. VIII, 2.

[7]Ingholt, *op. cit.*, 6, 13, 14.

[8]*Vinaya Texts*, i. p. 143, *Mahavagga*, i, 22, 18.

[9]Marshall and Foucher, *op. cit.*, 11, pls. XXIII, XL, XLII.

[10]Barua, *op. cit.*, Book III, pls. XXVI-35, XLV-45.

[11]Sivaramamurti, *op. cit.*, pl. V. figs. 18, 19, 22; Burgess *op. cit.*, XVI-6.

[12]Krishna Murthy, *op. cit.*, pl. VIII,3.

[13]Marshall, *op. cit.*, pl. 14, fig. 16.

[14]Cook, *op. cit.*, p. 226 : cf. pl. 30, A,B, etc.

[15]Charleston, *op. cit.*, pl. 14.

[16]Marshall, *op. cit.*, pl. 60, fig. 88, pl. 70, fig. 99, pl. 81, fig. 116, and Ingholt, *op. cit.*, 14, 35.

[17]*Culla Vagga*, V, 3,1; VI, 21,3.

[18]Marshall and Foucher, *op. cit.*, 11, pls. XXIII, XL and XLIII.

[19]Barua, *op. cit.*, Book III, pls. XXVI-35, XLV-45..

[20]Sivaramamurti, *op. cit.*, pl. V. figs. 18, 19, 22.

[21]Krishna Murthy, *op. cit.*, pl. VIII.4.

[22]Vogel, *op. cit.*, pl. IX-a; Auboyer, *op. cit.*, XIV, PL. IX, 66, 67, 68.

[23]Ingholt, *op. cit.*, IV. I, X.I., 89.

[24]Cook, *op. cit.*, 11,B, 30,B.

[25]Inghott, *op. cit.*, XI. I.

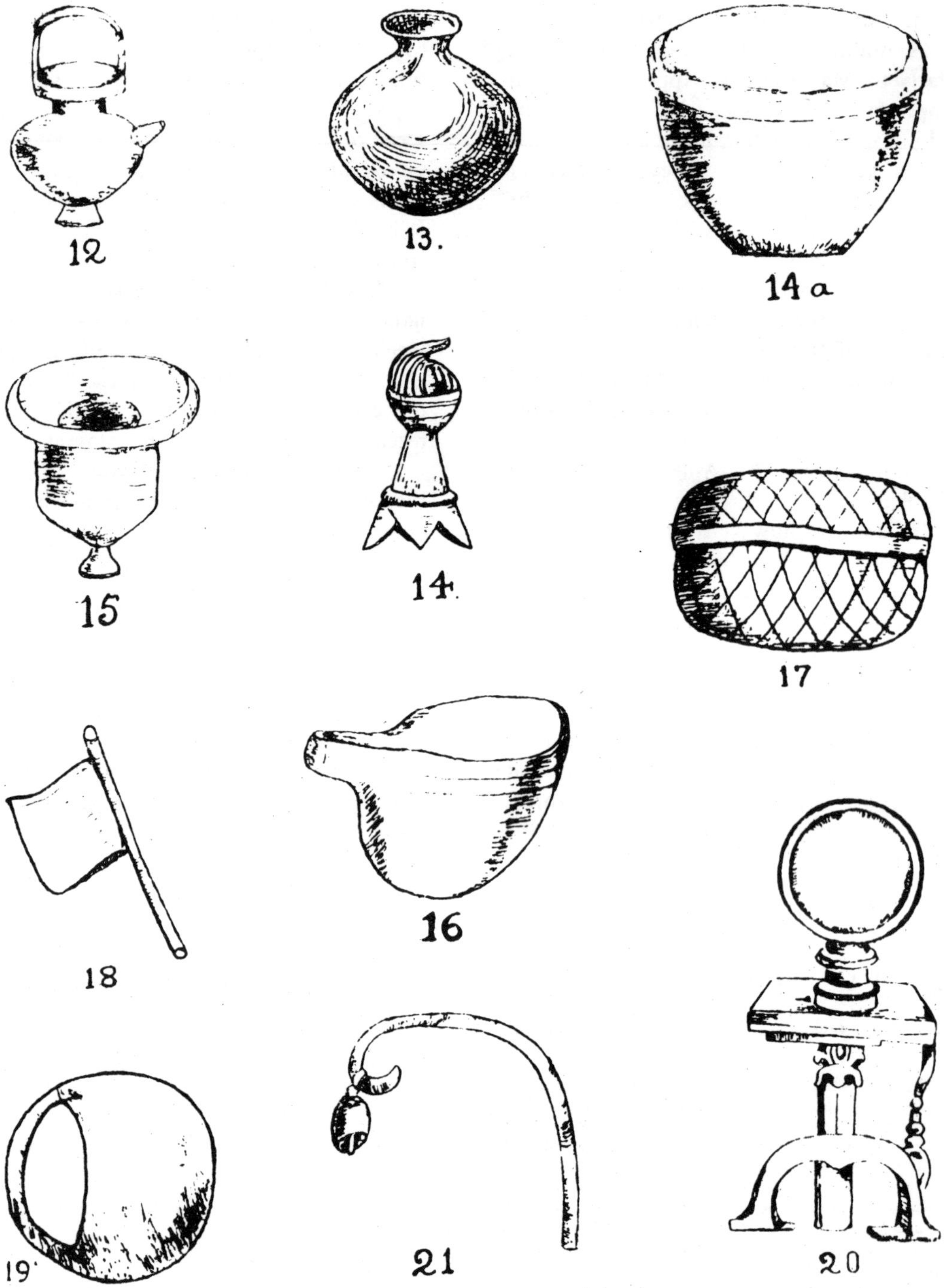

FIG. 2

(x) *Pots:* Two varieties of pots, namely the miniature pots and huge storage pots, are represented in the reliefs. In the panel representing "Bath of the infant Buddha",[1] Brahma and Vajrapani are shown pouring water with miniature pots, on the head of the infant Buddha. They have a spherical body and a round base. These may represent the *paribhojaniya ghatas* mentioned in the *Vinaya* texts.[2] The sculptures

[1]Ingholt, *op. cit.*, XI,1.

[2]*Vinaya Texts*, iii, p. 292. VIII, 5,3.

of Barhut, Sanchi, Amaravati and Nagarjunakonda depict many such miniature pots.[1] The huge storage posts occur frequently in the reliefs.[2] They are having externally thickened rim, spherical body and round base (FIG. 2, *13*). These storage pots can be identified as *udakamanika* or *paniyaghata* of the Buddhist texts.[3] Similar storage pots can be seen in the sculptures of Barhut, Sanchi, Amaravati, Nagarjunakonda and Mathura.[4]

(xi) *Incense burner of altars* : Thrice it is represented in the sculptures. The panel[5] representing "The Buddha's teaching" illustrates an incense altar being worshipped by two men. It has three legs and from its base, a shaft arises, tapering towards the top. Over this, stands a disc or a cup, the receptacle for the fire (FIG. 2, *14*), Again, a different variety of incense burner is met with in the panel illustrating the "coffin of the Budha" In this, it has rectangular base from which rises the shaft. The shaft is having a bulbous body in tiers and terminates into a disc or a cup.[6] The presence of such incense burners at the coffin of the Buddha incidentally suggests the social practice of keeping the light near the dead body. It is interesting to note that similar custom survives even to this day in many parts of India. Again in another instance[7] the incense altar has a solid round base from which a shaft rises and terminates into a cup or a receptacle intended for fire.

(xii) *Trough :* The example that occurs in the reliefs[8] has an ovoidal body with round or flattish base (FIG. 2, *14a*). It has a thick and externally rolled rim. Some times these troughs were provided with foot-rests (*pattamandala*).[9]

(xiii) *Krater:* Twice it is represented in the reliefs.[10] It is a Greek vessel in which, generally, wine was mixed with water. The specimens in the sculpture are moderately large with wide necks and bodies and pedestals. Owing to the rough representation, it is difficult to say whether they are provided with handles. The different varieties of kraters namely, kotyle-krater, column-krater, volute-krater, calyx-krater, bell-krater, etc., were known to the Greeks.[11] The one that is represented in the sculptures resembles bell-krater[12] (FIG. 2, *15*). This type of krater was available as early as the fifth century B.C. and became extremely common in the early part of the fourth century B.C.[13] It came to Gandhara along with the Greeks some time in second century B.C.

(xiv) *Wine-vat:* Wine vat appears on the toilet tray[14] representing 'Crowded drinking-scene' (FIG. 2, 16). Such Greek-wine-vats are generally used for mixing wine. The Greek *bikos* and the Roman *Seria* were smaller vats of the same kind but were used for storing salts, meats, figs. corn etc.[15]

(xv) *Wine-skins or wine-bags :* Wine-skin or wine-bags are represented in thereliefs.[16] They were known as *askos* in Greek.[17] Presumably the bag was made by sewing a number of skins together. Even to this day, similar bags are being used for storing *toddy*, country liquors, in many parts of India. The specimen represented in the relief may be *askos* known to the Greeks and probably came to Gandhara along with the Greeks.

WINE PREPARATION TECHNIQUES :

Two reliefs[18] representing crowded drinking-scene and an unidentified panel visualize the technique of wine preparation as known to the Gandharans. The toilet tray representing crowded drinking-scene illustrates in the middle register a large wine-vat, rising from acanthus leaves. In this wine-vat two men, one on the back of the other are treading grapes. While a lad in the centre draws off the juice in a tall flagon, to the left, another man is carrying a wine-skin on his back and emptying its contents into a krater. Thus, the whole thing indirectly reveals the technique of preparation of wine in those times. In another instance also, the reliefs depict the technique of the preparation of wine. In the centre, two men are standing inside a low tank, holding a pole with which to crush or to knead the grapes. Through the spout on the side of the tank the juice flows into a low bowl while a man standing

[1]Barua, *op. cit.*, pl. 4.5; Marshall and Foucher, *op. cit.*, II, pl. XL; Sivaramamurti, *op. cit.*, pl. LV, fig. 29 and V, fig. 21 ; Krishnamurthy, *op. cit.*, pl. VIII.10.

[2]Ingholt, *op. cit.*, V.2, XXII. 3, 33, 81.

[3]*Vinaya Texts*, iii. p. 98 : *Mahavagga* VI. 282.

[4]Barua, *op. cit.*, pls. XXXII-25, LXVI-79, LX, VII-80, etc. Marshall and Foucher, *op. cit.*, II, pl. XXIV; Sivaramamurti, *op. cit.*, pl. XXIV, fig. 3; etc.; Krishnamurthy, *op. cit*, XXI-4.

[5]Ingholt, *op. cit.*, XXI.4.

[6]Ingholt, *op. cit.*, 144.

[7]*Ibid.*, 302.

[8]*Ibid.*, 19 : Also see Marshall, *op. cit.*, pl. 72, fig. 104.

[10]Marshall, *op. cit.*, pl. 14, fig. 16, pl. 56, fig. 83.

[11]Cook, *op. cit.*, pp. 230-31; for comparison see pls. 12-C, 19-A, 44, 48A, 56B etc.

[12]*Ibid.*, pls. 48A, 56B.

[13]*Ibid.*, p. 231.

[14]Marshall, *op. cit.*, pl. 14., fig. 16.

[15]Seyffert, *op. cit.*, p. 684,b.

[16]Marshall, *op, cit.*, pl. 14, fig. 16; pl. 56, fig. 83.

[17]Seyffert, *op. cit.*, p. 684b.

[18]Marshall, *op. cit.*, pl. 14,fig. 16; Ingholt, *op, cit.*, 175.

at the left of the press seems to hold a fresh supply of grapes in his hands. From a bag suspended from from a tripod filtered juice drips into a tall wine jug standing on the ground.

OTHER HOUSEHOLD OBJECTS

Baskets : A rectangular basket with lid presumably made of Palmyra occurs in the panel[1] illustrating 'Monks and doners in Iranian costumes'. The basket has criss-cross decoration on the exterior (FIG. 2, *17*). The man holding it is an Iranian in Iranian costumes. In that case the basket he is holding may probably also be of Iranian origin.

Trays : The number of Gandhara toilet trays excavated at Taxila[2] are round and have frilled rims. They are assigned to the Saka-Parthian period and betray unmistakable Hellenistic influence.[3]

Fans : The sculptures[4] depict two varieties of fans, namely the square-shaped and the crescent-shaped ones. Thus in one panel[5] two examples of square-shaped fans, both held by monks occur. In both the cases, the fan has a side handle (FIG. 2, *18*). Again in the panel[6] illustrating the 'invitation of Srigupta' a fan with crescent-like form is met with (FIG. 2, *19*). In Amaravati sculptures and in the paintings of Ajanta, both the varieties found at Gandhara are available.[7] At Gandhara, the square-shaped ones have been favoured to that of the other form. The popularity of this square-shaped fan is continued in the sculptures of Nagarjunakonda[8] and even in the paintings of Ajanta.

TOILET ARTICLES

Mirror (Mukura): In the panel[9] illustrating 'conversion of Nanda,' the 'enticement scene' reveals the toilet scene of the bride of Nanda. She is shown being toileted. The *prasadika* is arranging her coiffure while herself adjusting it by looking in the mirror. A mirror and a small casket, probably containing scented oil, are seen kept on the tripod. The mirror has a round disc mounted on a handle which has a pedestal base[10] (FIG. 2, *20*).

In early Indian art, mirrors occur in the sculptures of Bharhut, Amaravati, Mathura, Nagarjunakonda,[11] etc.

Casket : In the same panel[12] by the side of the mirror can be seen a casket with knobbed lid. Probably it might have contained scented oil, one of the requisites of a toilet. In that case the casket may represent *taila manjusha* of Kalidasa.

Razor (ksura) : There is a solitary representation of a razor in the reliefs. The panel[13] illustrating "Three scenes from the story of Nanda" reveals a barber with his knife. The razor appears to have a curved terminal. The head of Nanda is being shaved with razor's edge. The razor depicted in the panel has close similarity with the modern ones. In Nagarjunakonda sculptures, a praralle1 example is met with[14]

Curved staff : In one instance[15] Dionysus is shown holding a curved staff (*thyrsos*)[16] with a bell suspended at its end (FIG. 2, *21*). It closely resembles the handle of a *kylix*.

CONCLUSION

Thus, the foregoing study of the domestic art depicted in the sculptures reveals the predominance of the foreign impact. In respect of the domestic vessels represented in the sculptures one can see the presence of the variety of Greek or Graeco-Parthian vessels. The Greek vessels like *Phiale* (saucer), *Carchesion* and *megarian* (bowls), *cyathus* (wine-cups), *holmos.* (goblets), *rhyton* (drinking horn), *amphorae, oinochoe* (flagon), *krater* (wine-vat), *askos* (wine-bags), besides Graeco-Parthian wine-cups (*kantharos*), appear in the reliefs. However, it does not mean that the indigenous traits are totally absent. We do find native *kujas,* spouted vessels, miniature or storage pots, and mugs resembling the metal tankards of the Kashmiris. The Buddhist monks and ascetics used bowls, *kujas* and spouted vessels suggestive of their religious use. Similarly, in other household objects

[1]Herold Ingholt, *op. cit.*, 418.

[2]Marshall, *op. cit.*, pl. 11, fig. 13, pl. 12, fig. 14, pl. 13, fig. 15, pl. 14, fig. 16, pl. 15, fig. 17 and pl. 16, fig. 18.

[3]Marshall, *Taxila*, vol. II, pp. 493-94.

[4]Ingholt, *op. cit.*, 74, 100.

[5]*Ibid.*, 74.

[6]*Ibid.*, 100.

[7]Sivaramamurti, *op. cit.*, pl. V, fig. 34, XLVI, fig. 26 : XL-2. Burgess, *op. cit.*, pls. XVI-1 : XVI-6.

[8]Krishna Murthy, *op. cit.*, pl. VIII, 18.

[9]Marshall, *op. cit.*, pl. 86, fig. 121.

[10]Seyffert speaking about the ancient Greek and the Etruscan mirrors informs that for mirrors the ancients used round or oval and square plates of melted and polished metal. In later times they were also made of silver. The Etruscan mirrors were highly ornamented ones (p. 395).

[11]*Archaeological Surgey of India, Annual Report*, 1925-26, pl. LVIII ; Sivaramamurti, *op. cit.*, pl. IX, fig. 17; Begram mirrors *vide* Auboyer, *op. cit.*, XIV, pl. IV, a,d : IX, pls. 73 to 75 ; Nagarjunakonda, Krishnamurthy, *op. cit.*, pl. VIII, 21.

[12]Marshall, *op. cit.*, pl. 86, fig. 121.

[13]*Ibid.*, pl. 81, fig. 121.

[14]Krishnamurthy, *op. cit.*, p. 469.

[15]Marshall, *op. cit.*, pl. 24, fig. 29.

[16]A staff carried by Dionysus and his attendants, and wreathed with Ivy and vine-leaves, terminating at the top in a pine-cone (Seyffert, *op. cit.*, p. 636b).

also one can see foreign elements like the *kylix*, Iranian baskets, Saka-Parthian toilet trays, etc. While the indigenous traits are perceivable in the articles like fans, mirrors, caskets, razors, etc., the leaning is more towards the Hellenistic influence in the material culture under study.*

K. KRISHNA MURTHY
Archaeological Survey of India,
Janpath, New Delhi, 110011

*This paper was read at the 4th Annual Congress of the Indian Archaeological Society during the Seminar held at Nagpur on 12th November, 1970. My thanks are due to Shri D.K. Malik, Artist, New Delhi who has prepared the line drawings of this article.

Anthropomorphic Ornaments in Early Indian Sculpture

Early Indian sculpture shows a profusion of ornaments. Both female and male figures display a fond desire for jewellery, but, it is in the case of the former that the yearning is especially conspicuous. Female figures are adorned with ear-rings, necklaces, armlets, bracelets, girdles and anklets. The most common designs are, however, floral or else, beads of all shapes and sizes form prominent constituents. Extremely interesting is the use of anthropomorphic forms in ornaments.

The earliest example is perhaps the Yaksha sculpture from Pitalkhora.[1] It shows a corpulent male figure with its arms upraised and holding a shallow bowl. Around the neck is a *graiveyaka* and another necklace formed by a string of gadrooned and collared beads with a large central gadrooned bead flanked by human faced amulets, the cord of the string passing through the ears. Engraved on the outer right palm is an inscription in the letters of the second century B.C. (FIG. 1, *I*.)

Another image, belonging to the same period, is that of a Yakshi, stated to have been found during excavations near the Qutb Minar at Mehrauli in 1912.[2] The much damaged sculpture shows a female figure standing under a tree and embracing the tree trunk with her left hand. She wears a torque and three pendant necklaces—the upper one has a clasp consisting of cylindrical beads separating two round human-faced plaques with a *nandi-pada* below (FIG. 1, *II*).

A third sculpture, the bust of a female figure, now in the Nasli and Alice Heeramaneck Collection, Boston,[3] is about a century later in date. It is from the Sanchi *stupa* and has been dated to A.D. 10-25. Falling between the breasts is a string of beads ornamented with two miniature statues of a woman. The left hands of the small figures are upraised and are possibly held in the same pose as that of the now damaged larger figure.

The excavations at Nevasa have led to the discovery of a terracotta pendant belonging to Period V (first century B.C.—second-third century A.D.). The pendant is in the form of a human figure with the head broken, and perforated through the shoulders and neck.

The paucity of the examples is an indicator of the rarity of the anthropomorphic form in jewellery in centuries preceding the Christian era. The picture, however, radically changes in Kushana art, especially in the Gandhara region. Not uncommon are Bodhisattva images adorned with necklaces having pendants in the form of two monsters flanking a jewel or two winged females[4] holding a gem. A good example is the Bodhisattva sculpture in the Musee Guimet, Paris.[5] The human figures occur not only in the necklace, but in the fillet and head-clasp as well. The fillet has a central clasp flanked by two flying figures carrying garlands and the head-clasp showing the anthropomorphic form of the Naga being carried away by the Suparna. In other sculptures, the head clasp is variously decorated with a standing couple kissing or the figure of a Buddha[6](FIG. 1, *III*, *IV* and *V*).

Apart from sculptures, excavations at Taxila[7] have brought to light several gold ornaments dated to the

[1] M. N. Deshpande, 'The Rock-cut caves of Pitalkhora in the Deccan', *Ancient India, no*, 15 (1959), p. 81.
[2] V. S. Agrawala, *Studies in Indin Art* (Varanasi, 1959), p. 102.
[3] *The Art of India & Nepal*; *The Nasli and Alice Heeramaneck Collection* (Boston, 1966), p. 23.
[4] H—Ingholt, *Gandharan Art in Pakistan* (New York, 1957). pl, 292.
[5] M. Hallade, *The Gandhara Style and the Evolution of Buddhist Art* (London, 1968), pl. 68.
[6] Moti Chandra, *Costumes, Textiles, Cosmetics and Coiffure, in Ancient and Medieval India* (Delhi, 1973), p. 35.
[7] Sir John Marshall, *Taxila* (Cambridge, 1951), pl 119 p. 632 and pl. 190, p. 625.

first century A.D. and adorned with human figures. A gold brooch (no. 98) shows the figures of Eros and Psyche, standing side by side and caressing each other. A circular gold medallion (no. 99) is decorated with a winged Eros reclining. Another gold brooch (no. 97) has the figure of winged Aphrodite or Psyche. A pair of gold ear pendants (nos. 11 and 12) has a double leech clasp ornamented at the centre with a female bust superimposed on a lotus rosette.

FIG. 1

Not only in the Gandhara region, but elsewhere also, Kushana art shows an abundance of anthropomorphic forms in ornaments. Girdles with round clasps are embossed with human figures with upraised hands.[1] A terracotta female figurine from Kausambi[2] wears an elaborate girdle adorned with figures of seated persons with upraised hands (FIG. 1, *VI*).

No. 46.80 in the Lucknow Museum[3] has a *lalatika* in the form of a pendant embossed with a human figure behind two galloping horses (FIG. 1, *IX*).

A statue from the Mat Devakula[4] depicts the headless torso of Shastana. He is clad in trousers and a long coat secured by a belt made up of square and round plaques, adorned with Scythian horsemen and tritons with forked tails (FIG. 1, *VII*).

No. B 82 in the Lucknow Museum, dated to the second century A.D. depicts the standing Bodhisattva. His *mukuta* shows the effigy of the Buddha seated cross-legged with the right hand in the *abhaya-mudra*.

Mathura Museum has preserved two Bodhisattva heads[5] which show a similar feature. A Bodhisattva head (no. 2367) has the *dhyani* Buddha in the crest flanked by a worshipper on each side. Another Bodhisattva head (no. 2336), of the 3rd century A.D. has the *dhyani* Buddha in the centre of the crown flanked by three *garudas* on the right and three on the left.

A Bodhisattva figure (no. A 45)[6] is embellished with armlets having plaques showing a human figure riding a conventional bird, probably a *garuda* or a peacock (FIG. 1, *VIII*).

These examples prove the great popularity enjoyed by anthropomorphic forms in Kushana ornaments. The popularity however, fades out with the advent of the post-Kushana era, a notable exception being the Buddha figure in the crown of the Bodhisattva images. Indeed, this gains added importance in Buddhist iconography, so much so, that at times, it becomes the only distinguishing feature of the Bodhisattvas.

This sudden efflorescence of anthropomorphic forms in the Kushana period poses a natural question as to its origin.

In a wider context, it is the Classical and Hellenistic period (about 475-100 B.C.) that is marked by 'the frequent use of human and animal motifs'[7] in jewellery. Spiral ear-rings often end in human and animal heads and to the disk type are added all sorts of human and animal pendants. Among the outstanding specimens is a Nike driving a two-horse chariot, now in Boston and a group of Ganymede with the eagle, in New York. Similarly, necklaces are often enriched with pendants in the form of heads or other motifs. (FIG. 1, *X* and *XI*).

The Scythic tombs,[8] dated from the seventh century B.C. to a little after the Christian era, have brought to light an astounding wealth of ornaments and jewellery. Whereas the 'animal style' marks the indigenous attempts at decoration, Greek influence[9] is also not wanting in the specimens recovered. Of the several objects attributed to Greek workmanship outstanding are those from Chertomlyk[10] and Kul Oba.[11] A necklet from Kul Oba[12] has the ends formed by two mounted Scythians. Equally interesting is a gold statuette[13] depicting two Scythians drinking out of the same horn (FIG. 1, *XII* and *XIV*).

A similar motif appears further eastwards. A necklace of the Late Chou dynasty (perhaps fourth century B.C.) said to have come from Loyang,[14] has a pendant in the form of two winged figures. However, in this case, stimulus from the west cannot be ruled out[15] (FIG. 1, *XIII*).

The specimens cited thus show that it was Greek influence which led to the use of human motifs in ornaments. The Gandhara region being a melting pot of cultures could have imbibed the influence either from the Scythians or else directly from the Greeks. The motif was then 'Indianized', and it was from this region that the influence spread to the other parts of the country.

As regards the concept of the motif, it is indeed difficult to explain. In the case of the earlier Yaksha figures, it may perhaps be said to symbolize the *mithuna* aspect or the generative powers of the Yakshas. The problem, however, arises in the case of the Bodhisattva images of the Gandhara school of art Here, possibly, the motif was used for purely decorative purposes and as such had no deeper significance.

HIMANSHU PRABHA SURAN
B4/113 Safdarjang Enclave,
New Delhi, 110016

[1] Bharat Kala Bhavan, Exhibit no. 694.
[2] E. H. Johnston, 'A terracotta figure at Oxford', *Journal of Indian Society of Oriental Arts* (1942), pp. 94.-102
[3] N. P. Joshi, *Life in Ancient Uttarapatha* (Varanasi), p. 187.
[4] V. S. Agrawala, *Indian Art* (Varanasi, 1955), p. 250.
[5] V. S. Agrawala, (*Studies in Indian Art* Varanasi, 1965), pp. 141 and 143.
[6] Joshi, *op cit.*, p. 211.
[7] G. M. A. Richter, *Handbook of Greek Art* (London, 1959), pp. 255-60.
[8] E.H. Minns, *Scythians and Greeks* (Cambridge, 1913), p. 149.
[9] *Ibid.*, pp. 261-91.
[10] *Ibid.*, pp. 284-87; pp. 288-89.
[11] *Ibid.*, pp. 287-88; pp. 289-91.
[12] *Ibid.*, p. 202; fig. 97.
[13] *Ibid.*, p. 203; fig. 98.
[14] W. Willetts, *Foundations of Chinese Art* (London, 1965), pl. 47.
[15] S. Lee, *A History of Far Eastern Art* (London, 1964), p.44.

Pella: Where Alexander the Great was Born

With Alexander, the stage of Greek influence spreads across the world, and Greece becomes only a small item in the heritage of the Greeks. The rise of Alexander was a great turning point, when an old chapter of history was finished and a new one begun. Alexander impressed the popular imagination of every race as a great conqueror, he subdued the East and came as far east as north-western India.

However, one can't comprehend a genius like Alexander without understanding the surroundings in which he lived. He must have been like any other man influenced by his environment. Much has already been written about Macedonians and about the campaigns and greatness of Alexander the Great, but very little is known about Pella[1]—the birthplace of Alexander.

The literary tradition concerning Pella consists of scanty and vague information. Before the rise of the Macedonian kingdom, it is the Athenians who speak to us of Pella and after its destruction by Rome, it is the Roman writers—especially Livy, who preserve the memory of Pella, the Macedonian capital of Greece, and for a while the Greek capital of the world, at the opening point of its Hellenization.

From the time of Archelaos, Pella grew rapidly in extent, population and importance. Xenophon in his *Hellenica* (V.2.13) mentions Pella as'the greatest' of all the cities in Macedonia. Philip II (359-336 B.C.) developed Pella into the most important centre of political life in the Greek nation. Eventually, Philip succeeded in uniting the Greeks under his control and they declared him the leader of the pan-Hellenic expedition. While it was Philip who prepared for the great expedition, it was Alexander, his son, who was destined to lead it beyond any foreseen limit (336-23 B.C.). The result was a world of Hellenization.

The city where Alexander ruled, Aristotle taught and Euripides died, was practically unknown until the last decade. A Greek archaeological team, under Photios Petsas aroused a world-wide interest at Pella in 1957. They discovered finds which may be confidently identified with Pella, the birth place of Alexander the Great.

Very little is preserved from the super-structure of the buildings, their furniture or other works of art at Pella. It is the floors which give evidence of the splendour, beauty and luxury of the houses. The houses with floors are covered with pebble mosaics,[2] in which figured representations. They are made of pebbles in their natural size and colour. Beads were used for details while special features were outlined with strips of either clay or lead. The eyes are almost missing in all the figures. They were, probably, precious stones and hence stolen at the first opportunity.

A mosaic, framed by a floral motif reminds of the well known motive group of Krateros in Delphi. It represents Alexander being saved at the moment by Krateros during a lion hunt somewhere near Susa in Persia (PL. XVIA). Here white pebbles are used mainly in several variations, for instance for shadows ash grey or buff pebbles have been used. Pebbles of honey colour and sand colour are used for the hair of Krateros as well as of Alexander.

In the architectural remnants, the building no. 1, as the excavator calls it, is of conspicuous importance. From the form of its Ionic capitals and other archaeological evidence, it must have been built in the last quarter of the fourth century B,C. when the importance of the capital demanded an expansion. The most conspicuous feature of the building is a series of open courtyards, running north to the south. The central court is paved with a pebble mosaic in a simple rhomboid pattern, framed by a spiral design, the other two are 'peristyle' courts with handsome stone columns of the Ionic order.[3]

Of particular interest are the brightly painted terracotta architectural ornaments, such as palmette antefixes (PL. XVIB). It will be quite congenial to point out at this juncture that these are the elements in the field of art which have marched upto India in the campaign of the world Hellenization and can easily be detected at Rampurva, Sanchi and Bodhgaya. A specimen from Rampurva (PL. XVIC) will suffice

[1]Pella is a Greek word, meaning a 'meadow' or pasture land. The scholars support the derivation of the name based on Hesychius gloss : *Pella lithos* which means a stony ground. Pella lies at a distance of about 37 km. north-west of Thessaloniki (the second city of Greece) on the way to Edessa.

[2]Mosaic generally means pavements, showing two dimensional, mainly white or dark, geometric and figured designs, and are made of natural, unshaped pebbles for the floors of private houses. The history of mosaic work in the classical world begins around *c.* 400 B.C. However, a more extended use of colour, dating from the late fourth and early third centuries, has come to light in houses at Pella, and northern Greece seems to have been the centre from which this technique passed to other lands.

[3]Ionic is the second order of Grecian architecture.

at this juncture. However, the similarity can't be underestimated.

Besides, the stamped roofed tiles, which offer the first definite epigraphic proof for the identification of this ancient city are also worthy of note.

The multitude of other finds include the marble hound of Pella. It belongs to the severe style (400 B.C.). Some Hellenistic marbles, Hellenistic vases and architectural members belonging to the period between 400 B.C. and the Roman times are lying in the Museum at Pella.

It was here indeed that in 350 B.C. Alexander the Great was born.

S. D. DOGRA

Delfon 56, Thessaloniki (Greece)

Book Reviews

A. Ghosh: The City in Early Historical India. Simla: Indian Institute of Advanced Study, 1973. 98 pp., excluding preliminary pages and 1 map. Price : Rs. 17·00.

This small and slim book from the pen of the ex-Director General of Archaeology in India is most welcome for several reasons. In the first place, Shri A. Ghosh belongs to that generation of scholars which have firm roots in Indian classical languages and Indian history. Secondly, he had the advantage of training in the old and new techniques of excavation, and above all because of his long association, first as an officer and then as the Director General of Archaeology and Editor of *Ancient India* and *Indian Archaeology—a Review,* he has intimate knowledge of all the facets of archaeology in India.

Shri Ghosh was thus eminently qualified to discuss the problem of urbanization in India, but before doing so, he also familiarized himself with the old and new theories of urbanization current in the West, particularly Europe and America. The result of his ripe knowledge of Indian archaeology and the theories and the current models, we have in this book and that too in a frank, and forceful words. For long, as Director General of Archaeology, Shri Ghosh had refrained from expressing himself on such vital questions as the authors of the Painted Grey Ware (even while he participated in a seminar on this subject at Aligarh), the existence of the palace-complex at Kausambi as early as 1000 B.C., and the survival of the Harappan tradition into Early Historical times, as well as the survival of this tradition in Indian culture today.

With regard to urbanization or the birth of cities, we have to keep before us two streams of thought. The first is Western. Here again a distinction is to be made between a town and a city, though this is known to very few persons in India. Towns grow (naturally), whereas a city has a municipality with definite boundaries and with various legal powers derived from a charter granted by the Government. To be declared a city, a municipality must attain a prescribed population figure.

From this point of view one might regard Dvarika, Takshashila, Pushkalavati and similar others which are said to be founded in the *Mahabharata* and *Ramayana* by kings as brand new cities, whereas others as towns; otherwise one may say that the concept of a city as opposed to that of a town, like that of a University, is foreign to India. But it is our tendency today, to take in an alien concept and try to apply it to things Indian.

Non-recognition of this distinction between a town and a city does not vitiate Ghosh's main thesis. Here he carefully examines Gordon Childe's ten criteria, as well as others formulated by Toynbee, Mumford, Sjoberg, and thinks that many of these are indeed arbitrary. In particular, he discusses the assumed prior existence of surplus food for the growth or foundation of a city and comes to the conclusion that 'a surplus does not exist in the air without a demand for it, that while the society must have the capacity to produce a surplus before it can have cities, there must be an organization to see that the surplus is produced and a machinery to ensure that the surplus is brought to where it is needed.' In the same way, one might say about the smiths and other industrial classes. These were never whole-time artisans, as the mill workers and many others are today. This has also been pointed out by M.J. Rowland in *World Archaeology,* vol. 3, 1971, pp. 210-26. Significantly, however, the existence of 'free travelling itinerant smith divorced from any social context is rarely found in ethnographic context'.

Of the other criteria enumerated by Childe, Ghosh finds it difficult to get well documented archaeological and literary evidence for the existence of monumental buildings and writing in the sixth century B.C., though some literary and traditional evidence might be cited for internal trade and a sensé of communal feeling (though once again the conception or definition of the latter would differ from country to country or culture to culture).

For the sixth criterion of Childe, viz., writing, while Ghosh can cite no evidence for its existence as early as the sixth century B.C., still his suggestion that 'a much more secular necessity—the maintenance of royal records—may be a reason for the introduction of the scripts' (p. 27). He admits that there is nothing to prove this suggestion, but if for a moment we accept it, then the question arises: "What are our earliest royal records?" Those of Asoka. Though these differ in content from those of the Achaemenians, still the Iranian stamp on them is undoubted. Thus, in this one respect at least, the Second Urbanization has had a foreign element.

After critically discussing this and other criteria Ghosh tries to apply them to twenty-five sites, shown in a specially prepared map. In both the list and the map Mahismati (Maheshwar) on the Narbada does not figure. But there is literary and also archaeological evidence to show that brick buildings, silver punch-marked coins, and a glass seal existed there before the third century B.C.

Here he is faced with two difficulties which the reviewer found some 15 years ago when he was asked by the Wenner Gren Foundation to prepare a paper for "Courses towards Urbanization". The literary evidence is unreliable, because it is not only stereotype but also comparatively late, as found by the reviewer in his study of the *Ramayana.* The archaeological evidence is woefully inadequate, so that hardly any of the criteria laid down by the Western scholars—such as fortification, monumental buildings, trade, writing, can be looked for at the sites selected by Ghosh. The only exception is Taxila. Even here not much is known of the Mauryan or pre-Mauryan city, whereas of the succeeding Indo-Greek we have a fairly good idea of the layout and a few important buildings. This state of things Shri Ghosh could have rectified himself during his 15 years of tenure as Director General of Archaeology, had he realized the importance of this vital knowledge. Even now it is not too late. Twenty-five years of vertical digging is quite sufficient. Let us dig now *horizontally* sites like Kausambi, Mathura and Ayodhya. In the absence of such a sure knowledge, Shri Ghosh concludes that a number of sites in north India had probably come into existence by the sixth century B.C. And the inspiration for this was neither Iranian, Central Asian, nor Greek, but purely indigenous, and not certainly Harappan. Here he specifically rules out the survival theory of Dr. S.C. Malik as absolutely unfounded.

Perhaps Ghosh is right. After thousand years of the existence of Copper-Bronze Age Culture practically throughout India, with the advent of iron, things began to take a different shape, first came the *Janapadas,* then the cities, and later empires. But in this development, did the chalcolithic cultures play no part ? If the distribution maps have any significance, then the distribution of P.G.W. only within the Ganga-Yamuna plains and north Rajasthan, that of the Navdatolian in western Madhya Pradesh or Malwa, of the Jorwe-Nevasa between the Godavari and the Krishna, and the Ahar or Banas in south-east Rajasthan does show the emergence of cultural units in northern India, say between 2000 B.C. and 1000 B.C. Though we do not know about the authors of these distinct regional cultures nor the language they spoke, these cultural units must have contributed to the idea of the formation of a *Janapada,* and such large sites as Inamgaon—with at least 100 or more one room huts, with its potter, goldsmith, lime- and bead-maker, and perhaps irrigated fields and incipient defence wall (quite suitable or efficacious against sling balls and stone-tipped arrows)—to the making of a town. Unfortunately little systematic work has been done outside Maharashtra, so that one might keep out of court the chalcolithic cultures so completely as does Ghosh from contributing to the idea of a city/town in the rest of India. However, Ahar (significantly known in tradition as *Tambavati Nagari*) with its large two or three room houses on a stone plinth and copper smelting technology and a life of at least 1000 years could have been another township in south-east Rajasthan. It must have had a stone fortification as well, whereas its large two-mouthed *chulahs* (domestic ovens) sometimes five or six in a row, do suggest some community life. These two instances should suffice to substantiate the claim of the chalcolithic culture in contributing to the formation of cities in the sixth century B.C. Otherwise we shall have to postulate or assume a a period of 1000 years of gestation. This seemed all right some 15 years ago when I first wrote, but now in view of our increased knowledge, particularly from Ahar and Inamgaon, it seems unjustified. Or we shall have to regard the emergence of cities in the sixth century B.C., as a third and independent urbanization, which had no roots in the past. This cannot be, because unlike the first, the chalcolithic cultures, as I have repeatedly said, were contemporary, both in time and space, with some of our late Vedic and Puranic dynasties. Anyway, this and other problems cannot be solved without well spread out, large-scale excavations.

As stated above, Ghosh categorically rejects Malik's derivation of the three Indian institutions, viz. (1)

the caste system, (2) the perpetuation by birth in a particular caste, and (3) memorization from the Harappan, as without any foundation. As for the third, a little thought would show that there is a continuous tradition of 2500 years which has helped the Brahmins to preserve unchanged the Vedas, and this tradition, cannot be linked with the Harappan as the present archaeological evidence suggests. Malik's illogical conclusions are the result of ignorance of Indian data, both literary and archaeological.

Likewise Ghosh has convincingly shown that there is insufficient evidence to regard the enormous mud-wall with a baked-brick revetment at Kausambi as very early, and a legacy of the Ha·appan. It is the duty of the excavator now to provide additional evidence, or give up his claim.

Ghosh also now agrees with the reviewer and many of his colleagues in holding the Painted Grey Ware as the work of the Later Aryans, and not of the Early Aryans, as first argued by Shri (now Professor) B. B. Lal. For, as shown by the reviewer, it is "democratically" unsound to rely on only one C-14 date, when all the rest, and that too from Ahichchhatra and Hastinapura, give much later dates. Secondly, not only the shapes of the three Painted Grey Ware pots, but also other objects of daily life, such as beads, bangles, bone points, have much more in common with the NBP Ware, than any of the chalcolithic cultures. Thus, in every way the Painted Grey Ware represents the dawn of Early Historical Period.

Shri Ghosh has produced a thought-provoking little volume, after deliberately keeping silent for so long. Let us hope he produces many more, for archaeology is not yet "overpopulated."

H. D. SANKALIA

Deccan College Postgraduate and Research Institute, Pune

C. Silvi Antonini and G. Stacul : The Proto-historic Graveyards of Swat (Pakistan). Rome : IsMEO, 1972. Part I, 524 text pages, including figures and 262 plates, both published separately. Price Lit. 40000.

Professors Antonini and Stacul have done a great service to the archaeologists by bringing out this profusely illustrated volume on the excavations of the graveyards of Loebanr, Katelai and Butkara. All these sites are situated in the valley of Swat river, near the centres of Mingora and Saidu Sharif in Swat, Pakistan.

Since these are voluminous books the authors have taken care to device an easy system of reference. From a brief account of the graves, one can easily find out the details of the associated funerary articles. For a comparative study of the archaeological material, this illustrated volume is very valuable. A high standard of figure drawings and their printing has been maintained. This volume is meant to be descriptive only to serve as a reference book. But the second volume, expected shortly, will discuss other aspects of the culture of these graves: viz., funeral rites, artistic production, chronology, etc.

As regards the finds, the authors report general damage to the graves due to erosion. Still, they have been able to reconstruct that there are two main types of g raves. The first type are two storeyed ; the lower cavity contains the burial remains but is not filled with earth. The upper cavity is separated from the lower one by a layer of schist slabs ; both the cavities are unlined. The second type is also like the first, except that the lower pit has a facing of unmortared walls made up of schist slabs.

The burials are also said to be of two types : inhumation and semi-cremation. There are examples of graves in which both the rites are present in a single grave. In both types, single, double or multiple burials are reported. The body was placed on the side, in a crouched position, with the hands placed near the head. The orientation of the body was determined with respect to the slope of the hills—with the head pointing towards the hills and the feet towards the slope.

In cremation, the semi-charred bones were put in a large jar closed by a lid. Sometimes small funerary objects were also placed inside the jar. Funerary objects were generally placed near the feet in the case of inhumations.

The wares encountered were Gray, Red and Gray Brown, both in thick and thin fabrics. Both wheel-made and handmade varieties were used. A great variety of types are available : stemmed bowls, pedestalled bowls, biconical vessels, bell-shaped vessels, beakers, bottles, jug and jars. Anthropomorphic terracottas and a variety of metal types like arrowheads, spearheads, disc-headed pins, etc., are reported. Both i·on and copper were in use.

As is well-known, there are serious differences

between the chronologies assigned to these graves by Dani and the Italian School. Dani has already published his criticism of the Italian chronology. It would be interesting to know as to what the Italian scholars have to say in return.

A large number of diverse analyses on metals, soils, organic remains, bones, etc., are in progress and will be published as separate studies. The data and the analyses will of course be so vast as to fill many volumes. But an integrated summary of all the results at one place will prove very valuable.

The present volume, we are sure, will prove an indispensable reference work on Pakistan archaeology for all the libraries and the interested scholars.

D.P. AGRAWAL

Physical Research Laboratory
Ahmadabad, 380009

D. Mandal : Radiocarbon Dates and Indian Archaeology. Allahabad : Vaishali Publishing House, 1972. 273 pp., 33 tables and 2 text figures. Price: Rs. 40·00.

In reviewing such a book three main aspects have to be critically evaluated : (i) methodology and the theme of the book ; (ii) academic conclusions ; and (iii) technical production of the book. Here we will concentrate only on (i) and (iii) aspects. Academic conclusions (ii) of the book need a very detailed discussion and will be dealt with here only cursorily.

(i) It is a book of only 273 pages but a lot of labour has gone into its making. In India where archaeological reports are so scarce, it is very difficult to interpret even the C^{14} dates meaningfully. Mandal has tried to collect information through insistent correspondence. As he gives a detailed information both on C^{14} dates and archaeological stratigraphy the book has become doubly valuable. He has discussed the chronology of each C^{14} dated site and given exhaustive tables of C^{14} dates.

At times he uses such ignorant expressions as 'even if dates are apparently not fully consisent but become consistent within the range of counting error they too have been treated as valid.' C^{14} dates are "true" only within the errors given But such lapses are exceptional. Amongst the archaeologists, he shows a relatively rare and clear understanding of the C^{14} technique and its errors. In this, his wife Basanti's role is more important than Mandal's cryptic acknowledgement concedes. She has used her knowledge of physics and maths. to good use in making the book more authentic.

The book's value is enhanced as the author has considerable experience in field archaeology. He has raised some basic queries on the fundamentals of stratigraphy in the tropical countries. (In fact, its a wonder as to how the author could complete this work as he is out in the field for the major part of each year !) A consideration of the role of soil-cover and faulting of strata would have been very useful in such a book.

The author's archaeological experience and logical reasoning has made the book a must for scholars, libraries and students' alike.

(ii) Mandal has propounded many time spreads ; some of which are quite controversial. For example, he brings down the date of the central Harappan (Mohenjo-daro) to *c.* 1700 B.C., ignoring the five C^{14} dates from level 4 (late) which would yield a compounded date of *c.* 2000 B.C. Obviously a sample collected from Mohenjo-daro in earlier excavations with vague particulars is less reliable than five samples from one layer collected by Dales !

This is quoted as an example of wrong methodology and not an attempt to contest his conclusions. It is natural that Mandal differs with several conclusions of mine given in the *Copper Bronze Age in India.* A large number of his objections will be explained by our exhaustive book on chronology (*Radiocarbon Dating and Prehistoric Chronology* by Agrawal & Kusumgar) which will be out by the time this review appears in print. Mandal bases his conclusions on 200 C^{14} dates, but now about 600 C^{14} dates are available. Therefore very soon he will have to revise his own conclusions. I will not go into academic arguments here as a review is not a place to settle such academic scores. His conclusions are based on facts and logic and deserve due consideration.

(iii) The weakest part of the book is its technical production. The wavy lines, printing errors and poor get-up mar the quality of the theme. At times, errors of punctuation, syntax and misuse of words make a jarring reading. Instead of the abstract in the Introduction, a chapter on conclusions would have been more appropriate. Figure 1 should have been in the concluding chapter and the map in the Introduction.

Keeping in view the difficulty of getting a good publisher in India even for a potentially good author, and the fact that it is his *magnum opus,* his book on the whole is a laudable attempt. I am sure, it will sell out fast and the second edition will be more excellent in all aspects.

The author deserves the gratitude of the archaeological community for this valuable contribution to scientific archaeology.

D. P. AGRAWAL

Physical Research Laboratory
Ahmadabad, 380009

Purushottam Singh: Burial Practices in Ancient India. Varanasi: Prithivi Prakashan, (1970), xii + 204 pp., 71 Plates and 2 maps. Price: Rs. 60.00

Burial was one of the established modes of the disposal of the dead in ancient India like most of the other countries with a hoary antiquity. Researches on this subject were undertaken as early as the nineteenth century by a number of scholars but until recently, the picture remained nebulous. During the last three decades or so, as a result of vigorous archaeological activity considerable data relating to ancient graves and their associated cultural horizons were collected in different parts of India. In the present work, which was originally submitted as a Ph.D. dissertation in the Banaras Hindu University in 1968, Dr. Singh studies and analyzes the archaeological material pertaining to the burial practices as obtaining in the Late Stone Age, Neolithic, Chalcolithic, Megalithic and Iron Age of India. In one of the chapters, he also examines the funerary (burial) systems of the present day tribals. The last chapter deals with summary and conclusions.

The author applies the term burial practices to following three modes of the disposal of dead: (i) inhumation in pits or pots; (ii) post-cremation; and (iii) post-excarnation burials, and examines the published data from various sites with accuracy and insight. In some instances he quotes other writers on the subject without giving his own views or comments, which the reader would like to know. For obvious reasons Dr. Singh does not take into account the literary evidence. In his opinion 'this line of enquiry has not led us to any appreciable results'; but one may not agree with him in this respect, as references to burial practices in Vedic and later literature do contain useful information applicable to some modes of disposal of the dead in protohistoric and historical times. He does not touch at all funerary memorials like *stupa* which seems to have originated as a grave mound.

His chapter on 'megaliths' dealing almost with all aspects of the subject is not without a few controversial points. He treats all the megalithic monuments of the Peninsula as a part of one unified culture-complex represented largely by (i) Black-and-red Ware and (ii) iron objects. Besides, there are other characteristic finds which are associated with the megaliths of the region. What is noteworthy is that he regards the megalithic folk as 'Dravidian speakers.' Yet he believes that the idea of megalith building came through the north-west.

If the author would have given some information on the non-tribal Hindu burials, which are not yet extinct, the work would have become more useful, for such practices represent the traditional *kula* or *janapada* (*desa*) *dharma,* recognized even by orthodox law givers. We are not definite whether the medieval practice of raising *chhatris* on the ashes has any distant cultural link with ancient post-cremation burials.

However, the work has its own merits. It is one of the well written and well documented books on the subject. The narration is up to date (till 1969), simple, brief and to the point. The approach is balanced. A remarkable aspect of Dr. Singh's writing is that he has been successful to a considerable extent in maintaining the spirit of objectivity. The utility of the work would have increased much more if some line-drawings were incorporated therein. The book on the whole is one of the most valuable contributions to Indian archaeology

M. C. JOSHI

Archaeological Survey of India
Purana Qila, New Delhi, 110011

S.B. Deo and J.P. Joshi: Pauni Excavations (1969-70) Nagpur: Nagpur University, 1972. 119 pp. excluding preliminary pages and index. Price not mentioned.

Field archaeology in India started more than a hundred years ago, primarily as a result of the exploration and identification of historical sites. From 1921-22 onwards, when Harappa and Mohenjo-daro were excavated, attention was also diverted to protohistory. In 1949, a definite shift towards prehistory was perceptible when F.E. Zeuner and V.D. Krishnaswami undertook the investigations of the Stone Age sites in India. In the following two decades, the leading field-archaeologists in India, who were never formally trained as prehistorians—H.D. Sankalia, B.B. Lal, G.R. Sharma, K.V. Soundara Rajan—threw most of their weight in favour of prehistory and protohistory. 'In the hands of stones and pottery historical archaeology is badly suffering', this I heard from a very senior professor in one of the archaeological seminars, held in 1958. *Indian Prehistory : 1964* (Poona, 1965), being the Proceedings of an all India seminar, clearly shows the directional changes which had already occurred during the preceding decade. Researches, conducted during the succeeding decade clearly show the hang-over of the preceding decade. Contents of the *Indian Archaeology—A Review,* published yearly by the Archaeological Survey of India unmistakably prove it. Thus, during the two decades after Independence, historical archaeology in India suffered a set-back.

The excavations at Pauni, a second century B.C. *stupa*-complex, located in District Bhandara, in the Vidarbha region of Maharashtra, when seen against this background assumes—greater significance. It marks a revival of the somewhat lost interest of Indian field archaeologists in historical sites. The excavations conducted on three different mounds at the site revealed the existence of baked brick *stupas*, built by the Hinayana sects. The trenches, most carefully dug, have shown beyond doubt that they were repaired and enlarged several times. The surviving sculptures indicate that *stupas* were embellished with a large number of stone pillars and slabs, somewhat repeating the richness and variety of Bharhut, both in representational art, including those of the *yakshas* but without Jataka stories, and epigraphical records of donors, exclusively belonging to the non-royal families.

The coins unearthed include silver and copper punch-marked variety, cast copper, and of Satavahanas, including one die-struck coin of Sri Satakarni, and Kshatrapa—all indicating the period during which this holy place was in most active worship—second-first century B.C., generally known as the Sunga-Satavahana period. From the lowest levels, painted N.B.P. Ware sherds were found. Structurally, the main *stupa,* about 40 metres in diameter with a superstructure bigger than that of Sanchi, and the other *stupas* exhibit a developed stage of skill since they have used both the 'box-technique' and 'tier-technique'. In one of the *stupas,* the excavators found for the first time a painted pot used as reliquary, deposited in a *kunda*-like construction with wooden *yasti* nearby. Probably, the excavators are right when they observe that Pauni 'must have played a commendable part in the transmission of Buddhism and Buddhist art and architecture further south, especially in Andhra Pradesh, which claimed such renowned centres as Nagarjunakonda, Amaravati, Bhattiprolu, etc.' as also south-western Maharashtra where Karle, Bhaja, and Kanheri caves also exhibit the same tradition.

It is a nicely written short report of a skilful excavation, conducted jointly by the University of Nagpur and the Archaeological Survey of India. Printing and production of the text, figures and plates are very good although the figures of scultptures (nos. 10 and 11) show bad printing and technical errors.

S. P. GUPTA

National Museum
Janpath, New Delhi, 110011

B.P. Sinha (Ed.) : Potteries in Ancient India. Patna : Patna University, not dated: 315, pp. including figures and plates. Price: Rs. 45·00.

The volume contains the proceedings of a Seminar on Potteries in Ancient India, organized by the Department of Ancient Indian History and Archaeology of the Patna University. It was perhaps the first seminar held specifically for discussing the problems pertaining to ancient Indian potteries. The publication of the volume will, therefore, be welcomed by scholars interested in this important branch of archaeology.

In his inaugural address, B.B. Lal has analyzed and emphasized the importance of pottery as a source-material in archaeological studies. It would, however, be imagining too much if we agree with Lal when he says that it 'throws light on almost every aspect of the past—social, cultural, religious, economic, political and *what not*' (emphasis added.—B.M.P.). He tries to substantiate his premises by citing examples of the Arretine Ware and amphorae from Arikamedu, jar from Lothal painted with a scene reminiscent of a *Pancha-tantra* story, painted scenes, motifs and graffiti on Harappan pottery, the Painted Grey and the N.B.P. Wares which have, respectively, thrown light on Indo-Roman contacts and import of Roman wine into India, possible beginning of *Pancha-tantra*, items of agricultural produce, dress and direction of Harappan script and food habits of the people during the period represented by the each example. Lal further maintains that the ceramic unity as exemplified by the distribution of the N.B.P. Ware represents, a complete cultural integration of India,' during the middle of the first millennium B.C. This, apparently, is rather subjective, and it will be hazardous to speculate so widely merely on the basis of pottery. He also touches upon various problems connected with ancient Indian potteries, correlation of ceramic evidence with that from literature, and need for technical studies.

In his introductory remarks, B.P. Sinha feels that in the absence of any epigraphic or numismatic evidence regarding the Vedic Aryans, the Epic period, the Asuras, Dasyus and Panis, mentioned in ancient Indian literature, pottery could perhaps be helpful in throwing some light. He has, of course, not specified who the Vedic Aryans were and what is the Epic period. He has also tried to highlight the problems relating to Black-and-red Ware, Ochre Colour Ware, foreign influence on Indian pottery, relationship between different contemporary ceramic industries, etc.

The papers presented at the Seminar dealt with a variety of problems. Barring S.P. Gupta's paper entitled 'Sociology of Pottery : Chirag Delhi, a case-study', and M.D. Khare's 'Study of Pottery—a new approach : ABC of Archaeology or A to Z of Archaeology', all the other papers were concerned with origin, nature and spread, technology, distribution and other problems connectcd with different ceramic industries or pottery-types, covering a vast chrono-cultural period. It is not possible to discuss the different viewpoints of the participants ; only a broad outline or the salient ideas of some of the papers has been touched upon.

S.P. Gupta on the basis of his meeting with a Delhi potter, discusses various apsects relating to pot manufacture including the procurement of clay, painting of the pots and various other socio-economic factors connected with pot-making. This is a novel approach to the subject although not strictly applicable in the context of ancient Indian potteries. Khare's paper is full of homilies and generalized suggestions in regard to the study of pottery. K.V. Soundararajan's paper 'The devolution of the peninsular 'Neolithic' culture—an analysis of ceramic influences' is a motley of abstract ideas ; the basic problems connected with the subject have hardly been touched upon by him. S.P. Srivastava's paper on the Black-and-red Ware from Ahar and Noh is mainly concerned with the description of the types and decoration in the ware ; his contention is that 'the painted black-and-red ware from Ahar......was the deluxe ware of the chalcolithic period while the unpainted black-and-red from Noh was the pottery of the common man.' This, as also the inference about the Painted Grey Ware being the pottery of the Aryans and of 'a superior kind' are highly speculative. The other papers dealing with the Black-and-red Ware, either from the pre-Painted Grey or the chalcolithic levels have been contributed by Purushottam Singh, R.C. Gaur, B.S. Verma and K.N. Dikshit. Purushottam Singh's paper on 'The problem of Black-and-red Wares in Indian Archaeology' is a succint summary of the researches on this interesting and important ware which is available in the Harappan context in Gujarat, Saurashtra and Kutch, in the chalcolithic levels in Rajasthan, central and eastern India, in the Gangetic plains in the pre-P.G. Ware and post O.C.P. levels, the megalithic and the early historical levels in central and western India and covers a time-range between the last quarter of the third millennium B.C. to the middle of the first millennium B.C. The associated antiquities found along with the chalcolithic Black-and-red Ware have been described by Naseem Akhtar.

The problem of the Ochre Colour Ware has been discussed by Krishna Deva ; he has tried to show that the Ochre Colour Ware using people in the upper Ganga basin are identical with the authors of the Copper Hoards and 'appear to have co-existed with the Cemetey H folk as well as the Harappan stragglers.' Dr. B.B. Lal has enumerated the results obtained by him on the basis of geochronological investigations. In his view, the sediments constituting the Ochre Colour Ware horizons 'may not be water-laid, and that flowing water may not be responsible for transporting and depositing it at the Ochre Colour Pottery sites' Likewise, the rolling and weathering of the ware is not due to prolonged water-logging and contact with river silt but due to 'the crystallization of soluble salts in the new environment.' The observations are significant, particularly in view of the theories which have been advanced on the basis of considering the Ochre Colour Pottery being waterlogged. A re-thinking on the problem of the O.C.P. is, therefore, necessary in the light of these observations. R.C. Gaur has confined himself to a description of the types of vessels in the ware recovered by him from Atranjikhera excavations.

B.K. Thapar has discussed the nature of the pre-Harappan wares. He has restricted himself to an enumeration of the pre-Harappan pottery found at Kalibangan, its classification into six fabrics on the basis of the surface-features ; on the basis of the correlation with different cultural assemblages, he concludes that 'the pre-Harappan communities appeared in northern Rajasthan somewhat later than on sites in Baluchistan and the lower Indus Valley, as though reflecting a 'sloping horizon' of cultural levels from west to east.' Vibha Tripathi has also dwelt on the same theme.

Not many papers were contributed on Harappan pottery. S.R. Rao's paper 'The Harappan ceramic wares and the devolution of the Harappa culture' or K.N. Dikshit's 'Nature of Harappan wares in Sutlej Valley' do not suggest any significant points.

The problem of the N.B.P. Ware, its technical aspects, origin and spread, and its regional characteristics were the subjects tackled by Sachchidanand Sahay, Sita Ram Roy, K.K. Sinha, H.C. Bhardwaj and R.C. Gaur, while the antiquities associated with the N.B.P. (with special reference to Bihar) have been described by Lala Aditya Narain.

Mention may be made of the papers by M.S. Pandey, Brajdeo Prasad Roy, and Shivaji Singh who have utilized literary references regarding potteryn Sushil Malti Devi's paper 'Potters and potteries i. ancient Indian inscriptions' is a useful compilation of data.

Of a different genre are the papers 'Roman pottery in India' by M.N. Deshpande, and 'Yakshi' or Kinnari pot from Begram and allied problems' by R.C. Agrawal, or the papers 'Spouted vessels in India,' by R.C. Prasad Singh and 'Dish-on-stand' by Madan Mohan Singh.

Generally speaking, the papers presented in the Seminar consist either of surveys of the work already done or being done or only give a broad idea of the problem. One of the contributors has presented as many papers as the number of wares available from his site. The arrangement of the papers in the volume also does not show any system or order ; it would have been more proper if the papers were arranged subject-wise . The omission of the title of the Seminar, the date when held and the year of publication is a serious shortcoming, since these serve as a datum. The volume also abounds in printing errors which detract attention. These shortcomings notwithstanding, the volume should serve as a useful compendium on the subject.

B. M. PANDE

Archaeological Survey of India
Janpath, New Delhi,110011

Amita Ray: Art of Nepal. New Delhi: Indian Council for Cultural Relations, 1973. 78 pp. and 103 pls. Price : Rs. 40.00.

The art of Nepal evokes a spontaneous response in the mind of an average Indian or a student of Indian culture because of its striking affinities with the art of India in theme and treatment. Of late, it has also started attracting votaries from other lands as well more so because Nepal seems to have become the Shangrila of tourists and travellers. In order, therefore, to cater to the needs of the increasing number of people, including those not initiated into the subject, the Indian Council for Cultural Relations has brought out this adequately-illustrated and moderately-priced volume. The volume, as the author says, has been designed and written as an introductory account with the aim of presenting an integrated study of the plastic arts of Nepal. Amita Ray has included, under the purview of the present work, the art of Nepal exhibited in the varied media such as stone sculpture, terracottas, bronzes, wood-work, paintings besides giving an account of the history, architecture and the religion and pantheon of gods and goddesses of Nepal.

Nepalese art is best exemplified in the variety of image types of the Brahmanical and Buddhist faiths, The various Saiva and Vaishnava deities, besides those of the other gods and semi-divine beings of the Hindu and Buddhist pantheons show a sequential development in terms of iconographic and artistic features, which, while displaying certain akinness with their Indian counterparts, still bear out the indigenous traits in terms of the distinctive art conventions of Nepal The period of hectic art-activity begins in the valley in about the fifth century A.D. ; in the *tarai* region of Nepal, it goes back to at least the Maurya and Sunga times, as is evident from the finds from Tilaurakot, Banjarahi and Paisia. The earliest sculptures, belonging to the times of the Lichchhavis reveal art-forms affiliated to the Guptas. However, discovery of a standing headless *yaksha* figure from Harigaon and another standing figure from the Gorakshanatha monastery in the Pasupatinatha temple seem to indicate that the sculptural tradition in the valley goes back to the beginning of the Christian era. Amita Ray rightly points out the akinness of the Harigaon *yaksha* figure with three well-known, free-standing Buddha-Bodhisattva images installed by the Friar Bala at Mathura, Sarnath and Sravasti. Yet another example is the seated Kirata (?) figure from Aryaghat, Pasupatinatha temple which, again, like the Gorakshanatha figure, is strongly reminiscent of the Kushan royal portraits. That the Kushan-based Gupta art wás characteristic of early Nepalese sculpture is also evident in the *kumbha* surmounted by a female head from Harigaon and in the nativity scene from Deo Patan. Amita Ray has, due to inadequate reference to the finds in the *tarai,* not considered the other early examples from Lumbini which has yielded a Bodhisattva bronze of late Kushan times, besides examples of later periods in stone and terracotta ; nor has she considered the early examples from sites like Kodan, Pipri, Kadzahawa, Lamtiya, Sisania, Sanagarh, etc.

Among the earliest dated examples from Nepal, which have been included by Amita Ray, are the sculptured reliefs of Vishnu-Vikrantamurti from Lajimpat and Mrigasthali which are datable to A.D. 467, Varaha from Dhum Varahi, datable to the sixth century, the bronze Vishnu (now in the Museum of Fine Arts, Boston) and perhaps also the bronze Siva image (now in the Indian Museum, Calcutta). According to Amita Ray, these earlier examples and those of the later times respectively bear out the distinct inspiration of the Guptas, Chalukyan and Pala art traditions. We, however, feel that the Varaha from Dhum Varahi seems to compare more with the Varaha figure in the so-called Varaha temple at Deogarh which is later than the Dasavatara temple datable to the sixth century. Amita Ray does not make it clear nor does she illustrate as to how the Chalukyan influence infilterated into the valley. We would also add that the Pratihara tradition, which does not seem to have been taken into account by Amita Ray, rather than the western Deccan, infuenced the Nepalese sculptor as is discernible in the Vishnu on Garuda from Changu-Narayana. In this context it may be relevant to speak of the influence of the Karnataka ornate style, which, according to N.R. Banerjee, is grafted on the Late Pala, 'or, in fact, Sena elaboration of the style in Nepal.'

In about the thirteenth century, with the increasing influence of the Buddhist or Brahmanical Tantric traditions, rigid iconometry rather than artistic considerations became dominant and the 'art slowly and inevitably became degenerated into stereotyped cultic forms.' The same is true of the bronzes of Nepal, most of which were prepared by the *retardataire* method even while the *cire-perdue* technique was also known to the Nepalese craftsman. Bronze images, particularly from the thirteenth century onwards, were turned out in large numbers to meet the needs of the increasing clientele and, therefore, perhaps exhibit, barring a few cases, certain rigidity and 'general fixation of the art form.'

Pride of place goes to the wood-carvings which are remarkable for their exquisite carftsmanship ; examples of these are available in various figures and architectural members used in the temples and palaces of Kathmandu, Patan, Bhatgaon and Vasantpur. These wood-carvings have as their subject both religious and secular themes in which are depicted vegetable, geometrical, human and animal forms. The earliest available specimens go back to about the thirteenth century, and it is still a living craft in Nepal. According to Amita Ray, the figures of divines and semi-divines on wood and covering the surface of the Brahmanical and Buddhist temples, unlike similar figures in stone or bronze are 'less bound down by rigid iconographic injunctions, and not unoften they breathe a secular air even.'

No less interesting are the Nepalese paintings, examples of which are the miniatures in Sanskrit or Newari illustrated texts, scrolls, wooden books and, what Amita Ray calls as the *mandala-patas.* The art of painting in Nepal was essentially and exclusively religious and hence is 'controlled and conditioned by a hieratic, sometimes even esoteric, religious order.' Despite the impact of the Tibetan paintings on the one hand and of the Rajasthani and Pahari schools of painting, the Nepalese paintings do not exhibit any spontaneity since the art was 'almost exclusively iconic and strictly controlled by monks and priests in the seclusion of temples and monasteries.'

This useful account of the art of Nepal is a welcome addition to the literature on the subject. Amita Ray has not merely discussed and described the examples of Nepalese art as isolated specimens or individual pieces, but has tried to present a unified picture by including architecture, religion and cults and socio-economic background in order to give a proper perspective to art. She has, however, not given due consideration to the evidence from Nepalese *tarai* which has been subjected to more systematic work in recent years and where interesting material and cultural remains have been brought to light. The importance of the area as a carrier of the influence to the valley, and, in certain cases at least, as the precursor to the art of Nepal, is beyond doubt. Likewise, the selection of examples is also inadequate and does not do sufficient justice to the rich art heritage of Nepal, particularly in regard to the bronze icons and paintings. No reference whatsoever has been made to the folk art either, or to the art of ivory carving, metal ware, etc.

A word may also be said here about lack of standardization of spellings of place names, and the discrepancies between text and captions of plates. For instance, it is not clear whether the correct name of the place is Nagaltole (p. 35) or Naugal Tol (p. 76 and fig. 32), Hadigaon (p. 31) or Harigaon (p. 75 and fig. 25). The figure of a devotee (perhaps Garuda-B.M.P.) from Kathmandu has been referred to as belonging to the ninth-tenth century in the illustration (p. 76 and fig. 32) and in the text (p. 32) as belonging to the fifth-sixth century. There are a few printing slips and a number of mistakes in the references cited. To cite a few examples out of the many : captions of figs. 55 and 56 have been transposed; fig. 75 has been wrongly placed while N.R. Banerji's articles (p. 14, n. 4 and p. 42, n.1.) have been published respectively in *Puratattva* and *Ancient Nepal* and not as given by the author.

A chronological chart, a map showing location of sites, and a bibliography, would have further added to the utility of the volume.

B. M. PANDE

Archaeological Survey of India
Janpath, New Delhi, 110011

Dharampal : Indian Science and Technology in the Eighteenth century. Delhi : IMPEX India, 1971. 182 pp. Price: Rs. 65·00.

In Indian history, the eighteenth century represents a period of transition from medievalism to modernity in the political as well as in the economic field. No doubt, this century marks an era of decline for India as a powerful political force and gradual ascendency of the colonial British rule, yet it is the period when the seeds of modern India were sown with the introduction of advanced European technology. During this span of time, the Indians perhaps never cared to understand or study any foreigner or foreign country, but the Europeans did observe the Indian way of life and our technical knowledge and skill.

It is on the basis of contemporary accounts of the Europeans, especially the British scientists and travellers, that Dharampal tries to visualize the scientific and technological progress of India in the eighteenth century. In doing so the author's aim has been to show that the underdeveloped economy of modern India is an outcome of neglect of native sciences and skills during the British period. On the basis of vital archival data reproduced in the book he tries to prove that only two centuries back Indians excelled in the field of astronomy, mathemetics, surgery, metallurgy and cloth dyeing, employed water mills for crushing the ore and drill plough in agriculture and produced intricate jewellery and waterproofing materials. The contemporary illustrations reproduced in the book have further enhanced its utility.

As a well documented work it is of immense value not only to the historians but also to archaeologists, especially in view of traditional metallurgical techniques described in the book.

M.C. JOSHI

Archaeological Survey of India,
Purana Qila, New Delhi, 110011

Smita J. Baxi and Vinod P. Dwivedi: Modern Museum, Organization and Practice in India. New Delhi: Abhinav Publications, 1973. XV+206 pp. and halftone illustrations. Price: Rs. 35·00.

Antiquarianism and ethnographical researches have played a key role in the growth and development of museums in India. In fact, most of the significant museums, particularly those at the archaeological sites, were established by the Archaeological Survey of India which had to improvise suitable modes of storing and displaying the excavated and explored material. Archaeological investigations were conducted solely by the officers of the Archaeological Survey of India who were largely art historians. This state of affairs has been recognized by the authors of the present work ; they have dedicated the book to art-historians.

The emergence of museology as an independent discipline is relatively recent and is the outcome of the establishment of different types of museums. It is, therefore, no surprise that the museologists of today consider the earlier museums as belonging to the 'store house phase' of museum development. According to the authors of the book, the museums are now no longer regarded as secluded store rooms but as '*instrument of education at every step*' (original emphasis—B.M.P.). It is to meet the requirements of the increasing tribe of museologists, engaged in pursuing these aims, that Smita J. Baxi and Vinod P. Dwivedi have pooled together their knowledge and experience in this joint endeavour, *Modern Museum*.

Modern Museum concerns itself with all the important facets of a museum and between themselves, the two authors have, in seven chapters, besides an introduction, described and discussed acquisition and registration, building and lighting, museum exhibitions and display-techniques, museum education and research, care and security of museum objects and the future role of museums. Besides, a select glossary and information on various connected aspects of the subject including a bibliography have been given in the form of Appendices.

The book has been 'planned as guide for the students of museology, the beginners in the profession and to the curators of the smaller museums.' It is a laudable attempt since it covers a very wide range of subjects : It is, however, in no way more useful than Aiyappan and Satyamurti's work published as far back as 1960. Somehow, the book reads like a compilation of articles published by the authors from time to time. The authors could have done well by weaving the articles into a continuous and interconnected whole. This lack of continuity makes inane reading. Though the authors have claimed that the book has been written as a text-book, the desired effect has not been achieved. In a book of this kind, purportedly meant for students of the subject, lack of background information, as a prelude to the subject, giving a brief history of the museums, is a serious lacuna. The Bibliography or the Glossary, again, show superficial and perfunctory treatment.

B.M. PANDE

Archaeological Survey of India,
Janpath, New Delhi, 110011

A. Flint-bladed sickle from Jarmo, Iraq.

[See p. 11] [Photo : Oriental Institute, Chicago.]

B. Lower Palaeolithic handaxes and cleavers from Garo Hills.

[See p. 19] [Photo : University of Gauhati.]

A. Middle Palaeolithic flake-tools (scrapers and points) from the Garo Hills.

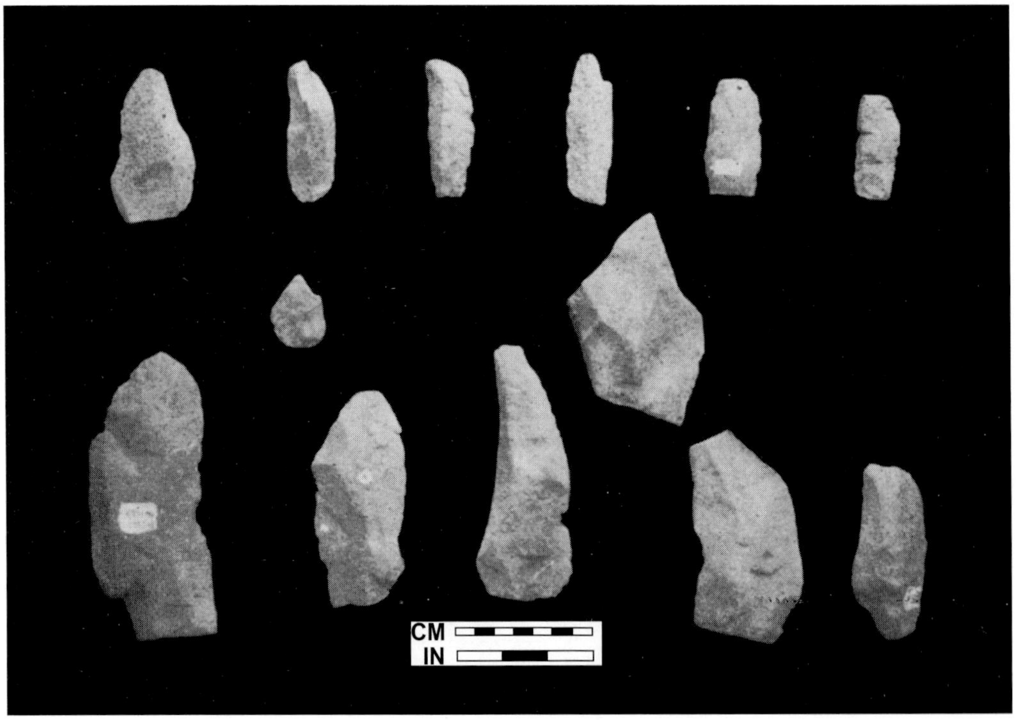

B. Upper Palaeolithic blades and burins from the Garo Hills.

[See p. 19] [Photos : University of Gauhati.]

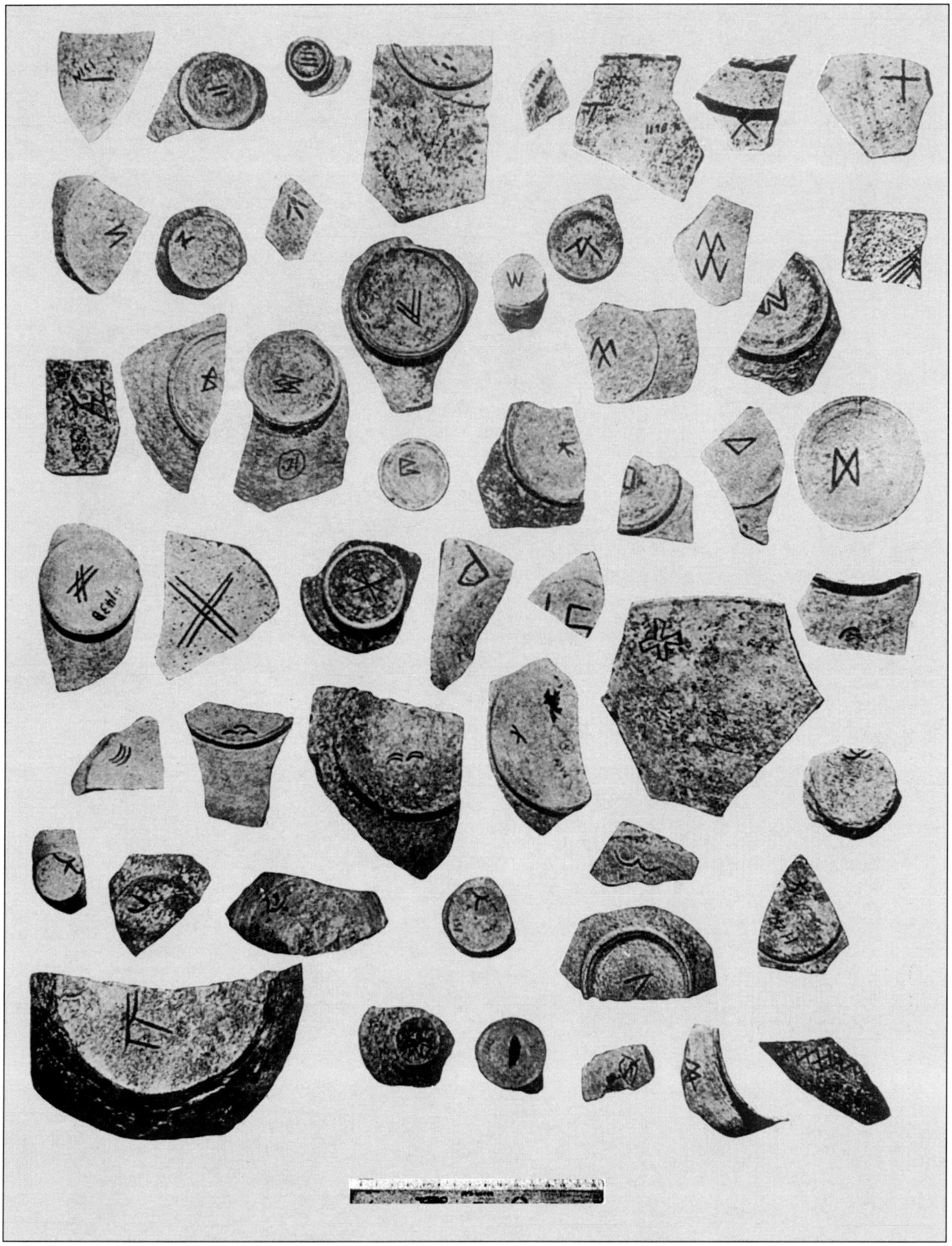

Marks on the pottery from the Quetta Valley (after Fairservis Jr.)

[See p. 22] [Photo : American Museum of Natural History, New York.]

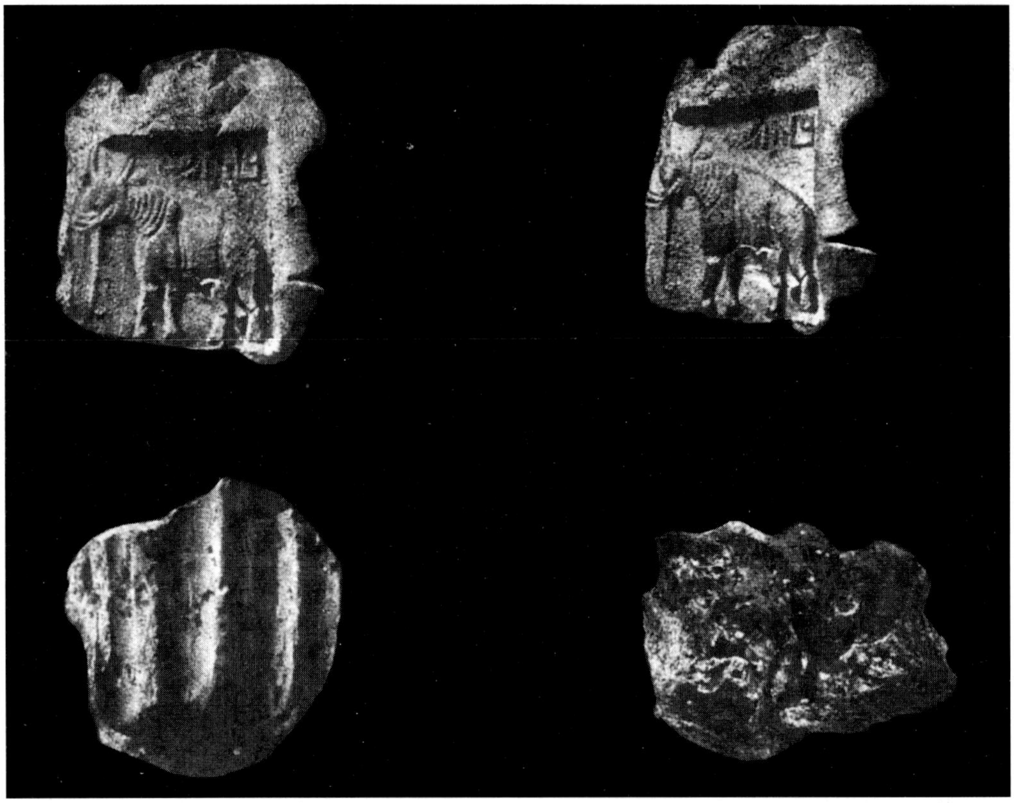

A. Terracotta sealings with impressions of reed, cord, etc. from Kalibangan.

B. Potsherd of the black-and-red ware, bearing a post-firing graffiti from Sanur.

[See pp. 23 and 24] [Photos : Archaeological Survey of India.]

A. Terracotta sealings with identical inscriptions from Kalibangan.

B. Cylinder seal and its impression from Kalibangan.

C. Steatite seal from Kalibangan.

D. Terracotta sealing from the warehouse at Lothal.

[See p. 23]

[Photos : Archaeological Survey of India.]

A. Potsherd bearing post-firing graffiti, showing overlap of signs from Kalibangan.

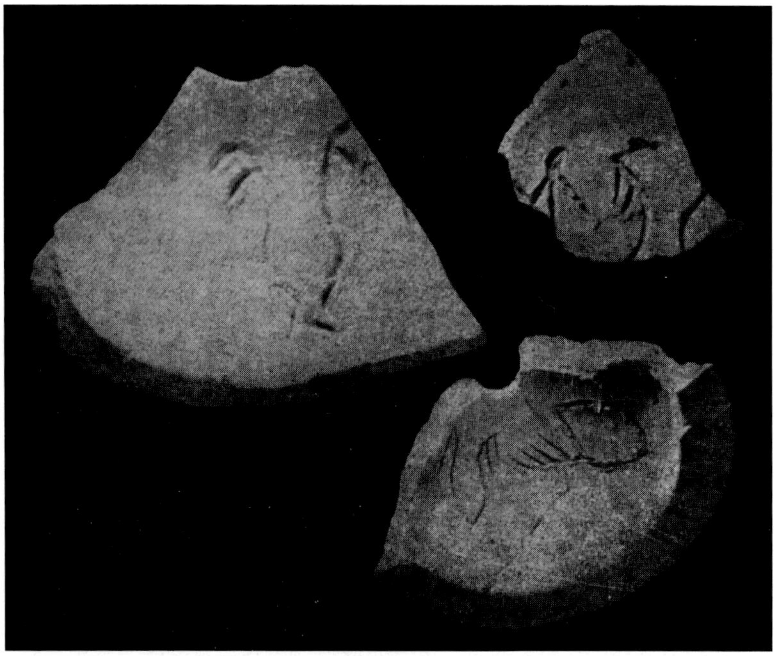

B. Post-firing graffiti on potsherds from Kalibangan.

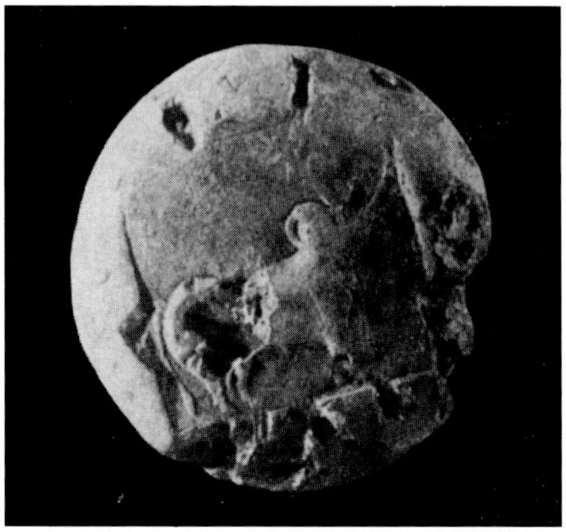

C. Terracotta from Kalibangan.

[See pp. 22 and 23]

[Photos : Archaeological Survey of India.]

Reserved slip ware from Surkotada.

[See p. 35] [Photo : Archaeological Survey of India.]

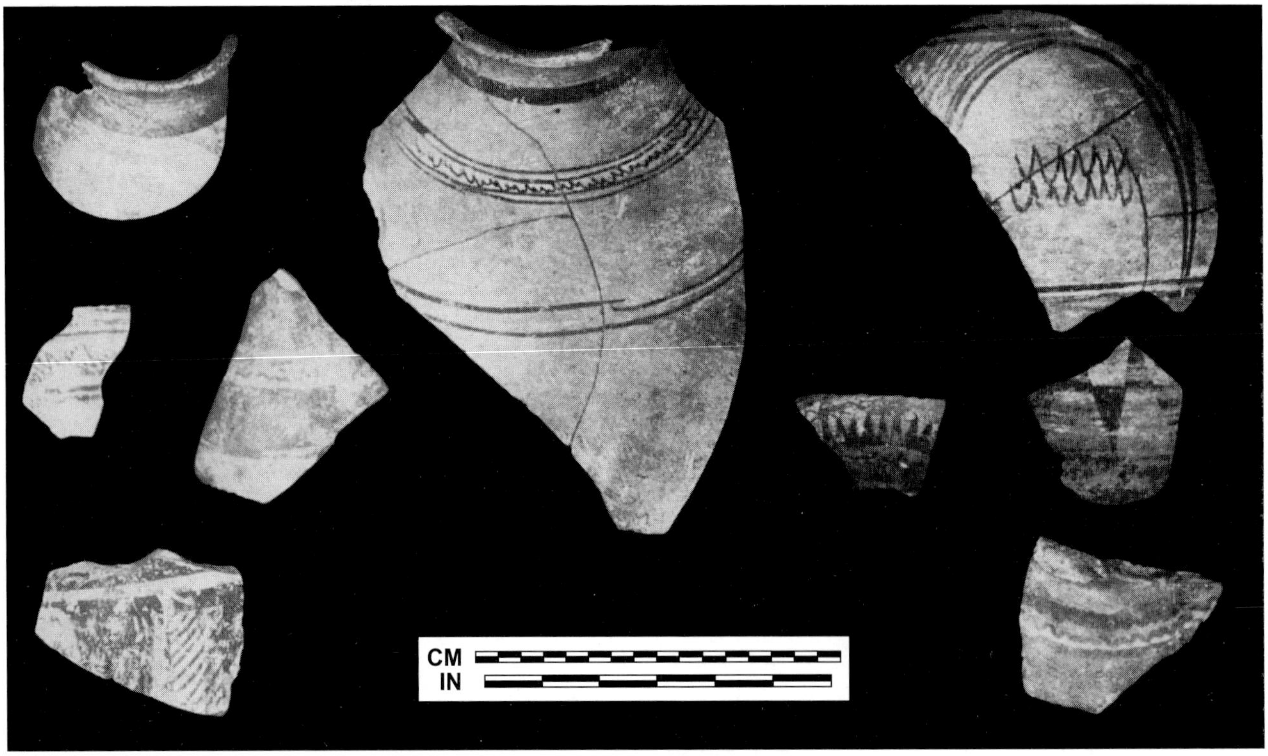

A. Polytone red ware from Surkotada.

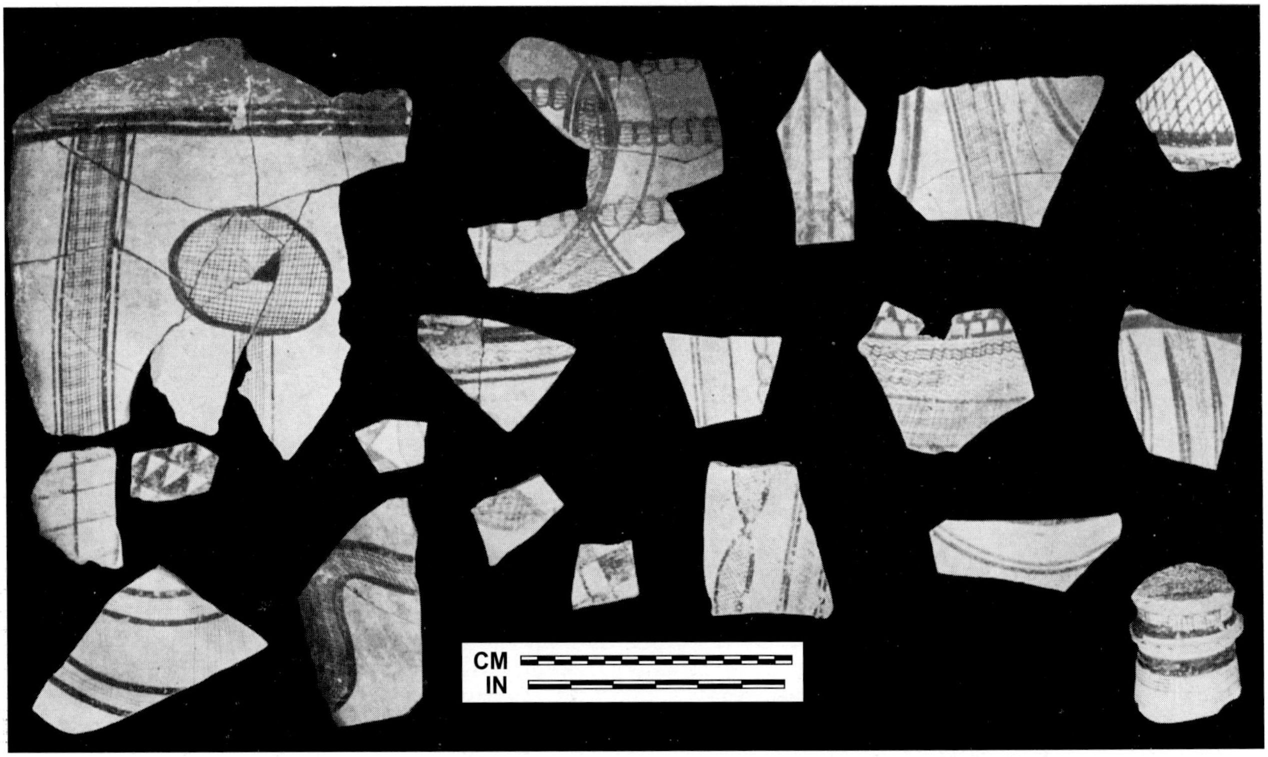

B. Cream-slipped ware from Surkotada.

[See p. 36]

[Photos : Archaeological Survey of India.]

A. House-remains of early Jorwe Culture at Inamgaon.

B. House-remains of late Jorwe Culture at Inamgaon.

[See p. 39]

[Photos : Deccan College, Pune.]

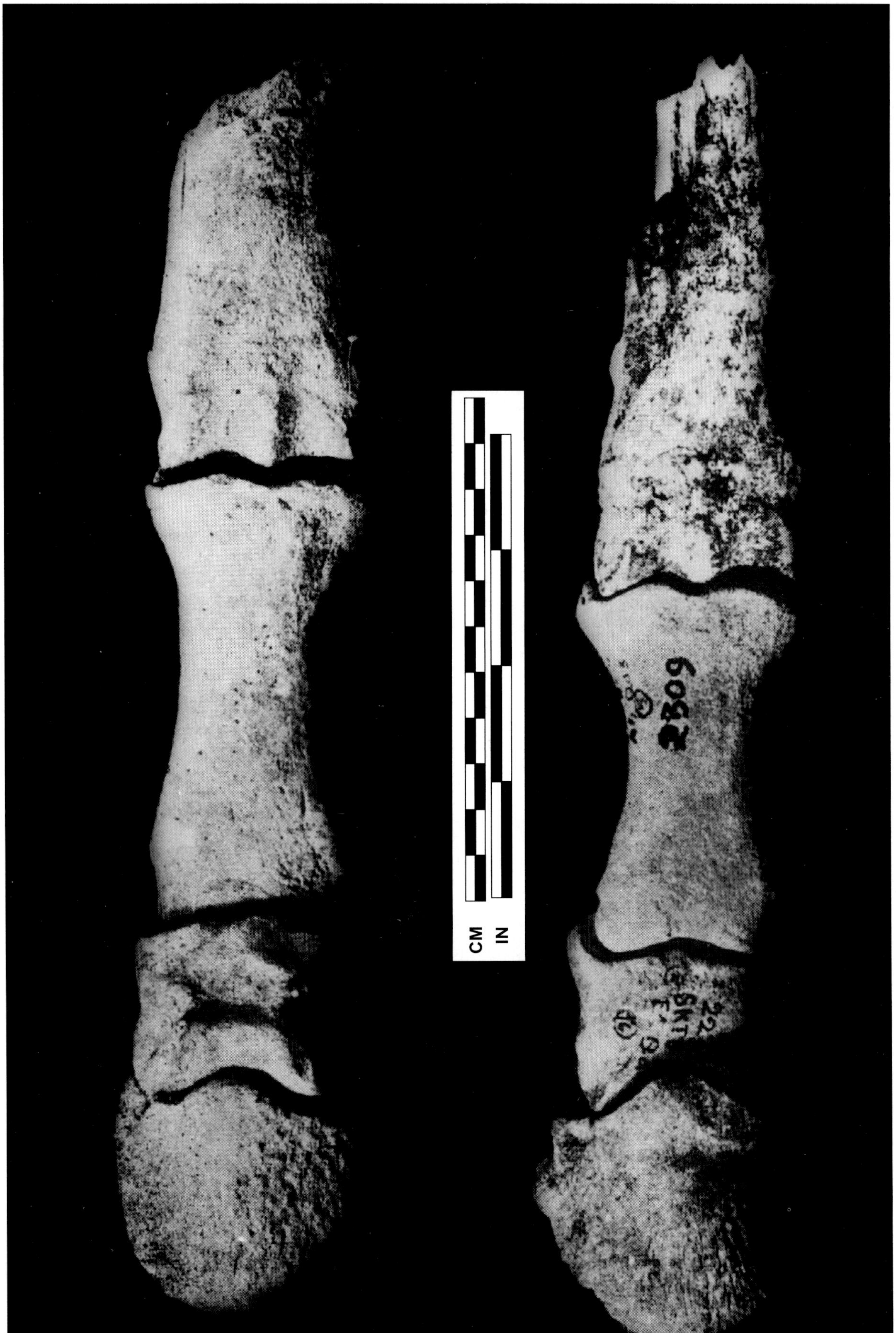

Canon bones and phalanges from Surkotada, arranged to show articulation.

[Photos : Archaeological Survey of India.]

[See p. 76]

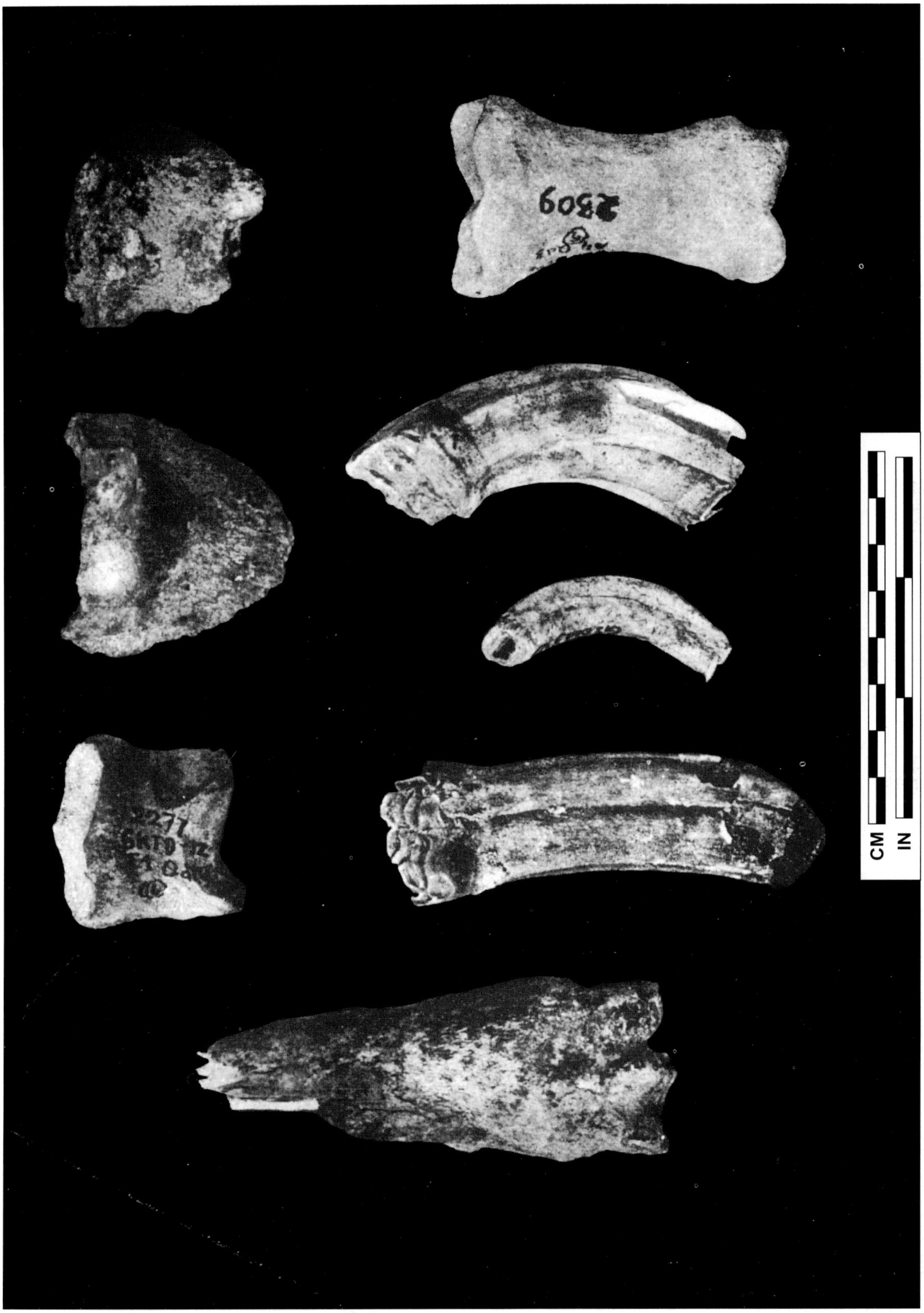

B. Bones of horse from Surkotada : top row (from left), canon bone, second phalanx, third phalanx; botton row, molar and incisor, of Equus caballus *Linn.*; the remaining of Equus asinus *Linn.*

[See p. 76] [Photo : Archaeological Survey of India.]

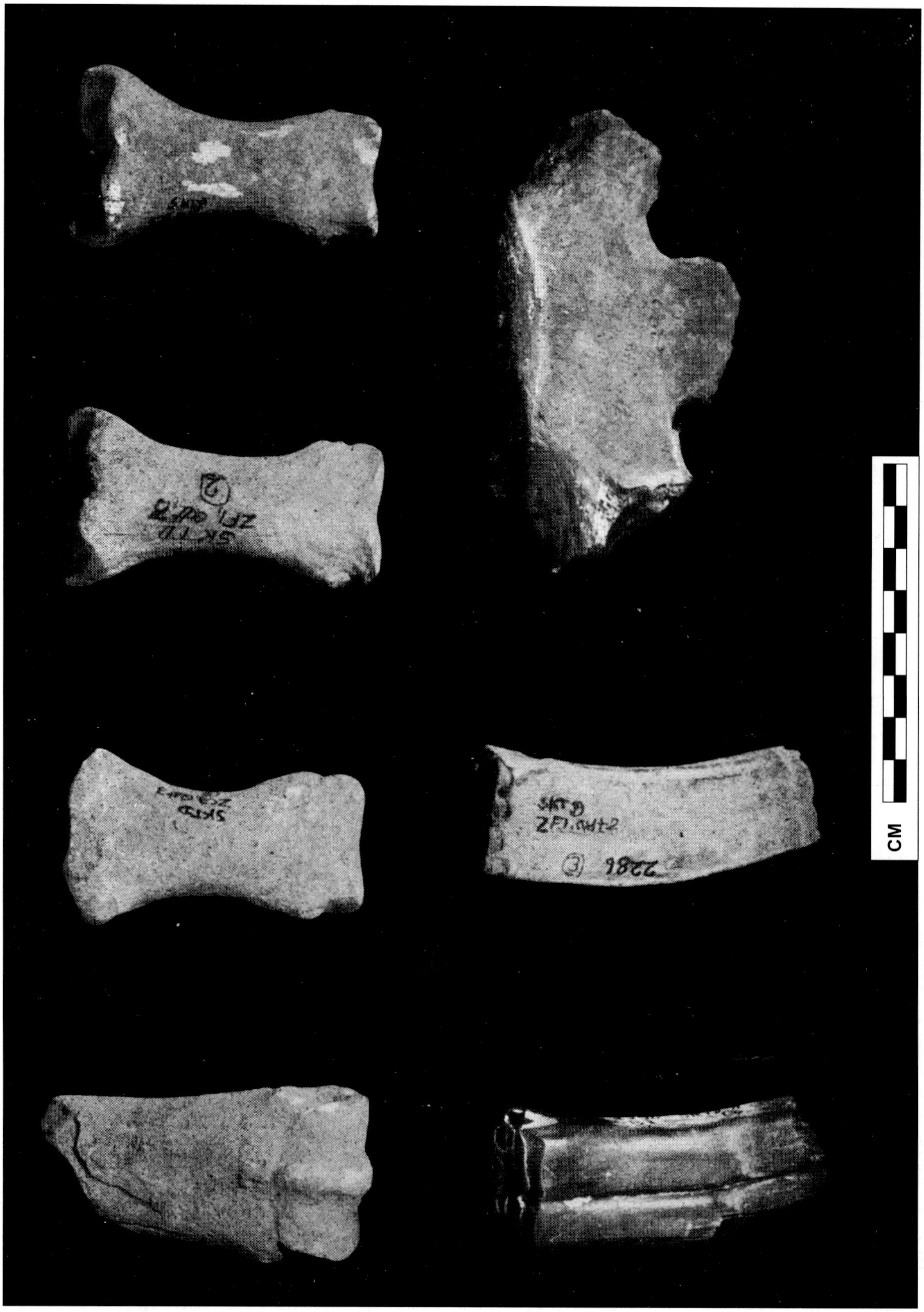

Surkotada : top row (from left), first one, canon of Equus caballus *Linn*. and bottom row, first two of Equus caballus *Linn*.; remaining examples of Equus asinus and Equus hamionus.

[Photo : Archaeological Survey of India.]

[See p. 76]

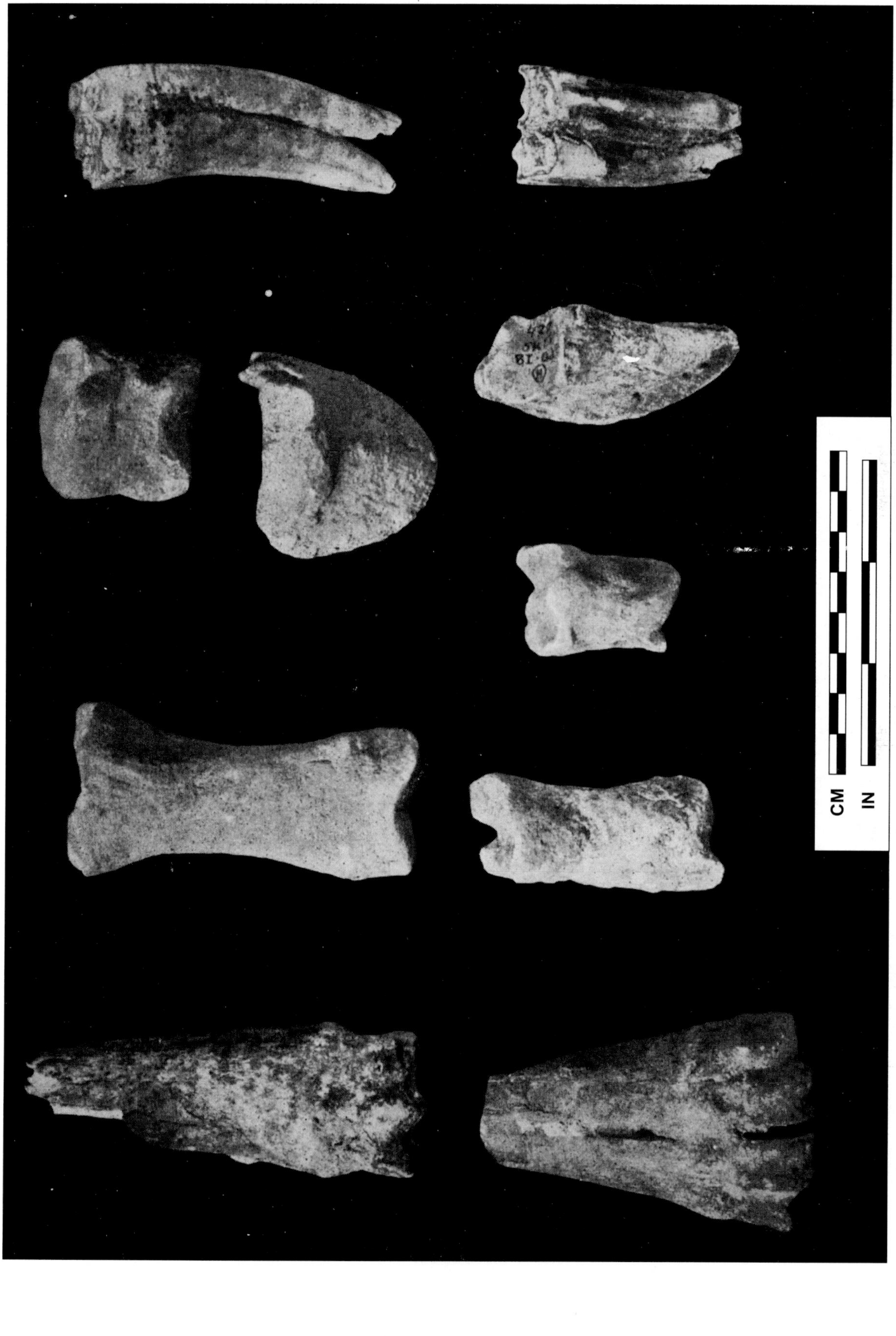

Surkotada : top row, bones of Equus caballus *Linn.*; bottom row, bones of cattle.

[Photo : Archaeological Survey of India.]

[See p. 76]

Noh: top row, a portion of charred lamp of clay, showing impression of rice husk x 2 ; middle row left, portion of charred lump of clay enlarged to show an impression of rice spikelets x 3 ; middle row, right, impression of rice spikelets to show chessboard pattern x 19 ; bottom row, two lumps of burnt rice husk enclosing charred rice spikelets.

[See p. 77]

[Photo : Birbal Sahni Institute of Palaeobotany, Lucknow.]

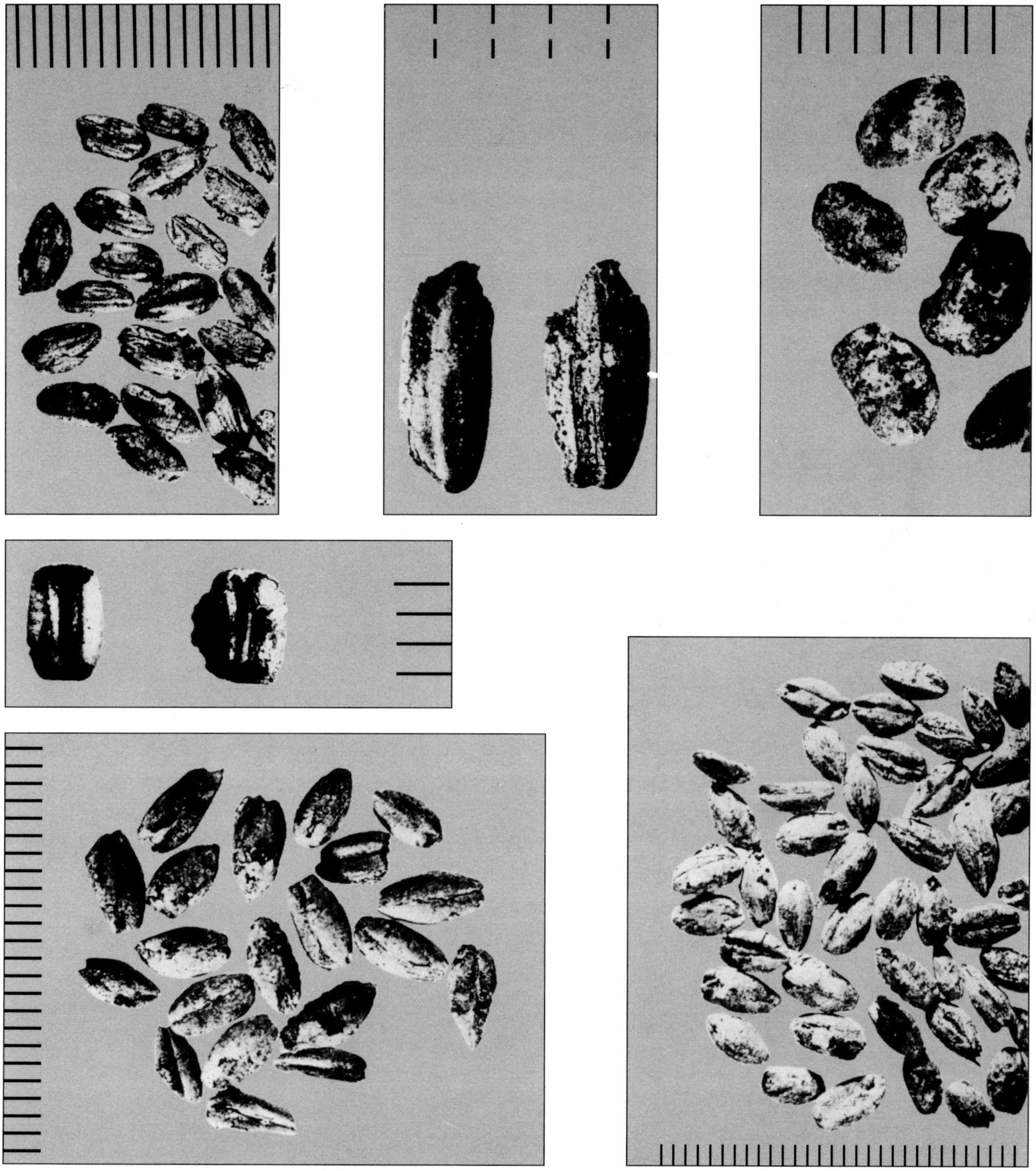

Noh: top row, (from left), charred spikelets of rice ; two charred kernels of rice enlarged, charred seed of Dolichos biflorus L.; middle row, charred seeds of Phaseolus mungo L; bottom row, charred kernel of naked barley (*Hordeum sp.*) and charred kernel of hulled barley (*Hordeum sp.*).

[See pp. 77-78] [Photo : Birbal Sahni Institute of Palaeobotany, Lucknow.]

A. Alexander being saved by Krateros during a lion-hunt, somewhere near Susa in Persia.

B. Palmette antefixes from Pella.

C. Palmette from Rampurva.

[See p. 106] [Photo : Author.]